CENTRAL
INTELLIGENCE
and
NATIONAL
SECURITY

Harry Howe Ransom

HARVARD UNIVERSITY PRESS
Cambridge, Massachusetts · 1958

PREFACE

A former Secretary of State has defined American foreign policy as "the grand strategy with which the United States proposes to deal with the main facts — the thrusts and the problems they present — of the outside world." (Dean Acheson, *Power and Diplomacy*, Cambridge, Mass., Harvard University Press, 1958, p. 2.) I do not quarrel with Mr. Acheson's definition, yet it leaves policy makers and American governmental institutions with a central task, more difficult now than ever before: getting at the "main facts" and understanding precisely the nature of the problems they present. Too often in contemporary as in past issues of foreign policy and national strategy, one man's fact is another man's fancy.

This book explores a major *terra incognita* of American government today, the national intelligence community, the primary role of which is to bring the main facts of the outside world to the attention of American policy makers. The new role of the United States in world affairs, the nature of the major threats to national security, and the time- and space-compressing effects of technology in the nuclear-missile age have combined to produce significant, though sometimes subtle, changes in American governmental institutions. In an age in which men of good faith profoundly disagree on the nature of the threat to Free World security, when statesmen debate about the specific requirements for national survival, and when, indeed, a strategic consensus does not exist among policy makers, those who are charged with *responsibility for decision* on a strategy for peace and security confront the intelligence community with the greatest possible challenge.

The decade since World War II has seen the creation and development of governmental machinery for producing integrated national decision. At the apex of the new governmental structure is the National Security Council, designed to give the President integrated advice and an integral intelligence for national security policy. The NSC's right arm is the Central Intelligence Agency. Under CIA leadership, the product of the intelligence community has become significantly influential in contemporary national decision making.

The purpose of this book is to explore insofar as is possible this shadowy sphere of government; to describe the growth and function of central intelligence in the United States since World War II.

Today the CIA presides over a massive and thriving intelligence community. Its prime responsibility is to collect, evaluate, and communicate information required both for decision making and for implementing national policy. CIA is the indispensable gatherer and evaluator of world-wide facts for the National Security Council. Yet to most persons CIA remains a mysterious, super-secret, shadow agency of government. Its invisible role, its power and influence, and the secrecy enshrouding its structure and operations, raise important questions regarding its place in the democratic process. One such question is: How shall a democracy insure that its secret intelligence apparatus becomes neither a vehicle for conspiracy nor a suppressor of the traditional liberties of democratic self-government?

CIA's invisible personnel nearly total in number those of the Department of State. CIA's annual budget in recent years — the figures are secret — may be as much as twice that of the Department of State. Additional hundreds of millions of dollars are expended annually by the other government intelligence units within the intelligence community. Yet even many serious students of public affairs, including members of Congress, possess little or no knowledge of the scope or the structure and role of central intelligence. Consequently an atmosphere of suspicion and prejudice envelops CIA.

No question has occupied the attention of policy makers in recent years more persistently than whether the United States is "behind," "tied with," or "ahead of" the Communist bloc on the diplomatic-military-economic fronts of the Cold War. While outer-space vehicles in the not distant future may assist the United States in seeking clearer answers to this question and the consequent policy requirements, primary dependence now must be placed upon an intelligence apparatus confined to the earth and its immediate atmosphere.

The requirement that policy makers know the world-wide facts of life, combined with the strategy and tactics of world communism, have drawn the United States, with some reluctance and perhaps with strain upon its moral purpose, into the hard, cruel, often savage underground world of realpolitik. Espionage and undercover political intrigue on a global scale have consequently become a part of America's arsenal for fighting the Cold War. American agents, in the open or under a variety of "cover," are at work around the globe on the mission of fact-finding or backstage political action. A kind of war in peace is an accurate description of the character of some of the activities that have been assigned to the contemporary central intelligence system of the United States.

Few question the assertion that United States foreign and military policies ought to be based upon "the facts." Given the explosive international setting of the mid-twentieth century, the importance of rationally determined policy and action cannot be overemphasized. Rational decision cannot be expected in the absence of essential information. The search for, and interpretation of, this information are primary missions of the massive intelligence apparatus now supported by the United States Government.

The potential rewards of an efficient intelligence system are great if the premise is accepted that the scientific approach — the use of systematic methods of research and analysis — may make possible the discovery of information by which statesmen not only can reach rational decision on current problems but can influence future world events as well. At least a good chance exists that a proper relationship between knowledge and action will produce national policy which is both rational and right.

No pretense is made that the following pages offer a complete picture of central intelligence, particularly of its overseas cloak and dagger and political action operations. This perhaps will never be written, at least not in this generation. But available nonsecret materials on central intelligence open the curtain of secrecy sufficiently wide to reveal the structure and method of the massive intelligence organization now at work in Washington and around the globe. From such materials, this book has been written.

Inherent and formidable difficulties confront any student of public affairs who sets out to describe the history, structure, and principal methods of the contemporary intelligence system in the United States. Careful *library intelligence* permits many of these difficulties to be surmounted. I hasten to add that I have never been a member of the guild of professional intelligence analysts. Indeed, were I privy, now or in the past, to secret information about central intelligence, I could not have written this book. But certainly the role and importance of central intelligence in national decision making, and its impact upon the American governmental process, are potentially too great to let this new phenomenon of American politics go without description and analysis. For to recall some neglected words in George Washington's Farewell Address: "In proportion as the structure of a government gives force to public opinion, it is essential that public opinion should be enlightened."

This book does not attempt to provide a substitute for existing standard works on strategic intelligence. I refer to books by authors experienced in intelligence. Included among these is George S. Pettee's *The Future of American Secret Intelligence* (Washington, 1946), an analysis of World War II deficiencies in intelligence, with suggestions for basic requirements for a post-war intelligence system. Sherman Kent's *Strategic Intelligence* (Princeton, 1949, 1951) is an outstanding work in the field. Written after the Central Intelligence Agency was established in 1947, Mr. Kent's book is an incisive discussion of intelligence as a kind of knowledge, as a type of organization, and as a unique activity. Roger Hilsman's more recent *Strategic Intelligence and National Decisions* (Glencoe, 1956) is a valuable contribution to the literature, based in part upon interviews with intelligence officials. Mr. Hilsman's purpose was to identify and analyze contemporary American intelligence doctrine and to speculate about the relationship between knowledge and action.

I am indebted to each of these authors for his pioneering work. Yet none of the works cited presents a detailed descriptive analysis of the contemporary intelligence community. The purpose of this book is to survey this uncharted ground. I do not offer a doctrine or theory of central intelligence, nor do I discuss in detail some of the more technical problems of strategic intelligence production.

My book is the outgrowth of materials originally prepared for use in the Defense Policy Seminar conducted by the

Defense Studies Program, Graduate School of Public Administration, Harvard University. Many participants in these graduate seminars over the past several years have contributed directly and indirectly to the substance of this book.

Acknowledgments

My thanks are due to colleagues in the Harvard Defense Studies Program, notably W. Barton Leach, originator and first Director of the Defense Studies Program, and Professor of Law at Harvard University. I also gratefully acknowledge the aid and co-operation of Defense Studies colleagues Edward L. Katzenbach, Jr., and Maury D. Feld. Acknowledgment is also due V. O. Key, Jr., Professor of Government at Harvard, whose suggestion that an earlier version of the material in the following pages might be developed into a book was an important stimulant to action. I thank also Sanford M. Dornbusch for his reading of the draft manuscript. Parts of an earlier version of this manuscript were commented upon also by Samuel P. Huntington, Walter Millis, George S. Pettee, and Walt W. Rostow. Their suggestions were highly valued. I alone, however, am responsible for the facts and interpretations herein. The indispensable person who endures the typing of manuscript drafts was in this case Rena Themistocles.

The traditional acknowledgment to the writer's "better half" has always appeared to me to be mere formalism. Now I understand why authors thank their wives and so acknowledge the major contribution of Nancy A. Ransom.

                                                                     H.H.R.

Defense Studies Program
Harvard University
Cambridge, Mass.
April 1958

CONTENTS

**CENTRAL
INTELLIGENCE**
and
**NATIONAL
SECURITY**

". . . we cannot continue to live and breathe the air of freemen without adequate intelligence; and intelligence of itself, no matter how good it is, is not enough; the cold facts have to be understood and used."

— House Committee on Military Affairs, 1946

"The fate of the Nation may well rest on accurate and complete Intelligence data which may serve as a trustworthy guide for top-level governmental decisions on policy and action in a troubled world, where so many forces and ideologies work at cross purposes."

— Hoover Commission, *Intelligence Activities, 1955*

"The acquisition of intelligence is one thing; the interpretation of intelligence is another; and the use of that intelligence is a third."

— Testimony of Lt. Gen. Doolittle before Senate Committee on Armed Services, 1957

I

INTELLIGENCE
in the Nuclear Age: Introductory

Each Thursday, from all over Washington, a small group of the highest government officials arrives at the White House for a meeting of the National Security Council.[1] This select group of Presidential advisers congregates at an oblong table a few steps from the President's office and adjacent to the White House rose garden.

At the appointed hour, the President or his Special Assistant for National Security Affairs introduces a subject for discussion from the carefully prepared agenda. If, as is usually the case with National Security Council deliberations, the question involves an appraisal of the objectives, commitments, and risks of the United States in pursuit of national security, the first step is a summary of foreign intelligence on the subject, presented by the Director of Central Intelligence out of the formidable resources of the Central Intelligence Agency and of the government-wide intelligence community.

The routine presence of the Director of Central Intelligence at National Security Council deliberations, and the primary place of the intelligence estimate in NSC proceedings, is demonstrable evidence of a new, vital, and somewhat unique role for intelligence in national decision making.*

* President Eisenhower's White House office routine has included an examination, early each morning, of daily reports from the intelligence community.

The intelligence estimate, injected in a crucial phase of national security policy making, is the end product of the now vast and complex machinery for gathering and evaluating information, presided over by CIA and encompassing the many separate intelligence agencies of government. The intelligence estimate available to the President and his advisers daily, as well as at NSC meetings, is the product of an intelligence community which employs thousands of individuals and expends hundreds of millions of dollars annually for activity ranging from library research to surveillance in the field.

Intelligence: Key to Decision

•Nothing is more crucial in the making of national decisions than the relationship between intelligence and policy, or in a broader sense between knowledge and action. Few Americans, even those reasonably well informed of public affairs, know of the existence and vital role in the contemporary Washington decision-making machinery of such groups as the Intelligence Advisory Committee, the Board of National Estimates, the Watch Committee, or the National Security Agency.•Indeed there is more misinformation and myth than need be about the key organization — the Central Intelligence Agency. Yet these are the agencies of the executive branch of American government that have evolved to meet the contemporary requirements for information and knowledge which, hopefully, precede and guide government policy and action.

Other agencies or adjuncts of government exist to produce information on operational requirements, such as the Pentagon's Weapons System Evaluation Group and its affiliate the Institute for Defense Analysis, the Army's Operations Research Office, the Navy's Operations Evaluation Group, the

Air Force's Office for Operations Analysis, and the USAF affiliate, the RAND Corporation. Intelligence is an important ingredient in, and by-product of, the work of these groups. Strictly speaking, however, they do not engage in national intelligence production.

What are some of the contemporary requirements for information? Today American bombing planes patrol the skies day and night, armed with hydrogen bombs capable of incinerating societies. Who is to give the word to these merchants of deterrence or destruction to attack or not to attack in a given situation? Intelligence plays a key role here.

In many parts of the globe, uneasy truces exist between Washington and Moscow, with opposing armed forces poised to attack or defend unstable territories or political structures. Who is to call the signals for attack or defense? Without requisite intelligence, the risk of ill-advised action increases.

If, for example, it is learned that nation X, an ally of the United States in the Cold War, has decided to invade by a certain date nation Y, politically hostile to the United States, American officials must decide upon a course of action. What shall be the basis of such a decision? And what will be the effect of alternate decisions upon nation Z? Decision makers look to the intelligence estimate, though it cannot always supply the answer.

Or let us suppose that it is learned that the entire fleet of Soviet submarines, armed with missiles of megaton power and a range of several hundred miles, have suddenly left their home pens. How do United States officials ascertain the meaning of this move, or the counter-measures required? Faulty intelligence could threaten national survival as much as enemy weapons.

All such questions directly or indirectly affect the survival of the United States. Survival in the nuclear age will test all

American instruments of government, our institutions, and our political processes. None faces a more severe and constant testing than the intelligence services. Important as is its function of around-the-clock daily watch upon world events, equally important is the central intelligence function of providing long-range estimates to policy makers. No development in American government institutions in recent years is more important than the evolution of the mechanism for producing the National Intelligence Estimate.

Intelligence and Policy Planning

Such estimates are of incalculable value to officials responsible for making plans and building and implementing programs for the security of the United States. Policy planners are required continuously to look into the future. Answers must be provided to such questions as: Will the Soviet Union continue as America's strongest and most hostile opponent in world affairs? In which of various ways and where will this hostility manifest itself in future periods? Will cracks in the Kremlin Wall widen or be patched up successfully? To what extent will unrest within the Soviet orbit become an important strategic factor? What are the timetables and the major trends in the development of Soviet military weapons of unprecedented power? What are the fundamental facts which should govern United States policy on armament limitation? What will be the significant trends in the drive for economic and political progress in the less developed areas of the world? What relative political, economic, and military strength will be maintained by former great power centers such as Western Europe (particularly Germany) and Japan? What future developments in Latin America will impinge upon the interests of the United States?

Central intelligence has the unenviable role of pointing

the way to the correct answers to these questions, of supplying information required to influence to America's advantage the trend of future events. The broad strategic doctrine of the United States must be geared to the best attainable intelligence forecasts. United States success in the game of competitive co-existence will depend heavily upon the quality of such intelligence, for the accuracy of the pictures drawn for decision makers of the future face of world politics has a profound impact upon the adequacy of United States planning.

The successful use of any of the major instruments of national policy also depends heavily upon the quality of the intelligence estimate. In the use of diplomacy, military power, economic pressure, propaganda, and psychological warfare, or any combination of these, accurate intelligence is a key to success, particularly in a period of Cold War. Thus a heavy burden of responsibility rests upon those who create the national intelligence estimates, those who sit as the Board of National Estimates or as the Intelligence Advisory Committee.

A sure way to court national disaster is to remain in the dark today about the present status, the capability, or the probable intentions of foreign nations, particularly potential enemies but also allies or neutrals in the Cold War. To avert this disaster, a massive American intelligence bureaucracy works around the globe to supply the federal government with the plethora of information required. At least twelve major departments and agencies of the government today are engaged directly in the intelligence process, with some ten additional units also engaged in some form of intelligence work. At the apex of this structure is the Central Intelligence Agency, overseeing and co-ordinating what has come to be known as the intelligence community.

A President, a Secretary of State or Defense, or a Congressional committee, may indeed make decisions apparently contrary to the intelligence facts. Yet never before have national policy makers had the benefit of such highly refined intelligence estimates. And the quality of the intelligence product presumably continues to improve. Certainly the institutional apparatus for the gathering, evaluation, and communication of intelligence has greatly expanded and improved in its first ten years under centralized direction.

Defining Intelligence

What is intelligence? Seeking a definition, a Hoover Commission task force surveying the national intelligence community in 1955 arrived at the following:

Intelligence deals with all the things which should be known in advance of initiating a course of action.[2]

This indeed is a broad conception of intelligence, describing an ideal situation which few decision makers, if any, can expect to find. Such a definition also suggests a completeness of the product which few intelligence estimators would claim to be attainable. As a highly placed Pentagon official once stated, "A decision is the action an executive must take when he has information so incomplete that the answer does not suggest itself." [3] Perfect intelligence would ease the pain of decision making. The ideal of the intelligence expert — of the intelligence community — is to supply the policy maker with complete and accurate information. If having this will not automatically produce a decision for the executive, it at least may increase the probability of the correct decision.

A somewhat less idealized and more useful definition of intelligence than the one cited above may be found in the

Dictionary of United States Military Terms for Joint Usage:

Intelligence — The product resulting from the collection, evaluation, analysis, integration, and interpretation of all available information which concerns one or more aspects of foreign nations or of areas of operations and which is immediately or potentially significant to planning.[4]

It is clear from such a definition that each of the many agencies of government concerned with national security will have its own particular intelligence requirements in order that its responsible leaders may make and implement decisions on plans and programs.

The pursuit of intelligence is the pursuit of information required for decision or action. The information gained, the product, is substantive intelligence. The same word, intelligence, often is used interchangeably, sometimes referring to the process, sometimes to the product.

The intelligence process, crude or refined, instinctive or conscious, is common to almost every level of human activity. When a man plans a vacation trip for his family or when a Secretary of Agriculture makes a decision on agricultural policy, an intelligence ingredient is part of the decision. Both types of decisions must be based in part upon factors in which precise predictions are not usually possible, such as the weather, or human behavior. The intelligence process and product required for national security policy making is infinitely more complex, yet it has characteristics common to any human decision.

This book is concerned primarily with what can be called national (or strategic) intelligence, which may be defined as high-level integrated intelligence covering broad national strategy and transcending the exclusive competence or needs of a single department.

The Knowable and the Unknowable

The primary goal of intelligence, as the definitions above suggest, is to provide foreknowledge, to supply national policy makers and operators with sound evaluations of the present and future status, capabilities, and intentions of foreign powers. In pursuing such information, a distinction must be made between the knowable and the unknowable, between what can be predicted with reasonable certainty or only in degrees of probability. It is one thing for central intelligence to be able to supply the President and National Security Council with the hard fact that the Soviet Union almost certainly possesses x number of ballistic missiles, with a maximum range and destructive power of y, and capable of being launched from z locations. It is even possible to make reasonably reliable estimates of such capabilities some years hence. Yet it is quite another thing to be able to give officials more than an estimate of probable Soviet intentions of using such weapons, or more than a qualified prediction of the probable effects their possession will have upon our own strategic capability or the actions of other nations. Even if this could be done, it is important to note here, the intelligence estimate does not automatically supply the decision as to what action should be taken by the NSC and the President in the light of such information.

The production of hard facts or qualified predictions is the end result of the intelligence process. This process involves the countless systematic steps by which raw data are collected, assembled, and refined into a useful information product which is to be communicated to intelligence consumers.

The body of information offered under the label of strategic, or national, intelligence to members of the National

Security Council as they deliberate national security policy issues is merely one element in the intellectual process by which responsible officials reach a decision or make policy. The intelligence ingredient in this process must compete with other factors to be considered and other "pictures in the mind" of the decision maker. These include not only his receptivity to, and faith in the accuracy of, the proffered intelligence estimate, but also his own assumptions, biases, perception, and knowledge from other sources and from experience. Indeed, in a sense, the official intelligence estimate must compete also with the sometimes unconscious evaluations made by the decision maker from his reading of the morning *Washington Post and Times Herald* or *The New York Times*. Indeed some of the oldest newspapers have borne the title, *Daily Intelligencer*.

Reliability of intelligence data and the reception accorded it by policy makers and operators are only two of many problems and questions about the intelligence function in foreign-military affairs. The purpose here is to survey some of the more important of such problems insofar as information is available on them. If, as the Hoover Commission of 1955 has stated, "The fate of the Nation may well rest on accurate and complete Intelligence data . . ." [5] these indeed are problems worthy of concern.

Leaders of World Communism today work relentlessly on two levels: the diplomatic and open level to gain any advantage in the Cold War by accepted means, and on the secret, subversive level to extend their power ever outward from the centers of the Communist movement. In the post-Stalin era, particularly, the methods of World Communism have seemed to become more flexible and subtle. In assuming the leadership of the Free World to combat the multi-pronged Communist efforts to expand the Soviet Empire, the United States has been forced to enter the underground world of secret intelligence in an attempt to compete with the Communists on equal terms.

The philosopher, the student of the administrative process, or the observer of the political process will find challenging and fundamental questions in the relationship between national intelligence and public policy. The descriptive analysis of central intelligence which follows does not attempt to perform the task of the philosopher or theorist of politics and government. A much more limited goal has been set — to describe contemporary central intelligence insofar as this can be done from nonsecret sources.

The following pages contain a descriptive analysis of the nature of intelligence, the development of centralized intelligence, the national intelligence community, intelligence in the military services and other major government agencies, top-level co-ordination of intelligence, the issue of secrecy and Congressional surveillance, and a discussion of some major problems of organization, procedure, and performance.

II

The Nature of
INTELLIGENCE

Intelligence, as previously suggested, is a term connoting both a process and a product. The nature of intelligence has been confused somewhat by a *mystique* surrounding the word and the activity. Misunderstanding abounds also from the many varieties and categories of sources for, and methods of, its collection. Some misapprehension also results from the fact that, as Sherman Kent has so well illustrated in his book *Strategic Intelligence,* intelligence is knowledge, is organization, and is activity. And the inclusion of special operations — secret political action overseas — within the jurisdiction of the intelligence system inevitably spreads additional confusion.

The intelligence process has been described in non-academic terms by Lt. Gen. James H. Doolittle: "The acquisition of intelligence is one thing; the interpretation of intelligence is another; and the use of that intelligence is a third." Yet the important point the General does not make is that these three basic elements in the process are, or should be, highly interrelated.

"There's nothing esoteric about the word 'intelligence,'" declared Allen W. Dulles, speaking as the Director of Central Intelligence.[1] This may be true to an experienced intelligence expert — Mr. Dulles has been active in intelligence work since World War I — but the layman is often confused by a myriad of descriptive adjectives classifying various types of intelligence according to its use or with reference to methods of collection. We find such categories as strategic, tactical, flak, target, air, photo, economic, radar, and electronic.

Categories of Intelligence

The three most useful categories are strategic (or national), tactical (or combat), and counter-intelligence.

Strategic intelligence is the broadest in scope. It refers to information regarding the capabilities, vulnerabilities, and intentions of foreign nations required by planners in developing the basis for an adequate national security policy in time of peace. It provides also the basis for projected over-all military operations in time of war. As Sherman Kent has put it:

> If foreign policy is the shield of the republic, as Walter Lippmann has called it, then strategic intelligence is the thing that gets the shield to the right place at the right time. It is also the thing that stands ready to guide the sword.[2]

It is impossible to set precise limits upon the scope and kinds of information needed in the strategic intelligence process. Basic elements include geographic, political, economic, scientific, military, sociological, psychological, and biographical factors, and many others.

Tactical, or operational, intelligence is sometimes termed combat intelligence because it usually concerns information required by a commander in the field engaged in tactical operations. The distinction between tactical and strategic intelligence, however, is not always clear-cut. For example, the movement of a Chinese Communist field army across

the Yalu River may be a piece of tactical intelligence vital
to the field commander, but it also may be important, high-
level "strategic" intelligence of major concern to the National Security Council. Indeed, a major field commander
today requires much of the same intelligence available to
the NSC.

Counter-intelligence denotes that phase of intelligence
activity devoted to countering the effectiveness of hostile
foreign intelligence operations. In essence it is a police function. More specifically its purpose is to protect information
against espionage, to guard personnel against subversion,
and to secure installations or material against sabotage.
Counter-intelligence is, in a sense, a negative, defensive
function. Sometimes, however, it turns up information of significance to those concerned with "positive" intelligence.

These various categories and distinctions in types of intelligence have precise meaning to the intelligence community. But the purpose of this book is to examine as a
whole the national intelligence organization and process
to which all types of intelligence contribute.

Steps in the Process

The intelligence cycle can best be described as the various
"steps" in the process. These are commonly grouped into
three general phases:

Collection — the procurement of information believed to
be pertinent, sometimes called "raw" intelligence data.

Evaluation and production — sifting, sorting, and judging the credibility of collected information, drawing pertinent inferences from its analysis, and interpreting such inferences in keeping with the requirements of the planners,
policy makers, and operators.

Dissemination — communicating the intelligence findings

in forms most suitable — oral, graphic, or written — to appropriate planners, decision makers, or those responsible for implementing decisions.

All links in the chain must be securely fixed or the intelligence system will be ineffective. A nation may have an efficient system for collecting intelligence data but its evaluation or the inferences drawn may be faulty, as may be its system for dissemination to the proper consumers. American experience in World War II, from its very start in Pearl Harbor to the end of the conflict, was characterized by a loose and sometimes ineffective organization for utilization of available intelligence. Certainly the use of intelligence immediately prior to the attack on Pearl Harbor can be described as "casual." [3]

It would be misleading, however, to picture the intelligence process merely as routine steps in a well-defined cycle as outlined above. A more accurate picture is to be had by considering intelligence production in comparison with the inductive method, or with any intellectual process in which there is a high degree of "feedback" and interrelationship between the elements of knowledge and the "steps" in the process. Certainly the collector of raw data needs guidance from the policy maker as well as from the evaluator. Channels of communication must always be kept open among the collector, co-ordinator, and the consumer. Certainly the collector and collator must have some idea what the intelligence consumer needs to know. The consumer, in turn, must be supplied with enough basic facts in order to recognize that certain elements in the picture are missing. This is only to suggest the limitations of viewing the intelligence process as a clear-cut performance of routine isolated tasks.

Procuring Raw Intelligence

Because the intelligence process is indeed a dynamic, interacting process, there is no clear-cut starting or stopping point. Yet it may be said that the first *general* step in the process is the procurement of data, of so-called raw intelligence. The process may be compared to a huge jigsaw puzzle, the solution to which is complicated by the fact that many of the pieces submittted to the puzzle solver do not fit at all into the picture. Data collected by the nation's far-flung intelligence operations cover a multitude of items in varying stages of rawness and with varying degrees of relevance to the problem faced by the analyst.

The secret movement of Soviet submarines through the Skagerrak or out of the Kuriles may be of immediate strategic import. The removal of permanent naval delegates from the Russian Communist Party's Central Committee, on the other hand, may lack immediate critical importance but yet may fit significantly into a long-range study of the relative position of Army, Navy, and Air Force officers in Soviet strategic planning.

The size of this year's graduating class at a Moscow engineering institute must be included in any long-range estimate of Soviet capability for industrial expansion. A public announcement in *Pravda* of a railroad being laid in a heretofore barren area may stimulate a drive for collection of information on this area to ascertain whether a landing field, a steel mill, or a uranium mine may lie at the end of this iron rainbow. It should be clear that intelligence — strategic or tactical — involves more than military secrets, clandestinely gathered. The movement of freight cars, discovery of a new oil field, or development and application of a new industrial process are of interest to intelligence agents all over the world. The influence of such facts, usually gathered from "open" rather than secret sources, may be just as significant to our military-foreign policy planning as a spectacular May Day public demonstration in Moscow of a new model of the Bison (long-range bomber).

"A cable from the State Department regarding political developments in a country is intelligence," as Allen W. Dulles has observed.[4] So, too, are scientific, technical, military, and other data, whether collected from an American B-29 aircraft flying along the East German border with a long-range camera, from a translation of a Russian scholarly journal, from interviews with refugees or political defectors from Iron Curtain countries, from such highly technical methods as particle-analysis, micro-analysis, from electronic information-gathering devices, or from intelligence agents, operating either in the open or secretly. Intelligence, like knowledge, knows no boundaries either as to substance or source. Yet the procurement of data to be fed into the intelligence mill is a vital management function of the various intelligence agencies of government. The intelligence apparatus would soon become useless if the raw data were gathered at random. To be efficient, data gathering must be planned and purposeful. Those who collect, evaluate, and assemble intelligence reports must be keenly aware of the important unanswered questions in the mind of the decision maker.

Sources

World War II taught Americans that, in the words of William J. Donovan, "good intelligence was no more mysterious than McGuffey's *Second Reader* and just about as sinister."[5] During the war, agents of the Office of Strategic Services learned that a few minutes spent with the brakeman of a freight train destined for Occupied France produced more useful data than Mata Hari could learn in an entire evening. And in the war, for example, an item in a society column of a German garrison-town newspaper revealed the location of a German division which the Allies had been seeking.

Reflecting on his days as an attaché of the British Foreign Office, Harold Nicholson recalls how very little information of value he could have conveyed to the fictional Slav countess who might have approached him on the Baghdad Express offering, in return for valuable information, a half million dollars, safe passage to Chile, and the favors of the lady herself. "There was little I could reveal to her which her employers could not have gathered from the London press."[6] The professional spy's more fruitful target is not the young attaché, Nicholson suggests, rather it is the "worker in some munitions factory, the dock hand at Scapa or at Kiel, even the Flemish peasant tilling the land and counting the military trains as they rambled along the railway embankment above him." Even such sources generally produce less useful information than that pieced together by research and analysis far behind the front lines of secret intelligence operations.

In gathering raw intelligence data the decline of the classical espionage agent is unmistakable. There are far more scholars and scientists, lawyers and former college professors who work a nine-to-five day at intelligence jobs in their Washington offices than there are current-day secret agents. The undercover foreign agent still exists in large numbers and sometimes can supply the vital link in the information chain. The major part of the intelligence function is performed by the college graduate or Ph.D. sitting at his desk creating a mosaic from multi-colored data gathered from around the globe, most likely from nonsecret sources.

The shift of emphasis from spying to scholarly research and analysis has been due in part to the increasing complexity of war and society, in part to the increasing effectiveness of state security systems, and in part to the vast scope of the information needed by the intelligence consumer.

One intelligence expert, Ellis M. Zacharias, a World War II Deputy Director, Office of Naval Intelligence, some years ago wrote that in the Navy 95 per cent of peacetime intelligence came from open sources, another 4 per cent came from semi-open sources and only 1 per cent, sometimes less, was obtained from secret agents. Wrote he, "There is very little these confidential agents can tell that not accessible to an alert analyst who knows what he is looking for and knows how to find it in open sources." [7] Since those words were written, ten years of the Cold War have elapsed. During this time, intelligence operations by secret agents have undoubtedly increased, though it is debatable whether the facts they supply have increased accordingly. Yet the fact remains that the great proportion of intelligence is gained from nonsecret sources.

A rough breakdown of the recent peacetime sources of United States national intelligence probably would indicate the following magnitudes as to sources and collectors:

Clandestine operations, secret sources, secret agents	20 per cent
Press, radio, tourists, published documents and other standard sources	25 per cent
Routine reports, Department of State and other government agencies abroad	25 per cent
Military attachés, accredited by foreign governments and from routine military operations	30 per cent

Much material which may have been given a security classification by government agencies, such as the cables of foreign service officers or reports from other government agencies operating in foreign nations, is nonetheless collected
by overt, above-board methods, and would normally be
available to anyone with a well-organized information-
gathering system.

Secret Sources

While it is clear that 80 per cent or more of intelligence
raw material in peacetime is overtly collected from nonsecret sources such as newspapers, libraries, radio broadcasts, business and industrial reports, or from accredited
foreign service officers, the importance of secret sources
should not be underestimated.

Current methods and sources of that 20 per cent of material gained through various forms of espionage by United
States central intelligence cannot be described here in more
than very general detail. If the total operations of the national intelligence community are carried on, as they are,
with a high degree of secrecy, its espionage activities are
inevitably classified as TOP SECRET. One United States Senator declared that it "almost chills the marrow of a man to
hear about" clandestine activities of American CIA agents.[8]
In addition to the hazardous activities of American foreign
agents in hiding or masquerading under various guises or
cover in foreign nations, scientific advances in electronics,
photography, and various forms of communication are being
brought to play in the intelligence process. Recall, for example, the Russian allegation a few years ago that the United States was drifting balloons across Soviet territory, carrying special cameras to photograph Russian installations and
industry. Again, reliable information is scarce on such meth-

ods and devices, although it can be assumed that effective use is made of them. Electronic intelligence, long-range and micro-photography, and other possible devices suggest to the imagination many possible uses.

Allen W. Dulles has publicly revealed, for example, that there are "certain types of special projects of a unique and important nature which this agency [CIA] undertakes from time to time in the research and development field." [9] Mr. Dulles disclosed this much to Congress in requesting authority to make five-year contracts with manufacturers for special devices, some of which undoubtedly would seem to be science fiction come true.

Espionage activities of American intelligence agents are unavoidably and rightly obscured in secrecy. It remains the most romantic aspect of intelligence and provides stimulus to the imagination of Hollywood and television script writers. But the serious work of cloak and dagger operations must be planned and carried out with the greatest of efficiency. A United States secret agent caught in the act of certain kinds of espionage obviously could cause serious diplomatic and political difficulties for this country if a plausible disavowal could not be made. It would obviously be a waste of effort and money — and possibly of human life — to attempt to procure information from behind the Iron Curtain which might be available otherwise from a translation of *Pravda*, or from monitoring a Russian radio broadcast.

Duplication of intelligence effort, and overlapping jurisdiction in foreign areas cause problems for a multi-agency intelligence system, and have pointed to the need for central intelligence. Similarly, there also may be a danger of overemphasizing the value of information obtained from secret sources. Unless properly directed, undercover agents can furnish masses of trivia and useless information or may even fabricate data in order to meet their "quotas" or in order to remain in the employment of a government agency. Here, indeed, is a vital, if "dirty," business which must be handled with great delicacy and finesse by a nation little experienced in such matters.

Effective and trustworthy undercover agents may, of course, be valuable to the intelligence process. The tale of the combination valet and German spy who served Britain's Ambassador to Turkey during World War II has been oft repeated and the results perhaps exaggerated, but few will deny that it was the kind of investment which might have repaid handsomely the German intelligence system.

But the investment did not in fact pay off because of a fundamental difficulty which plagues all intelligence systems — the problem of credibility of source and data. The British Ambassador in Ankara was a career diplomat with the story-book name of Sir H. M. Knatchbull-Hugesson. His valet at the time was a man known only by the name of Cicero, who obtained and offered to the Germans at very high price photographs of very secret documents, some of which included details of Allied war negotiations and strategy. The Germans purchased these documents (with counterfeit British sterling notes, as it turned out) but skepticism and disagreement, and competition between rival Nazi intelligence agencies, dominated their evaluation in Berlin and the Nazis downgraded their validity. The purloined papers were viewed by the Nazis as documents deliberately "planted" by British agents.[10] At any rate, placing an undercover agent of this sort is often a very long-range project.

Another example is the Dutch watchmaker who was dispatched to Scapa Flow in 1927 and whose detailed wartime reports on the British harbor defenses enabled the German Navy to slip its submarine *U-47*, commanded by Lieutenant Prien, into the highly protected British Harbor at Scapa. The *U-47* sank the battleship *Royal Oak* as she lay at anchor, on October 14, 1939. A point to note is that it was a dozen years before the watchmaker sent his first report.* Reports of intelligence agents may not always result in such spectacular success or even contribute much original information. But they often return excellent dividends by confirming intelligence gathered by other means or by pointing up leads which can be followed by other collection methods.

Aside from the difficulties and long-range planning involved in procuring reliable personnel and locating them in a fertile area, manifold problems are encountered in collecting secret information. For usually it is this information which is held under the greatest security by a foreign nation. In the mid-twentieth century it is difficult to place agents in the heart of a foreign government or in vital areas of a military training or research and development establishment although this has been successfully done and evidence is continually revealed that it is being attempted. Internal security procedures have gained in efficiency in recent decades, particularly in totalitarian systems of government. And many of the devices, such as electronic equipment, which may seem to facilitate clandestine procurement of data, also aid those charged with the security of such information.

In the contemporary atmosphere of tight state security systems, heavy reliance in international espionage is placed upon that immeasurable secret asset, the defector in place — that is, the disloyal American, Canadian, Englishman, or Frenchman who is willing to supply secret information to a foreign nation. Or the defector might be a Communist who

---

* Because the United States is a latecomer to clandestine operations on a world-wide scale, it is confronted by a disadvantageous lead-time factor. Thus it may be some years hence until its network of secret agents is firmly entrenched in rewarding locations.

has broken with the Party without its knowledge but who remains in a position to supply an American central intelligence officer with secret documents or oral reports. In the former category, examples include the cases of Klaus Fuchs, Julius and Ethel Rosenberg, Morton Sobell and others, all of whose activities were eventually detected. Their cases provide chapters in an espionage story undoubtedly not yet finished. In the latter category, American central intelligence utilizes today any person who can be enlisted as a trustworthy defector in place (as well as the publicized defectors who flee the Communist orbit) but on these there are no details for obvious reasons.

Totalitarian governments maintain very efficient counter-intelligence systems, and their disregard for the conventional civil liberties, honored in most Western nations, enable these agencies to operate with deadly effectiveness in peace as well as in war. The United States Director of Central Intelligence paid tribute to the effectiveness of Communist counter-intelligence when he declared, in 1954, "It's the toughest job intelligence has ever faced — getting good information from behind the Iron Curtain." [11] American intelligence pipe-lines to the Kremlin are scarce, if they exist at all.

The never-ending problem of "getting good information from behind the Iron Curtain" is often heightened by diplomatic factors. The affair of Commander Lionel Crabb, famous British frog-man who mysteriously vanished near the Soviet cruiser *Ordzhonikidze* at Portsmouth, England, in 1956, provided considerable embarrassment to Her Majesty's Government. And the Russians did not hesitate in charging that Crabb was in the employ of United States naval intelligence. The Soviets also generated much anti-Western propaganda over an alleged attempt by United States intelligence agents in 1956 to tap the main underground cables between Moscow and Soviet military headquarters in East Berlin. A 1,000-foot long tunnel was dug into the Soviet zone and an elaborate telephone exchange was set up and reportedly attached to Soviet wires. The Russians accused United States agents of doing this. The Soviets, for their part, have been far more embarrassed by exposure of their more extensive operations in Canada and Australia, to say nothing of their apparent espionage forays from the Soviet Embassy in Washington and from the United Nations headquarters in New York City and from other espionage *avanpost*.[12] The problem is not only to avoid detection in covert operations but to be able plausibly to disavow connection with adventures in espionage which are exposed or which fail.

An example is the widely publicized case of Colonel Rudolph Ivanovich Abel, an officer of the Soviet Russian State Security System, the "GB" (*Komitat Gosudarstvennoi Bezopasnosti*), roughly analagous to the American CIA. He was arrested in the late summer of 1957, arraigned in a Federal Court in New York, and indicted, convicted, and sentenced on charges of operating a military and atomic espionage ring for the Kremlin in the United States for many years. He had been living in Brooklyn under cover as an artist and photographer, using assumed names. His indictment charged that he, with several co-conspirators, had sent secret defense information to the Soviet Union. Such data apparently was transmitted (presumably as microphotographs) to Russia in containers cleverly fashioned from bolts, nails, coins, pencils, cuff links, and other devices of modern espionage.[13] At the time of his indictment, Colonel Abel was ignored by accredited Russian diplomats in this country, who implicitly were "plausibly disavowing" connection with his activities.[14] Another revealing case was that of Yuri A. Rastvorov, who operated an extensive Soviet spy ring centered in Japan under the cover of a special Soviet "Mission." He defected to the West on January 24, 1954.[15]

The use of "legal" cover by secret intelligence agents is a well-established practice. This is done by both sides in the Cold War. J. Edgar Hoover has testified that foreign intelligence agents

... seek admittance to the United States on diplomatic passports. They seek assignments to some official foreign agency and thus conceal themselves under the diplomatic cloak of immunity. To further avert suspicion, a high-ranking espionage agent may very well be employed as a clerk or in some minor capacity in a foreign establishment.[16]

Replying to Congressional inquiry, an unidentified Executive agency also has reported on individuals in the United States from Iron Curtain countries, either as officials or employees in foreign embassies or the United Nations. This report indicated that some forty-five of these individuals "have records of active work for the intelligence services of their respective countries." [17]

Some modern techniques of espionage in the Cold War were disclosed in the spring of 1958 when two Oxford University undergraduates were prosecuted by the British Government for violating the Official Secrets Act. The two students, in fulfilling National Service obligations, apparently took part in secret intelligence operations of the Royal Navy. Their duty, according to details published in the Oxford undergraduate magazine, *Isis*, — for which article they were being prosecuted — involved participation in Iron Curtain "frontier incidents" deliberately provoked by the British.

A plane or sea craft crosses the Iron Curtain line. The purpose of such provocations is to obtain intelligence about the nature of Russian military defenses, tactical behavior, and communication procedures and secret codes. Such provocations allegedly occur on land and sea and in the air. Thus it becomes clear that many of such incidents, often reported in the press as "unprovoked" Russian attacks upon Western forces "accidentally" encroaching on Soviet territory, are incidents deliberately provoked for intelligence purposes. Details emanating from the trial of the Oxford students are found in *The Times* (London), on May 22, 1958.

Traditional American Misgivings

Little reliable published information exists, understandably, about current United States secret operations in gathering intelligence data from foreign nations, or in backstage political maneuvers. One United States Senator, for example, designated by the Senate to keep informed of the program and activities of the national intelligence community, has indicated a strong hesitancy about asking such questions of CIA for fear that he might, in his own words, "obtain information which I personally would rather not have...." [18] The existing super-secrecy about these and other aspects of CIA operations overseas has the necessary advantage of protecting such activities from exposure that would rapidly dry up sources of vital information. Yet it also has the effect of arousing public and Congressional suspicion.

Traditional American misgivings about government support of espionage activities are illustrated in an experience cited in the memoirs of former President Harry Truman. Shortly after becoming Chief Executive in 1945 he had a discussion with the Director of the Budget, who brought up the matter of an item of twelve million dollars in the President's special fund. It was for unvouchered use in intelligence operations outside of this country. "I told Smith [Harold D. Smith, Budget Director] I did not want the fund enlarged and that I wanted a study made of all the agencies and services engaged in intelligence work. I told him what my thinking was on the subject of our intelligence activities and my misgivings about some of the fields of these activities. I again wanted to make one thing clear: 'I am very much against building up a Gestapo.'" [19] Here was an expression of traditional American misgivings about government-sponsored espionage.

As Hanson W. Baldwin also has suggested:

To most Americans the idea of an espionage system — a spy system — is abhorrent, at least in time of peace. The Office of Strategic Services [World War II] and the adventures and accomplishments of its agents did much to "sell" the public on the wartime necessity of espionage, yet there is still a native repugnance to the permanent establishment of a peacetime system. It smacks too much of duplicity and hypocrisy and poses hidden danger to the social system. It implies an "unfairness" foreign to the American mind, and some details of any intelligence system unquestionably are a "dirty business." [20]

This was written in 1947. The intervening years doubtless have brought an increasing awareness of Soviet international espionage and perhaps a wider public acceptance of the argument that the United States needs its own international espionage network. But the suspicion still lingers. Indeed, Mr. Baldwin himself has been a leader among journalists advocating a closer Congressional surveillance of the Government's foreign intelligence operations. [21]

In contrast to the period prior to World War II, today the United States is expending tens of millions of dollars annually for espionage equipment, research, travel funds for agents in foreign lands, radio monitoring of foreign broadcasts, purchase of bits of information from foreign informants, and many other activities in the intelligence process unknown to but a few American officials. As has been said, "the spy business is booming." This may be an inevitable outgrowth of a dozen years of Cold War, yet its compatibility with the American democratic system is open to question.

Overt Collection Methods

The value of overt collection methods has been suggested by President Truman in commenting on the ease with which Soviet Russia is able to gather intelligence about the United States. Writing of the 1951 Senate investigation of the dismissal of General Douglas MacArthur, he stated, "for the price of a good clipping service an enemy of the United States can acquire untold items of information about our plans and intentions and even about our installations and our equipment." [22] Mr. Truman added that if a potential enemy wanted to know even more, he could hope for nothing better than a Congressional probe of foreign-military policy. Said the man who had access to most of the nation's top secrets, "Then he will probably receive at no extra charge all the information he wants."

The open societies of Western nations stand in sharp contrast to the closed system of Soviet Russia. United States intelligence agencies seeking foreign data obviously do not enjoy these advantages outlined by the former President. Many officials today feel that the American system makes the Soviet intelligence process far too easy. The Director of Central Intelligence in 1954 stated, "I would give a great deal if I could know as much about the Soviet Union as the Soviet Union can learn about us by merely reading the press.

"Sometimes I think we go too far in what our Government gives out officially and in what is published in the scientific and technical field. We tell Russia too much. Under our system it is hard to control it." [23] Yet as previously suggested, the United States in pursuing vital data from behind the Iron Curtain does not resort entirely, or even largely, to clandestine operations. The Communists are notorious boasters, apparently prone to advertise widely their accomplishments and product. They have not been timid, for example, in boasting in recent years about their progress in the field of long-range bombers, missiles, earth-satellites, or other achievements in science and technology. One major task of our intelligence process is, indeed, to attempt to verify or disprove the facts behind such chest-thumping. Like their Western opposites, the Communists have a proclivity for talking, and their public, and perhaps some private, communications are well monitored by the American intelligence community.

It should be clear, then, that most of the information collected in the American intelligence process is obtained by methods and techniques which involve no greater risk or difficulty than those arising from the handling of massive amounts of data. The wide scope of the problem is illustrated by the fact that as many as five million words monitored from foreign radio broadcasts are processed into a one-page daily summary of Soviet propaganda highlights for the busy policy maker. Such a process may be compared with that of mining nickel ore — the concentrate may be no more than 0.03 per cent of what must be dug out, but the end product is essential and worth the effort. Such an analogy may be applied not only to the monitoring of foreign radio broadcasts but also to the over-all process of central intelligence.

To recall again William J. Donovan's remarks, at the end of World War II, intelligence is not the "mysterious, even sinister" thing it is sometimes imagined to be; rather, he said, it is mostly a matter of "pulling together myriad facts, making a pattern of them, and drawing inferences from that pattern." [24]

The premium is actually not so much on whether the facts are overtly or covertly gathered or even how many facts are collected. The emphasis in this first step — the collection phase — of the process must be on developing a purposeful collection plan. Here guidance from the policy makers is essential. Keen analysis by intelligence community administrators of long-range information requirements is vital. To say that the information needed in the process knows no boundaries as to source and substance is not to say that masses of information can with good effect be collected indiscriminately.

Functional Categories

The existence of certain functional categories of intelligence is helpful in maintaining a purposeful collection plan. Three general functional categories of information have been suggested. These are basic descriptive or general information type of intelligence; current reportorial or current estimate category; and speculative-evaluative or the forecasting or warning kind of intelligence.[25] Such categories are, of course, highly interrelated and the same mass of intelligence data will normally contribute to all of them.

Basic descriptive intelligence is that contained in the numerous and constantly revised intelligence encyclopedias available both to policy makers and to intelligence analysts.

These several categories have been refined in Sherman Kent's trail-blazing book, *Strategic Intelligence*. The descriptive element is referred to as "the groundwork which gives meaning to day-to-day change and the groundwork without which speculation into the future is likely to be meaningless." [26] The basic descriptive function is, therefore, performed by the intelligence community in the production of the government's own special set of secret encyclopedias. Rather than being organized alphabetically in the fashion of an ordinary encyclopedia they are organized by nations or by special categories, and further subdivided into introductory national surveys, advanced surveys in depth and *spot intelligence* such as: "How good is the water supply at an air base in Saudi Arabia?"

This basic descriptive element is embodied in the National Intelligence Survey (NIS), a publication series which succeeded the Joint Army-Navy Intelligence Studies produced during World War II (JANIS). NIS has been published and continually revised since 1948. The advent of warfare potentially total in nature or the prospect of an endless era of Cold War or competitive co-existence has made it necessary that foreign-military policy planners have information available dealing not alone with military forces, terrain, and general political factors. All-inclusive basic descriptive studies, also, are needed for such purposes as foreign aid planning, economic, political, and psychological warfare, effective diplomacy, propaganda, strategic bombing plans, and military government planning.*

The National Intelligence Survey inevitably must go to press from time to time, thus in a sense stopping the clock while national and international events continue their dynamic process. This makes necessary the *current reportorial* category of intelligence which can give policy planners and decision makers up-to-date information. While the "basic-descriptive" category may contain a very full biographical account of the Soviet Russian leader Nikolai Bulganin it would be a current reportorial function to be able to answer

---

* For more details on the National Intelligence Survey, see below, pp. 103–104.

a query from the Secretary of State: "What is Bulganin's position today in the political power structure of the Soviet Union?"

Another example of *current reporting* was the detection of unexpected radioactive dust on September 3, 1949, by the Air Force Long Range Detection System. This system has been set up with the specific purpose of obtaining intelligence on Soviet developments in atomic energy, and its discovery in September 1949 was given the highest priority for scientific analysis. The results led to a dramatic presidential announcement on September 23 that the Soviets had succeeded in detonating an atomic bomb. This kind of reporting fulfills both the requirements of keeping the basic descriptive element up to date and of alerting policy makers to developments which might affect the national interests. In addition to this, it also provides what has been called "a bridge between the past and future." [27] The past is embodied, essentially, in basic descriptions of the National Intelligence Surveys. The future is represented in that function of intelligence which puts the greatest demand upon the capacities and talent of intelligence analysts. And it is this function in which the work of the intelligence expert is most fallible — the *speculative-evaluative*, or forecasting function. It is one thing to be able to forecast the rate of production of Soviet long-range bombers over the next two years. Even here, in the experience of very recent years, the intelligence community has been wrong.[28] But it is quite another thing to be able to predict with certainty the future intentions and actions of leaders of foreign nations or even of American leaders.

The *speculative-evaluative* category is that very important and difficult element in the intelligence process devoted to forecasting the future and giving adequate warning to responsible officials of government. In a perfect grand strategy, it is often argued, the unexpected never happens. It seems clear from the record of the past dozen years that neither American intelligence nor strategy has even approached such perfection. But it is the function of this third category of intelligence to develop a very elaborate set of *indicators* which permit the operation of an efficient forecasting or warning system. Efficient gathering and processing of raw data obviously is a vital first step in the performance of this function, just as the existence of reliable national surveys provides the middle ground for competent forecasting.

An example of an indicator in a warning system would be the movement of Russian submarines through the Dardanelles. This normally could be considered an indicator of a possible Russian adventure. It would have been established in advance as an indicator based on previous surveys of the Soviet strategic potential, particularly the Russian capability to wage submarine warfare. Undergirding this would be prior analyses of the previous history of Soviet courses of action, an estimate of probabilities and the likelihood that the Russians would behave according to historical patterns, and among other things an appraisal of the existing state of international affairs. Other indicators of possible aggressive action could be the mobilization of troops in Russia, tightening of food rationing, increases in the frequency and violence of propaganda broadcasts, or the revision of Russian secret codes.

Such indicators, added to others, would have real significance, however, only in the light of previous knowledge of a nation's capabilities, specific vulnerabilities, and the leaders' interpretations of these factors. This latter must be based upon a continuing study of a nation's basic ideology. Knowledge of the strategic potential of other states involved would also be essential. Possessing such knowledge, intelligence specialists ought to be able to read the latest indicators and make at least educated guesses as to the probable course of action of a foreign nation, or at least of prospective trends and tendencies. But the impossibility of making a forecast on a basis of certainty is readily discernible.

It is important to stress here the critical importance of an integrated collection plan as a first step in the eventual production of sound estimates or speculative forecasts of another nation's capabilities and intentions. An effective set of indicators which can be applied promptly to a foreign power's actions might be termed the apex of the intelligence process triangle. But it must be re-emphasized that such indicators, to have validity, can be established only on a base of detailed and accurate descriptive studies coupled with the latest significant intelligence reports. An intelligence prediction or estimate based upon a foundation of sand, of bias or hunch, can destroy the effectiveness of a national policy generated by such an estimate.

Processing the Data

In discussing the collection and sources of intelligence data the question of its processing — evaluation and analysis — inevitably has been anticipated and discussed indirectly. Clearly the functional categories of intelligence influence the collection of the raw data, just as they have effect upon its processing — the second step in the intelligence process.

The collection of the massive amount of data described above, for the functions also described, is only the beginning of the process. A second problem is properly warehousing and meaningfully digesting this wide assortment of data.

Although much information is accumulated and filed by an intelligence agency with an immediate purpose in mind, much additional data must be kept as insurance against future requirements. It is comparable to the problems of the institutional library, which must continue to acquire books and documents for possible future use while satisfying pre-determined needs. The best libraries are those which can afford to, and do, anticipate the present and future require-ments of the scholarly community. So an efficient intelligence system must be able to anticipate the present and future needs of foreign-military policy planners.

The processing stage in intelligence procedures, although vital to the usefulness of the final product, is to a certain ex-tent a mechanical process. It is, in effect, essentially a prob-lem of librarianship, albeit a highly specialized one. It is librarianship involving a careful interplay of modern ma-chine handling of data and human judgment. This judgment must be injected into the processing of the data to determine whether, for example, digests of material will suffice or the entire mass of the original data should be retained. Similarly the cross-referencing system must be skillfully organized so as to insure a balance between security and the maximum utilization of existing information. So, too, must there be an efficient system of cataloging all the material which exists in the various departmental intelligence libraries. With the con-temporary emphasis accorded such a collective security system as the North Atlantic Treaty Organization, an inter-allied system of cataloging and exchange of material also must be a working reality.

Although no published details are available, the Central Intelligence Agency employs modern systems and devices for processing and handling data. The use of electronic de-vices for handling, cataloging, and cross-referencing data has not been overlooked as an efficient, though fallible, method for rapidly supplying essential data to intelligence analysts. Although automation has undoubtedly been incorporated to a degree into the central intelligence process, an electronic library will be unlikely to serve as a substitute for competent human judgment at many of the crucial steps in the intelligence process.

Establishment of a central library for the national intelligence community was ruled impracticable in 1955 by the various intelligence units of government and by the Hoover Commission. The 1955 Hoover Commission, however, urged that all intelligence units within the Defense and State Departments adopt a single-index system based upon the intelligence subject-code used by the CIA and the Air Force.[29] The cost of a more unified system may be high but the best intelligence data are useless if kept buried in forgotten safes or if one agency is unaware of essential data held by another department. Incompetent or careless management in processing raw data could result in a serious breakdown of the entire intelligence cycle, just as the whole system might be made inefficient by improper cross-referencing or interdepartmental ignorance of information existing within the intelligence community.

Evaluation and Analysis

Although in a strict sense evaluation of intelligence takes place at the point of collection and continues all during the process, the primary responsibility for evaluation and analysis may be separated out as another step. This occurs after information has been gathered, indexed, and boiled down into manageable form. Evaluation at this stage is one of the most critical phases in the intelligence cycle. Both source and content of each item of information requires careful evaluation as to reliability and accuracy. While it is true that the originator of an item may evaluate the source, content evaluation is usually reserved for an intelligence middleman whose sole job may be evaluations, or for the central intelligence topical specialist. Also, at another crucial stage, the presentation of the intelligence product to the consumer, another re-evaluation in effect may take place. In the intermediate stages, to be described below, evaluation and re-evaluation also occur.

A method of achieving some measure of standardization and also protection of clandestine sources that has been employed in the intelligence process is a letter-numerical evaluation system. Sources may be evaluated by letters A through D, for example, and contents by numbers 1 through 4, all in descending order of reliability and accuracy.[30] For example, an "A" source would be one of known reliability; a higher letter of the alphabet would designate a less reliable, or not reliable source. Material with a "No. 1" content designation would be considered authentic; a higher number would indicate the material to be "probably false" or "disproved." The most frequent complaint from intelligence consumers is that this system is too mechanical, that is, they would like to know more about the source of material as an aid in their own evaluation of the contents. Another complaint is that too frequently a middle-ground evaluation, such as "undetermined" is given. The counter-argument is that consumers should trust the intelligence experts who do the evaluating. And, of course, secret intelligence sources, particularly persons, must be protected from disclosure. Both positions suggest a fundamental and perhaps never to be resolved controversy between intelligence specialists and the makers and implementers of policy.

A continuing question is: "How far do intelligence analysts go beyond presenting the 'facts' "? Professional intelligence men can be heard to say in private: "Having a high-grade intelligence product is fine, but if the consumer doesn't believe it, if you aren't able to 'sell' your product, you might just as well not have collected it, evaluated it, and presented it." A growing professional group in Washington of highly competent intelligence specialists undoubtedly meet with frequent frustration when national policy is made seemingly without regard to the intelligence available. It is perhaps impossible to prevent policy preferences of the intelligence corps from coloring the entire intelligence process, from its collection to the final step of communication to responsible policy makers. Yet an efficient intelligence system must try to maintain a spirit of objectivity throughout the process.

Inevitably, however, policy preferences do tend to work their way into the processing of raw data, and into the evaluation of reliability of source and accuracy of specific information. Decisions all along the line must be made on how the data is to be analyzed, about its significance to United States national interests, and about the best form in which to present it to policy makers. The decision must often be made as to whether to present the raw data or an analytic digest of it that would point up several events it may portend. It also must be decided often whether and how data should be collated with other relevant information, coupled, at some stage, with an overlay of data on United States policy. Or must implications as to United States policy (and strategic capability) always be left to the politically responsible decision maker? Such complex questions pervade the intelligence process and will be discussed below.

The difficulties and scope of the evaluating process may be illustrated, for example, by the report of a large-scale movement of Soviet armor into East Germany. Such a report would be forwarded immediately with the necessary evaluation to the appropriate military commanders, to an Indications Center in Washington (a perpetual guard-duty apparatus established under the Watch Committee within the intelligence community), and to other interested consumers. The report would then be followed by an analytical report indicating whether this movement allegedly was occurring in conjunction with military maneuvers or whether it was a secret Soviet military operation; whether East Germans were staging uprisings; whether similar military movements were being encountered elsewhere within the Soviet orbit; whether the Soviet tanks were being accompanied by air forces and infantry; and whether the pattern of such movements had ever occurred in the past, and so on. The full-blown evaluated report which would be sent to the President's desk or to the National Security Council, to be meaningful, would have had to be further matched against other diplomatic and military events around the globe in order to be of full use as an indicator of events. Had such an Indications Center existed at the time of the Pearl Harbor attack, there were sufficient "indicators" to have sounded a government-wide alarm.

Recall also the example previously mentioned of the 1949 Air Force report on existence of radioactive dust in the atmosphere. President Truman writes that "the scientists went to work and analyzed the data. The Air Force specialists, the AEC's [Atomic Energy Commission] experts, and consultants called in from the universities went over the available information." Mr. Truman adds that their collective findings were then reviewed by a board of scientific authorities and the end result was the conclusion that between August 26 and August 29 "an atomic explosion had been set off somewhere on the Asiatic mainland." [31] It was the analysis in this case rather than the raw data that produced the ultimate finding. And note, also, the large number of participants in the evaluation process.

Not all or even most of the data collected are the type eagerly sought by decision makers. A truly efficient intelligence system will anticipate the needs of policy makers without wasting effort in attempts to gather every fact under the sun. Doubtless intelligence men on more than one occasion have been confronted with the policy planner's exasperated question: "Why haven't you got information on this?" Likely as not the same policy planner had failed to give previous guidance to the collector on his possible future needs. So the intelligence process must produce considerable information that is fed into bound volumes as insurance against future requirements. During World War II American strategic planners found that the cupboard was almost disastrously bare of *basic descriptive* information on many crucial parts of the globe where American forces had to fight. One intelligence expert has complained of a World War II tendency to weaken intelligence program planning by "a heavy schedule of miscellaneous customer demands." [32] Too much energy can be channeled off, it is claimed, into spot studies and answers to requests on a "crash" basis rather than upon attention to carefully researched long-range projections.

The importance of long-range intelligence projections cannot be overestimated. The long lead-time in developing and producing new weapons systems, for example (four years is not unusual in this regard), puts a heavy burden on intelligence. As the Chairman of the Joint Chiefs of Staff testified in 1956, military-foreign policy planning involves "estimating capabilities of weapons and intentions of the enemy 4 or 5 years in advance." [33] Indeed, technology continues to require projections of ever-increasing range.

A somewhat separate problem in the intelligence process is that of dealing with hypothetical questions involving the intentions of foreign leaders. This is in the previously mentioned category of "unknowable" intelligence, as contrasted with a question, for example, about prevalent diseases in

Saigon, Indo-China. A question of the unanswerable variety might be: What will be Chou en Lai's policy toward Indo-China, or South Korea, in 1965? Obviously Chou himself may not know what his policy will be under future conditions which he himself would have difficulty in predicting. Yet an estimate of probabilities may have some relevance, for example, to officials planning a long-range program of military and economic aid to Asian nations.

Intelligence analysts faced with such a question must move out of the factual into the speculative-evaluative arena. Few intelligence men will claim that an infallible forecast can be given to speculative questions. But policy planners can benefit from knowledge at least of the courses of action which seem most likely to be open to leaders of other nations. Leaders of the intelligence community claim that efficient collection, evaluation, and analysis can provide at least educated guesses in answer to "unknowable" questions. This, they argue, is preferable to policy making based upon untutored hunches.

Expectations of the intelligence community remain high, but Americans should not expect the impossible. As General Walter Bedell Smith is reported to have said prior to becoming Director of Central Intelligence in 1950, "America's people expect you to be on a communing level with God and Joe Stalin. . . . They expect you to be able to say that a war will start next Tuesday at 5:32 p.m." [34] Certainly America's people can expect a performance better than that rendered by the intelligence system in the first week of December 1941, in which there was a major failure in the final and crucial step of the intelligence process — dissemination of known information to the commanders who badly required it in a hurry.

Dissemination of Intelligence

Of the lessons from Pearl Harbor none was greater than the importance of proper and timely dissemination of intelligence.* For intelligence, by definition, is foreknowledge. It is information which should be known in advance of action — action by our own policy makers or action by a potential enemy. Clearly a most essential and crucial step in the process is dissemination of the intelligence product.

A principal though not entirely convincing defense of the Army and Navy commanders at Pearl Harbor made during the Congressional investigation of the December 7, 1941, attack was that they were not kept informed of the information available in Washington. A major difficulty appeared to lie in a Washington penchant for security. Brig. Gen. Sherman Miles, then Army chief of intelligence, testified that no distribution outside of Washington was made of decrypted Japanese diplomatic messages in order to protect the famed "Magic" system of cryptanalysis.[35] That is to say, a natural desire existed to safeguard the fact that Japanese diplomatic codes had been broken. The desire to protect Magic also contributed to General George C. Marshall's decision to alert Pearl Harbor through commercial telegraph rather than by telephone.[36] The result of this decision was that an RCA messenger (Japanese by birth) bearing General Marshall's message to the Pearl Harbor commander was on his two-cyclinder motor-bike covering his rounds when the bombing attack sent him scurrying for cover. He delivered the message around noon on December 7.[37]

Intelligence today is disseminated to decision makers and operators, through briefings, daily digests, and routine routing of summaries and estimates. Effort is made to maintain rapport between intelligence collection and analysis and

---

* For a fuller discussion of Pearl Harbor, see below, pp. 54–58.

policy making and operations. To this end, as we have seen, every meeting of the National Security Council during the Eisenhower Administration opens with a briefing by the Director of Central Intelligence, and this is likely to become a precedent. President Truman used to start each work day with a briefing by the Director,[38] who gave the Chief Executive a daily digest of the most important and up-to-date intelligence. And presumably all theater and area commanders and important United States officials overseas are kept up-to-date on national intelligence. Dissemination of national intelligence estimates now is made even to major party presidential and vice-presidential candidates, following precedent established in the Eisenhower-Stevenson campaign of 1952.

The present popular currency of intelligence is illustrated by the following exchange between a Congressman and the Secretary of the Air Force in 1957:

Mr. Whitten. . . . Where do you get your figures on what Russia has? How are they fed up to you? I know with your multitude of duties you cannot bring them together. . . .

Secretary Quarles. . . . I get almost daily reports from our own Air Intelligence Office in the form of brief digests of information they have acquired or the intelligence community has acquired during the previous day. Then, of course, I see the Intelligence Digests and what we call the National Intelligence Estimates which are prepared by the whole intelligence community working as a team under the Chairmanship of the Director of the Central Intelligence Agency. . . .

Mr. Whitten. . . . do you, as Secretary, on occasion submit requests for specific information or things of that sort?

Secretary Quarles. Yes. I have done so. For example, we came to the view a year or a year and a half ago that our intelligence on guided missile work in Russia required a much more thorough study made of it. . . . a very comprehensive report was prepared. Now you should qualify these reports this way. They bring together bits of information of very many different kinds and from very many different sources. Then they compile the best educated guess of what the evidence shows has been done or what capability they give the Soviets for doing things. Capability for doing things is, of course, different from a demonstration that they will do it or conclusion that they will do it. But, generally speaking, we take the view that we should, if possible, be prepared to meet what they are capable of presenting to us. That is, in a sense, the philosophy of these reports.[39]

This exchange between a Congressman and an armed service Secretary reveals the currency if not the credibility of intelligence reports in the policy-making and administrative process. Intelligence estimates theoretically play a major role in determining the allocation of national resources to contend with the capabilities and probable intentions of potential enemies. In practice, the estimate is sometimes inadequate, or even more often, accurate, but disregarded. The importance of the estimate, whatever its reception, makes clear the necessity that every step in the intelligence process be performed with utmost skill and efficiency. It also suggests the need for a rationally designed organization for effective conduct of the process. Today's organization for intelligence is based in part upon modern strategic intelligence doctrines. But this structure also inevitably is influenced by intellectual traditions and by the historical development of the intelligence function.

UNITED STATES INTELLIGENCE
— Historical Background

On the eve of World War II, the United States intelligence system was highly compartmented, largely unco-ordinated, and almost starved for funds. There was no central intelligence. In previous wars the armed services had greatly expanded intelligence staffs, relying heavily upon civilian specialists, and at the war's end returned to a general neglect of the intelligence function. Prior to World War II, according to General George C. Marshall, our foreign intelligence was "little more than what a military attaché could learn at a dinner, more or less, over the coffee cups." [1]

Even though neglected as an important function of government by the United States, the concept of intelligence and of its importance to the strategy of any operation, civil or military, is as old as society itself.

Intelligence: An Ancient Function

The Bible records that Moses was instructed to send what in effect were intelligence agents "to spy out the land of Canaan." [2] In the sixth century, B.C., Sun Tzu, a Chinese military theorist wrote, in *On the Art of War*, ". . . what enables the wise sovereign and the good general to strike and conquer and achieve things beyond the reach of ordinary men, is foreknoweldge."

45

In the Mongol invasion of Europe during the thirteenth century, Subotai, a disciple of Genghis Khan, utilized the well-organized intelligence system of the Mongols in his spectacular advances westward. As one authority has noted, "Whereas Europe knew nothing about the Mongols, the latter were fully acquainted with European conditions, down to every detail, not excepting the family connexions of the rulers." [3] The pattern of history suggests that aggressive, expansionist organizations have the best-organized intelligence systems. Foreknowledge is indeed essential to those who would seize the initiative in international affairs. It has been of equal importance to nations on the defensive, but has been somewhat more neglected by them.

The literature on intelligence is filled as much with complaints of its failures as with its successful exploits. This is exemplified in the words which Shakespeare put into the mouth of King John: "O, where hath our intelligence been drunk? Where hath it slept?" With reference to King John's plaintive query, one observer has commented, "knowing the two classic methods of Intelligence, he might well ask!" [4]

If spying is indeed an ancient activity, the "classic methods," as suggested in the previous chapter, have become less and less useful, although by no means completely abandoned. Intelligence has become a more scientific enterprise. And as government bureaucracies have become more tightly organized and presumably more honorable, there is less information for sale to spies than in earlier times. The task of the intelligence agent has become increasingly difficult over the centuries. Spies themselves are perhaps a shade more reliable than in medieval days, when a Bavarian Duke instructed his son in 1428, on the eve of a military expedition: "Whosoever wants to wage war well, must look out for good intelligence, much of it, and of various kind; but you must not trust them [the spies] and not tell them what you intend to do on the strength of their findings." This was to suggest, perhaps wisely, that one's own spy in those times might with sufficient information easily become the opponent's spy.[5] The development of a professional corps of American "spies" with what amounts to civil service status in the mid-twentieth century tends to eliminate this hazard. Yet the purveyors of secret information will perhaps always remain suspect. Even the "gentlemen spies" are not true gentlemen; the "double agent" is still known to exist.

Library shelves bulge with memoirs and accounts, often a mixture of fact and fiction, of the activities of spies and counter-spies over past centuries, particularly dealing with wartime exploits. Yet as a function of government, the gathering of foreign intelligence in the eighteenth and nineteenth centuries tended to be haphazard, with professional diplomats going one way (tending with some notable exceptions to shun spying) and military general staffs another (tending to give little attention to the diplomatic consequences of the work of commissioned spies). The conflict between diplomacy and espionage has continued to this day.[6]

One major exception, among others, to the haphazardness of national intelligence systems in early times was the intelligence apparatus maintained in the reign of Queen Elizabeth in sixteenth-century England.

The Elizabethan intelligence system was the highly personalized domain of the Queen's principal State Secretary, Sir Francis Walsingham. He developed to a high degree the art of foreign intelligence, utilizing his personal fortune as well as official financial provisions to maintain several score agents in foreign lands. Walsingham's motto was "Knowledge is never too dear," and he concerned himself not only with his spy network but with the codes and ciphers by which vital information was secretly communicated. As one authority has put it, "Under Francis Walsingham, no power in Europe, not even the secretive Venetians, had a more efficient system of security and counter-espionage, such that 'not a mouse could creep out of any ambassador's chamber but Mr. Secretary [Walsingham] would have one of his whiskers.' " [7]

The creation of an institutionalized and systematically organized intelligence service in modern times is widely credited to Frederick the Great. Under him, and with the later assistance of Wilhelm Stieber, the Prussians carefully developed an intelligence system as a vital general staff function. It was operating with some efficiency and on a widespread basis in the late nineteenth century. Similar intelligence services were developed by other European nations, patterned on the Prussian military model. Late in the nineteenth century, Europe had become a vast network of spies and counter-spies. Few hotels, restaurants, and other places of recreation in major European cities did not have secret agents operating in disguise. As Roger Hilsman has written, ". . . the whole continent began to look like the stage of a comic opera with hundreds of secret agents dodging in and out of the scenery as they played the lucrative and, in peacetime, not-too-dangerous game of spy and counter-spy." [8]

Such activities were apparently deemed necessary to support a general staff system. Also, an accelerating military technology and the competitive war plans of Continental powers required an increasing amount of information. As Walter Millis has pointed out, some of the information which Captain Dreyfus was wrongfully accused of transmitting to the Germans was technological, dealing with the design of a new artillery recoil mechanism; another item pertained to

France's War Plan XIII being developed by the French general staff. As in the case of the Prussians, all the great powers began to develop elaborate intelligence systems.

American Neglect of Intelligence

The United States, on the other hand, pursuing a more aloof and independent foreign policy, relied chiefly upon its diplomatic agencies and military attaché system for the collection of whatever information seemed necessary from foreign nations. One example is the fact that the United States Consul General in Havana in 1897–98, General Fitzhugh Lee, was praised by the captain of the Battleship *Maine* for his helpful "spying" activity.[9] It was through such open channels that most information was obtained, but there was no organization for co-ordination of separate information collected by the War, Navy, and State Departments.

According to its own official history, the United States Army was "slow to recognize the importance of military intelligence and backward in its use in the solution of military problems."[10]

During the Civil War, Allan Pinkerton, a famous detective, was hired as chief of intelligence for General McClellan's Union Army. Pinkerton (using the *nom de guerre* of "Maj. E. J. Allen") and his agents were adept at ensnaring bank robbers and railway bandits, but possessed little competence in military intelligence. Consequently it is now known that his estimates of Confederate troop strength were greatly exaggerated, a fact which bolstered the excessive caution with which McClellan planned his Peninsula campaign. Pinkerton was later replaced by a more experienced intelligence officer, Col. Lafayette C. Baker.[11] Although the Confederacy supported many spies and counter-spies, its intelligence service was even less well organized and more poorly co-ordinated than that of the Union. The point is that military men experienced in strategic intelligence were almost nonexistent at this stage of the nation's history, although the concept of intelligence was age-old, and although organizations, such as the Cavalry, often performed a combat intelligence function.

When the United States became involved in World War I, Army intelligence was a tiny section buried within a division of the General Staff, consisting of only two officers and two clerks.[12] With reorganizations, the Military Intelligence Division had grown into a staff of over 1,200 officers and civilians at the time of the armistice. Its duties, however, ranged widely, including internal security and censorship. By the war's end, the government was indeed intelligence-conscious, and twenty officer-specialists of Army intelligence accompanied President Wilson to the post-war Peace Conference.[13]

The Military Intelligence Division of the General Staff evolved from the Bureau of Information in the Adjutant General's office. The duties of the Division, as assigned in August 1918, were ". . . to maintain estimates revised daily of the military situation, the economic situation, and of such other matters as the Chief of Staff may direct, and to collect, collate and disseminate military intelligence." [14] Collection of information remained the responsibility of the military attachés. A year after the war's end, 88 officers and 143 civilians were employed in the Military Intelligence Division of the Army.[15] This number was rapidly cut back in the subsequent years of international retrenchment and isolation.

Intelligence clearly was neglected in the decades between the two world wars. But concepts of the proper function of intelligence were not wanting. Writing in 1920 a brigadier general who headed American wartime Army intelligence,

Marlborough Churchill, expressed the fundamental concept: "National strategy," he wrote, "must be based upon national policy. It is obvious that national policy must depend upon correct predictions concerning the international future, and that, after the national policy and strategy have been determined upon, war plans can never be satisfactory unless they are based on correct detailed information." [16] But such a concept of intelligence was not adopted and vigorously pursued. Both Army and Navy intelligence hobbled along in the 1920's and 1930's, rarely attracting the most promising officers and receiving only meager Congressional appropriations. Many Congressmen tended to look upon the military or naval attaché as an officer being sent on a luxurious vacation at the expense of, and with no benefit to, the American taxpayer. Some veteran Congressmen, perhaps habitually, today still closely question military budget requests supporting the attaché system.

Intelligence and World War II

In the War Department this situation as America entered World War II was, in the words of General Eisenhower "a shocking deficiency that impeded all constructive planning. . . ." [17] A basic requirement for the needed intelligence, a "far-flung organization of fact finders" was nonexistent. General Eisenhower further comments:

Our own feeble gesture in this direction was the maintenance of military attachés in most foreign capitals, and since public funds were not available to meet the unusual expenses of this type of duty, only officers with independent means could normally be detailed to these posts. Usually they were estimable, socially acceptable gentlemen; few knew the essentials of Intelligence work. Results were almost completely negative and the situation was not helped by the custom of making long service as a military attaché, rather than ability, the essential qualification for appointment as head of the Intelligence Division in the War Department.[18]

One consequence was the rather low esteem in which many commanders held military intelligence.* Sir John Slessor, one-time R.A.F. chief, recounts an illustrative incident at the time of the allied planning for the invasion of North Africa. Intelligence estimates were, of course, an important consideration in the formation of such plans. Expert advice was required concerning the location of the enemy, his strength, and his likely reaction to alternate situations. This was the job of the intelligence staff. But, as Slessor recalls, some of the American officers on this joint planning effort "tended to take a robustly independent line in these matters — 'to hell with the G2 guys — I don't give a damn what they say — that is what he'll [the enemy] do.'" As consequence of this attitude, General Eisenhower found it necessary to issue an order that official intelligence estimates were to be accepted for planning.[19]

The Department of State, inherently a prime collector and user of intelligence, also was poorly equipped to produce or cope with the volume and types of information required *circa* 1941. Dean Acheson, when Under Secretary of State, testified to Congress in 1945 that until World War II, the Department of State's "technique of gathering information differed only by reason of the typewriter and telegraph from the techniques which John Quincy Adams was using in St. Petersburg and Benjamin Franklin was using in Paris."[20] In 1909, the Department of State had only four persons whose function was classified as Intelligence. By 1922, this figure had

---

* Perhaps some commanders were persuaded by the dictum of Clausewitz that most of the information obtained in war is contradictory, false, or of doubtful validity.

risen to a grand total of five, and by 1943, to no more than eighteen. In any one of these periods, of course, the great majority of State Department personnel were working in intelligence, broadly construed.

It is commonplace to blame Congress and its inadequate appropriations for the sorry state of American strategic intelligence in the years between the two World Wars. But the crux of the problem was the lack of recognition, within the State and War and Navy Departments, of the importance in peacetime of co-ordinated foreign intelligence. A more fundamental cause of intelligence neglect, of course, was the temper of the times — a period of isolation from world affairs, of governmental retrenchment, of America viewing itself as the world's moral bastion, and of a military policy of passive defense, centered in the Western Hemisphere. Whatever the reasons, Congress in the 1920's normally appropriated less than $200,000 annually for Army intelligence. Compare this with the Army's 1958 budget request for $125,000,000 for intelligence.

A similar situation existed in the Navy. The Office of Naval Intelligence had in 1934 a permanent civilian force of only twenty persons, and only two officers and a clerk were assigned to twenty countries of Latin America.[21] In fiscal years 1934 and 1936 Congress expressly forbade the Army to maintain more than thirty-two military attachés.[22]

Comparing British and American military intelligence talent early in World War II, General Omar Bradley has stated "the British easily outstripped their American colleagues."[23] Worse than that, commented General Bradley, misfits were sometimes assigned to intelligence. Recall also the "Old Man's" advice to the young commander Melville Goodwin in Marquand's fiction: "Put the prima donnas in Intelligence, but keep them out of Operations."[24]

In some segments of the military organization, the intelligence section became a dumping ground for officers unsuited for regular command assignments. This reveals much about the professional military attitudes in the past regarding an intelligence career. As General Bradley and others have recounted, the day was saved in wartime by the incorporation into intelligence units of numerous civilians with special knowledge or talents. The Navy, with its predilection for general line (i.e., sea duty) officers, similarly was a discouraging place for able officers to pursue an intelligence career.

The Impetus of Pearl Harbor

When a message that Pearl Harbor was under attack by Japanese planes reached Secretary of the Navy Frank Knox in Washington on Sunday afternoon, December 7, 1941, he exclaimed "My God, this can't be true. This [message] must mean the Philippines!" The Navy Secretary's reaction may seem to symbolize the failure of strategic intelligence as America was plunged into World War II. But the point is not so much that intelligence was not available, as it is that to political and military officials even in possession of suggestive intelligence the attack was inconceivable. Pearl Harbor is an intelligence lesson burned into the minds of planners of national strategy, general staffs, and responsible commanders in the field.

Pearl Harbor provided the stimulus for the development of a centralized intelligence community and a revitalization during and after the war of military intelligence personnel and the intelligence process. There is no need to review here the events leading up to Pearl Harbor nor to describe the attack itself. This has been done in 25,000 pages of official transcript of testimony and reports and in numerous books. The reams of official testimony were produced by seven separate official inquiries and a post-war Congressional investigation which itself turned out 39 volumes (15,000 pages) of hearings and a 573-page report.[25]

Some of the conclusions from this mass of testimony and reports will always be debated, but one fact is indisputable — the Japanese achieved complete surprise in the attack.[26] If intelligence is, as previously stated, foreknowledge, Pearl Harbor was, then, a complete intelligence failure. It was a top-to-bottom failure of the intelligence system — or lack of system. But it was particularly a failure in intelligence communication and receptivity.

At the top, the commanders — civilian and military — failed to utilize efficiently the intelligence available.[27] At the bottom it will be recalled that the United States Navy's destroyer *Ward* detected at 3:50 a.m., December 7, and sank at 6:45 a.m. a submerged submarine in a forbidden zone near the Pearl Harbor entrance. But the *Ward's* reports were virtually ignored. It is an often told tale, also, that a cloud of planes, the first Japanese attack force, was detected by an Army mobile radar unit at 7:02 a.m. as they approached from the north. Such warnings again fell on unbelieving ears and were shrugged off.

Granting that an aggressive nation has an incentive for having the best possible intelligence, the Pearl Harbor raid nonetheless was for the Japanese in one sense a brilliant success. In the long run the raid may have been, as carried out, strategically unwise, tactically incompetent, and politically disastrous. Indeed there were better strategic targets at Pearl than the ships. Permanent installations and oil tanks strangely went unscathed. The Japanese made no attempt to knock out the two Pacific Fleet aircraft carriers, which were at sea. In concentrating on Battleship Row scant attention was paid to cruisers and destroyers. In retrospect it is clear that from the viewpoint of long-range strategy, the choice of targets at Pearl was unwise. As more than one observer of military affairs has remarked, "The loss of our battleships at Pearl Harbor advanced U.S. naval warfare by a good ten years!"

But the Japanese did choose the battleships. And of the 94 vessels of the United States Navy situated in the harbor, Japanese pilots clearly knew what they wanted and where to find them. The Japanese were well briefed not only about ship locations, but about the Sunday morning habits, and week-end liberty tradition of the American Navy. With complete surprise, the Japanese hit their chosen targets.

The voluminous testimony and commentary available on the Pearl Harbor episode indicate that the not inconsiderable suggestive intelligence available prior to the Japanese attack was simply not believed. The imminence of war was widely felt, but both Japan's capabilities *and* intentions were wrongly assessed. In the minds of many responsible leaders, Hawaii was thought to be too far distant from Japan; the Japanese Navy technically incapable of launching such an attack; Japanese military aviation insufficiently skilled for such an action; and the risks of failure were believed to be too great for Japanese war-making strategists.

The basic intelligence problem, then, as now, was only in part a matter of sufficient information. What mattered most were the pictures in the minds of responsible decision makers. The Secretary of the Navy's exclamation "this can't be true" suggests the root of the matter.

With the clairvoyance of hindsight it is always easy to be an armchair intelligence expert. Yet the intelligence lessons of Pearl Harbor are painfully clear, and the post-war development of a centralized intelligence community reflects some of these lessons. Few question the necessity today of having a centralized system which guarantees, in theory at least, that properly evaluated and co-ordinated and timely information is brought to the attention of all responsible officials. The concept of an intelligence system which serves — to use Henry L. Stimson's phrase — as a "sentinel on duty" at all times is now unanimously accepted in official Washington.

Recognition of this concept, however, has not solved all the problems of intelligence. For the warning function, it will be recalled, is only one of our intelligence requirements and there remain questions of doctrine, organization, and personnel. These are all involved in facing the problem of balancing enemy capabilities with enemy intentions. In December 1941 few believed that Japan had a *capability* for the Pearl Harbor attack. They had it. But even fewer, if any, concluded that Japan had the *intention* of such an attack. The problem then, as now, is a tendency to create policy and plan actions based upon what potential enemies will probably do (what we would do if we were they) rather than adequately assessing everything they *can* do. The fusing of capability and intention will always create a dilemma and will suggest the limitations of any intelligence system. Yet it was clear that a better apparatus was required for intelligence assessments of such problems than existed in 1941. During the war and in the post-war period, particularly, a beginning was made in applying the intelligence lessons of Pearl Harbor.

In the words of the 1955 Hoover Commission, "The CIA may well attribute its existence to the surprise attack on Pearl Harbor and to the postwar investigation into the part Intelligence or lack of Intelligence played in the failure of our military forces to receive adequate and prompt warning of the impending Japanese attack." [28]

With the clairvoyance gained from a dozen intervening years, the Hoover Commission task force in 1955 concluded what others have concluded about the Pearl Harbor experience: namely, that information necessary to anticipate the attack was available to government agencies but that the breakdown came in its evaluation and dissemination. Thus appropriate decisions were left unmade and timely instructions were not given to responsible commanders in the field.

Analysts of the Pearl Harbor episode have cited the lack of a high-level joint intelligence group and the absence of a high echelon organization for national estimates and an indications center. The latter deficiency was painfully evident on December 6, 1941, when raw intelligence reports — the intercepts in "Magic" (the broken Japanese code) of the Japanese ultimatum — were read but neither properly evaluated nor acted upon. As previously suggested, there was no joint intelligence group or Intelligence Advisory Committee to evaluate, analyze, synthesize, and promptly disseminate the available information. There was no "Watch Committee" or National Indications Center such as exists today, with trained sentinel eyes perpetually scanning the globe. Nor did a National Security Council exist to act in concert upon the basis of information known to some, but not all, high officials.[29]

The Beginnings of Central Intelligence

Five months before the Japanese attack, President Roosevelt had in fact moved to correct obvious national intelligence deficiencies. The President summoned Colonel (later Major-General) William J. Donovan to draft a plan for a new intelligence service designed for the requirements of global war. "You will have to begin with nothing," he told Donovan. "We have no intelligence service."[30]

Colonel Donovan was soon appointed as Coordinator of Information, with instructions to collect and analyze all strategic intelligence information and data and to furnish the results to the President and other interested agencies.[31] Amidst a maze of red tape, Donovan was attempting to organize and to ascertain the precise mission of his new agency when war came. There is a widely told, perhaps apocryphal, story that strategic intelligence activities were considerably delayed on the eve of war because of an inability to find office space for new intelligence agencies.

Joint Intelligence: The Wartime Organization

With the formation of the Joint Chiefs of Staff in February 1942, it quickly became apparent that co-ordinated intelligence was needed in order that the Joint Staff might function effectively. Plans for combined interservice and interallied military operations necessitated the formation of a Joint Intelligence Committee as an agency of the Joint Chiefs of Staff. Members of the JIC included representatives of the Office of Naval Intelligence, Military Intelligence Service (Army), Assistant Chief of Air Staff (Intelligence), Department of State, Office of Strategic Services (OSS), and the Foreign Economic Administration. This committee was the wartime *ad hoc* answer to the need for centralized intelligence, although most intelligence operations were performed by its constituent members. The Joint Intelligence Committee's role was to synthesize intelligence received from all sources for use by the Joint Staff and Joint Chiefs. Much of its work in co-ordinating intelligence activities was carried on by specialized subcommittees. These included: Technical Industrial Intelligence, Topographical Studies, Joint Studies Publication, Archives, Weekly Summary Editorial Board, and Publications Review.

Under stimulus of the Joint Intelligence Committee, a government-wide effort was made to co-ordinate the strategic intelligence system in the field and in Washington. Joint Intelligence collection agencies, staffed from Army and Navy intelligence offices and with a heavy influx of civilian specialists in various fields, were set up in military theaters of operation. Their functions were to co-ordinate intelligence collection and dissemination, and to maintain effective liaison with the field and with a Joint Intelligence Agency Reception Center in Washington. Such joint collection groups were established in the Mediterranean, Africa-Middle East, India-Burma, and China theaters of operation. A more effective integration and dissemination of the resulting joint intelligence product was effected in 1943 when publication was started of the Joint Army-Navy Intelligence Studies (commonly referred to as the JANIS series), which were encyclopedic volumes covering a vast field of intelligence on enemy capabilities, targets, terrain, and other factors.[32]

Jointly and individually the wartime intelligence services, amidst some confusion, duplication, and much interagency conflict, sometimes measured up to the high standards set by the combat forces in the field. Some notable successes were the Navy's communications intelligence code-breaking performance at Midway Island, which led to the location and ultimate defeat of the Japanese Imperial Navy's carrier force; the thorough and skillfully executed deception plan before the Allied invasion of Normandy in June 1944, which kept German defense disastrously off balance; the generally excellent beach studies developed for the Pacific campaign; the identification of the German guided missile development center at Peenemunde; and the achievements of OSS described below. A notable individual performance also was given by Allen W. Dulles, who later became Director of Central Intelligence in 1953. Operating from Bern, Switzerland, in the period 1942–1945, he built up a combined political action and intelligence network employing hundreds of informants and operatives reaching into Germany, Hungary, Yugoslavia, Czechoslovakia, Bulgaria, Spain, Portugal, and North Africa.[33]

But there were perhaps an equal number of intelligence breakdowns during the war. Combat intelligence erred disastrously at the Battle of Savo Island (an Australian Air Force observer failed to inform the Navy that Japanese cruisers were approaching) and at the Battle of the Bulge — the German surprise offensive in the winter of 1944 in the Ardennes area. Some strategic intelligence analysts are said to have overestimated the strength of the Japanese Manchurian forces, which aided the "get Russia into the war" advocates. German ability to recuperate from Allied bombings of its industrial centers was underestimated.[34] In many cases, however, intelligence was blamed for what in fact may have been blunders or failures of judgment by military commanders in the field or by policy makers in Washington or London.[35]

Intelligence supporters, using hindsight, claim that some Office of Naval Intelligence and Air Forces intelligence estimates suggested to the Pentagon and the White House early in 1945 that Japan, with her fleet and air force virtually immobilized for lack of oil, could not long survive. The fact seems to be that there was no system for developing truly national composite estimates. Decision makers accordingly listened to some intelligence experts while turning a deaf ear to others and finally decided that Russia be brought into the war with Japan, a large-scale invasion planned, and atomic bombs dropped at Hiroshima and Nagasaki. A majority of intelligence experts apparently believed that naval blockade and bombing could not alone produce unconditional surrender prior to the date set for invasion (March 1, 1946).[36] But the point is that a system for a truly composite intelligence estimate did not exist.

Office of Strategic Services

The government's closest approach to a central intelligence system during World War II was the widely publicized, now almost legendary, Office of Strategic Services. At least two legends are attached to OSS. One, to which its detractors adhere, pictures it as a catch-all group of scholars, socialites, Wall Street operators, and adventurers, recruited to perform a variety of roles under the vague rubric, "strategic intelligence." This legend suggests, without distinction among its various separate functions, that OSS generated more romantic activity than hard intelligence product useful for strategic or operational decision.

The other legend, perhaps the more accurate, portrays OSS as giving the United States, with its new world leadership responsibility, invaluable experience in meeting the variety of problems involved in operating a modern central intelligence system. In spite of its fumbles and the inevitable confusion surrounding any new Washington agency in the wartime emergency, OSS, according to this legend, offered a constructive experience for a nation with little prior experience in the various functions which ended up within the OSS jurisdiction.

It is difficult to paint an accurate picture or make an objective evaluation of OSS because its official history remains unpublished and because most of the sources on its multifarious activities are ephemeral, contradictory, or under security classification. Also, there were many sides to OSS, from pure research to the wildest kind of secret operation. It seems clear, however, that the most publicized of the operations of OSS — of the "cloak and dagger" type — produced in many ways the least significant long-range results. And perhaps the melodramatic publicity given to the activities of OSS secret agents in World War II is largely responsible for many of the prevailing myths about the nature of central intelligence.

The popular heroes of the wartime OSS — those who play the major roles in motion pictures and in television scripts about OSS — are the secret agents who worked behind enemy lines or the secret operatives whose function was essentially counter-espionage. But the most significant work was done by those unheralded college professors, lawyers, and others who worked tirelessly in the research units, in the analysis of economic objectives, and in other operational analysis and technical groups within OSS. These groups contributed much data on which successful wartime operations were based, and developed techniques useful to contemporary intelligence research and analysis.

This is not to suggest that the often heroic overseas espionage and political action work of OSS agents was not of incalculable value to a nation naïve in such activity. The point is that the popular tendency to identify cloak-and-dagger activity as the principal and most important role of a central intelligence system has distorted the public picture of the nature of intelligence.

When the Joint Chiefs of Staff assumed responsibility, after its formation in 1942, for co-ordinating military intelligence, a function performed by the Joint Staff and various JCS committees, Colonel Donovan abandoned further serious attempts to operate, as under his original mandate, an over-all government intelligence co-ordinating agency. His

Office of Coordinator of Information soon was transformed into the OSS, a combined research, foreign espionage, and special operations agency. With the creation of OSS early in the war, the United States became engaged for the first time in intensive strategic intelligence research and extensive espionage and political action operations on a world-wide scale. OSS was the by-product of total war. Its purpose varied from the gathering, evaluating, and synthesizing of information about the capabilities and vulnerabilities of enemy nations, to the conduct of a wide variety of destructive operations behind enemy lines.

Colonel Donovan's OSS blossomed and spread throughout Washington and the world in something of a Gilbert and Sullivan manner. By war's end some 12,000 OSS workers were engaged in every kind of work believed to be strategically important. OSS personnel comprised a hodge-podge of Americans believed to have some talent for the frontierless game of strategic intelligence and special operations. OSS was, in fact, an assemblage of college professors and Hollywood stunt men, Wall Street bankers and Chicago bartenders, football players and missionaries. "There were men who did careful scholarly work; men who did sensationally dangerous work; and men who did absolutely nothing except travel around the world on a high priority at government expense." [37] An indication of the scope of OSS activity is seen in its budget estimate for the fiscal year 1945: fifty-seven million dollars.

Undeniably, OSS bore the imprint of Colonel Donovan's energy and imagination. He has been described as "a mobile unit of the first magnitude"; with the power to "visualize an oak when he saw an acorn"; a man who traveled fast, hatching new schemes at each stop, and surprising no one if he, in effect, "left one morning and returned the previous afternoon." [38] This explains in part the fact that OSS engaged in the widest variety of enterprises, calling for more different skills and personalities than any other American government organization previously existing.

The OSS performed these many functions while ostensibly serving the Joint Chiefs of Staff in collecting and analyzing strategic intelligence and implementing specific special operations related to Allied objectives in the war. To perform one of its major if less publicized functions, OSS built up an extensive, and in large part effective, research and analysis branch in Washington. This unit worked to supply policy makers and operators with essential facts and intelligence estimates.

The nucleus of OSS leadership was Colonel Donovan and his administrative assistants drawn largely from New York City law firms and financial institutions, and the so-called group of "100 professors" recruited early in the short life of OSS. The academicians brought the research techniques of scholars to bear upon the wartime requirement for strategic information. The roster of academic personnel who served OSS is long and distinguished. Their product was in many instances outstanding and the techniques of analysis they developed valuable to the post-war intelligence system.

But, as previously suggested, OSS became more widely known for its special operations, a term covering espionage, counter-intelligence in foreign nations, sabotage, commando raids, guerrilla and partisan-group activity — in conjunction with such as the French *maquis*, Italian anti-fascists, anti-Nazis within Germany, *Kachins* in Burma — and in various other forms of psychological warfare and underground operations. In essence, OSS assumed operational responsibility in a field previously ignored and scorned by many diplomats and military professionals.

Since no official report on the wartime activities of the Office of Strategic Services has been published,[39] opinions on the effectiveness of its special operations in specific areas have varied and the evidence is sketchy. OSS work was of prime importance in the invasion of North Africa. In Europe and the Middle East, OSS agents seem to have generally held the confidence of theater commanders to whom they were responsible. General Alexander M. Patch, commander of the U.S. Seventh Army, is said to have obtained from OSS agents some 60 per cent of the intelligence used for planning the invasion, with only a small force, of Southern France. General Eisenhower later applauded the close co-ordination between resistance groups and field operations.[40] In the Far East, with the exception of Burma, the quality of the agency's operations was more questionable and apparently OSS activity was less successful. General Douglas MacArthur reportedly added to its difficulties in this area by placing stringent restrictions and controls upon OSS agents in his theater.[41] The OSS was also banned from operations in South America, a jealously guarded jurisdiction of the Federal Bureau of Investigation's Special Intelligence Service (described below).

"Much balderdash has been written about the 'brilliance' of the work of OSS," writes Hanson W. Baldwin with reference to its special operations, "some of it was brilliant — particularly in Switzerland and some of the work in China and Southeast Asia — but much of it was inefficient, some of it was stupid, and for a considerable part of the war, we were dependent upon the British for much of our secret information." [42]

Neither the Joint Intelligence Committee, on which OSS was represented, nor Colonel Donovan's Office of Strategic Services functioned to provide the projected single integrated intelligence clearinghouse so badly needed during the war. Much intelligence confusion prevailed in Washington, as a dozen or so agencies conceived of intelligence as one of their jobs. Baldwin, among others, attributes the confusion and administrative bickering to the "opposition of the old-line agencies," apparently referring to resentment or jealousy of OSS by War, Navy, and State Departments.[43] Among those affected by the lack of unified, centralized American intelligence estimates during the war were our Allies, who were befuddled by a myriad of very active United States intelligence agencies and operations and confused by the conflicting estimates turned up by various American agencies. This bustle of intelligence activity, according to Baldwin, not only promoted inefficiency, embarrassment, and confusion, but also gave "aid to the enemy." [44]

Yet there were important instances, in both the European and Pacific theaters of the war, in which OSS gave anything but comfort to the enemy. One friendly observer of OSS has written: "On the whole the record is impressive. OSS contributed measurably toward victory and in some instances — as in the wangling of German surrender in North Italy — it was a decisive factor." [45]

Until a detailed objective history of OSS is published, it is possible to make only a general estimate of its value and significance to the evolution of a post-war central intelligence system.

The primary point to be made about the impact of OSS upon government intelligence is that it brought recognition that scholars and the best of scholarly techniques have a fundamental role in uncovering the facts required for national decision. In one sense OSS had, in this regard, the effect on national defense planning which the New Deal's acceptance of intellectuals in the 1930's had upon domestic government planning. The recruitment of hundreds of academicians to staff the various OSS units in Washington and in the field had both a direct and indirect impact. The direct effect was the realization, at least by some persons, that scholarly analysis in many cases could be more rewarding than espionage. The indirect effect was that OSS competition provoked all the armed service intelligence organizations — Army, Navy and Air Forces — to seek out the same kind of academic talent employed by OSS. The net result: vastly improved armed service intelligence organizations.

Since many alumni of OSS presumably today serve the intelligence community, either on a full-time basis or as consultants, the over-all intelligence experience gained in the four hectic wartime years remains highly valuable. A fundamental lesson, too, was learned by the fact that the government, in World War II, had to call upon individuals who essentially were amateurs in strategic intelligence. This produced the conviction that in the post-war central intelligence system, reliance would have to be placed upon intelligence agents who are prepared to make this work a professional career and not a casual hobby.

Invaluable experience also was gained through OSS in intelligence procedures and methods of operation. Techniques of collection, either secretly from within the boundaries of foreign nations, or overtly from systematic analysis of nonsecret data, were tried and tested during the short existence of OSS. Important lessons were learned in an environment which cannot be duplicated today in the Virginia countryside. The wartime experience also allowed the development and testing of techniques of evaluation of sources, interpretation of information, and synthesis of masses of data into an intelligence estimate useful to policy makers. And finally, the existence of half a dozen major intelligence agencies during the war provided a laboratory for experiments in one of the most difficult of all problems — one which was, and remains, acute — the co-ordination of government-wide intelligence effort.

The World War II operations of OSS also provided rewarding experience in the more technical aspects of central intelligence. The strategic requirement for the right kind of maps of areas around the globe resulted in the establishment of an OSS Map Division, which produced thousands of essential maps in the period 1942–1945. Winston Churchill is said to have preferred OSS maps to all others during the war. At the Quebec Conference, the British Prime Minister reportedly called President Roosevelt to his room and pointing to OSS maps on the wall, said, "See, I've got them, too." At any rate, the contemporary, large-scale mapping program of the government rests in part upon the foundation hastily constructed by the OSS during the wartime emergency. Another technical field in which wartime OSS experience was of benefit was in the planning of strategic bombing targets. An OSS Economic Objectives Unit, stationed in London, and working closely with Army Air Forces operations analysts and British intelligence specialists, helped to work out optimum maturity targets for the selective bombing of ball-bearing, oil production, fighter-plane and other vital facilities within the Nazi realm. The contemporary Strategic Air Command target systems, so important to American retaliatory capability, owe much to the achievements, and mistakes, of OSS personnel in World War II. Still another technical field in which wartime experience contributed much was the always difficult communicating of secret information, and the monitoring of secret messages of foreign nations. An elaborate world-wide radio network was operated by OSS during the war, contributing valuable know-how for this specialized function.

Recognizing suddenly the need for thousands of intelligence agents as the war began, the United States was faced with the problem of recruitment and training. Although, as previously suggested, recruitment for the over-all OSS was done in a somewhat haphazard fashion, a serious effort was undertaken to develop assessment and training techniques for candidates for overseas intelligence work. This was particularly true for those individuals selected for hazardous behind-the-lines missions in theaters of war. Psychiatrists and psychologists developed techniques for predicting the performance of intelligence agents in stressful situations. These assessment techniques provided the underpinning for some of the current intelligence personnel doctrine. This difficult task undertaken by OSS psychologists and psychiatrists of assessing the qualities of persons recruited by OSS and predicting their behavior on a variety of assignments is described in detail in *Assessment of Men.*

Finally the wartime OSS experience brought the United States face to face with the still difficult problem of inter-allied intelligence co-operation. No organizations of government are more security conscious than those concerned with intelligence. This innate characteristic of intelligence agents and agencies confronts allied governments with crucial problems in coalition wartime effort. As previously suggested, the wartime experience in inter-allied intelligence was anything but smooth, yet if nothing else, World War II acquainted the allies with the nature and magnitude of this problem, and the OSS experience, because of its multifarious inter-governmental activities, undoubtedly taught valuable lessons in how to cope with this continuing problem.* In sum, the American experience with OSS during the war,

---

* Indeed, although the collective security concept is a cornerstone of the Free World's defense system, inter-allied sharing of intelligence information remains, as of 1958, one of the more serious weaknesses of the alliance system.

aside from OSS' contribution to allied victory, resulted in a net gain for the United States in knowledge of some of the basic requisites for a central intelligence system. For the range covered by OSS — research and analysis, espionage, and overseas political action — is covered also by the intelligence community in the contemporary environment.

Post-war Reorganization

At the end of World War II, it was evident to those in the Executive Branch and in Congress that permanent changes were required in national intelligence organization. Wartime arrangements had been largely *ad hoc* and sometimes makeshift. In the words of former President Truman: "The war taught us this lesson — that we had to collect intelligence in a manner that would make the information available where it was needed and when it was wanted, in an intelligent and understandable form." [46]

When Mr. Truman became president in 1945, he was painfully aware of the imperfect co-ordination of national intelligence. No single official existed who was responsible at the White House level for national intelligence. No truly national intelligence, in fact, existed, at least by present-day standards. Reports would flow across the President's desk on the same subject at different times from various agencies. These intelligence reports often contradicted each other.[47] The result was that the President had to act as his own intelligence evaluator, or, out of frustration with conflicting estimates, simply had to play his own hunches.

President Truman apparently did not believe that the OSS at the war's end provided the answer to the problem of co-ordinating intelligence at the White House level. He ordered that the OSS be disbanded on October 1, 1945, apparently because of pressures from the armed services, the

FBI, the Department of State, and the Bureau of the Budget. Another influence was undoubtedly Mr. Truman's own apparent prejudice against cloak and dagger operations by the United States. To continue an international spying organization in peacetime seemed somehow un-American in the atmosphere of the immediate post-war period. The President, however, was not without advice as to how to establish a permanent central intelligence service.

Centralization vs. Confederation

William J. Donovan, for one, had devised a detailed plan for a post-war centralized intelligence agency as early as 1944 and submitted it to President Roosevelt. The Donovan plan was transmitted to the Joint Chiefs of Staff for review. There it came under the careful and critical scrutiny of the professional military officers. The Navy studied the Donovan plan with particular care and with considerable skepticism and concluded that while there was much intelligence duplication to be eliminated and much better co-ordination to be effected, the degree of merger of intelligence services proposed by Donovan was not desirable. Too much centralization was considered not feasible because, in the words of the Eberstadt Report, ". . . each of these [armed services and civilian] departments requires operating intelligence peculiar to itself." [48] The Navy's views on centralized intelligence were formulated largely by Rear Admiral Sidney W. Souers, then Deputy Director of Naval Intelligence. The Navy proposed, in fact, a "Central Intelligence Agency" to co-ordinate foreign intelligence activities and to synthesize "departmental intelligence on the strategic and national policy level." [49]

This position, which in effect called for a confederation rather than complete centralization of intelligence, gained the general concurrence of the Army. At the Department of State, Secretary James F. Byrnes reportedly maintained that his department should have predominant control over any national strategic intelligence agency.[50]

In the midst of the controversy over the degree of centralization of intelligence, the OSS was rapidly being dissolved. Its highly skilled Research and Analysis sections and its Presentation section (intelligence briefing and reports) were transferred to the Department of State. Espionage and other covert operations fell under the temporary jurisdiction of the Army, where they were largely held in limbo to await a more permanent policy and operational directive.

The proposals for tight centralization and unification of intelligence, symbolized by the Donovan plan, versus the federalization proposals embodied in the Navy's position were the basis for lively debate in the 1945–1947 period. The question of how best to organize the national intelligence function was one of the many battles of the Potomac which ran concurrently with World War II and continued during the two years immediately following. Shadowing the debates was a fear in some quarters that an institutionalization of the wartime roles of the OSS would in effect amount to the establishment of an American *Gestapo*. The armed services were concerned lest their intelligence services — grown to considerable size during the war — be swallowed up by a centralized agency out of touch with the needs of the separate armed forces. The armed services also feared the establishment of intelligence units which would be partially under their jurisdiction but would also have the power to report directly to a centralized agency. Intelligence or counter-intelligence which was not reported "through channels" was feared. In spite of such fears the larger realization existed that a centralized system was badly needed to produce a truly national intelligence product, an effective warning system, and agreed-upon national estimates.

The post-war dispute over organization for national intelligence was a major side issue of the great debate over defense "unification." Pressures for greater centralization of the national establishment collided with organization concepts which placed great value on the principle of federation and of decentralization.

A powerful naval figure's view on centralized intelligence in 1945 is recounted in the Forrestal diaries. In March 1945 Secretary of the Navy James Forrestal asked Admiral Ernest J. King for his views on a proposed single, centralized intelligence agency. King replied that while such an arrangement was perhaps logical, it had inherent dangers. He feared that a centralized intelligence agency might acquire power beyond anything intended, and questioned whether such an agency might not threaten our form of government.[51] This view coincided with the Navy's position strongly opposing the more extreme defense unification proposals being made during this period.

The armed services, particularly the Navy, argued effectively for only limited centralization and in the end the intelligence system which evolved was, like the national defense establishment, the product of a compromise between the competing organizational concepts — centralization *vs.* decentralization. And, as in the case of most such compromises, it left unsettled the issue of how much central direction and control was to be exercised by the central agency. Such an issue has continually surrounded the Office of the Secretary of Defense since 1947; similarly it has involved the role of the Director of Central Intelligence. In the latter case, however, less public debate has been heard on the issue.

The Compromise

The referee in the post-war organization disputes turned out to be the Bureau of the Budget, which had on its staff administrative analysts specializing in the problems of intelligence organization. On January 22, 1946, President Truman issued an Executive Order — the result of much work by the Budget Bureau [52] and other agencies — establishing the Central Intelligence Group. This new group, the forerunner of the present-day CIA, operated under an Executive Council — the National Intelligence Authority — composed of the secretaries of State, War, and Navy and the President's personal representative, who was Admiral William D. Leahy. Rear Admiral Sidney W. Souers was named first Director of Central Intelligence and he was succeeded six months later by Air Force General Hoyt S. Vandenberg. The Central Intelligence Group, representing a compromise of views held by the various governmental agencies concerned, started out primarily as a holding company co-ordinating the work of existing departments. It was authorized, however, to perform services which the National Intelligence Authority determined could best be performed centrally. As a national intelligence collation group, it rendered intelligence service to the President and his cabinet, as well as to the co-operating departments.

Under this new organization the President began, in 1946, to receive a unified daily digest and summary of important international intelligence. With an almost audible sigh of relief President Truman records in his *Memoirs:* "Here, at last, a co-ordinated method had been worked out, and a practical way had been found for keeping the President informed as to what was known and what was going on." [53]

Yet the intelligence millennium had not arrived, although President Truman rightly was pleased with the progress made. Centralized intelligence was soon more substantially established and organized under the National Security Act of 1947.*

---

* For a general blueprint, by Allen W. Dulles, for post-war central intelligence, see Appendix A.

Secretary of the Navy James V. Forrestal, who fought a hard and successful fight against the degree of defense unification advocated by many powerful persons in the 1945–1947 period, sounded a nearly unanimous note when he told a Congressional committee considering defense unification:

> We do need a central intelligence agency . . . we do need to have some machinery for collecting accurate information from the rest of the world, because . . . the speed, the tempo, and the fluidity of events in the world today very definitely require some central source here that is trying to evaluate those events for the various departments of government that are charged with our security.[54]

Both the National Intelligence Authority and the Central Intelligence Group were formally dissolved in the historic unification act, by which Congress created a National Security Council, a semi-unified defense establishment, and the Central Intelligence Agency (CIA). Significantly, however, the principle of federation prevailed over the concept of tight centralization in shaping the structure of the intelligence community.

IV

THE CENTRAL INTELLIGENCE AGENCY:
Basic Functions

In 1947 a Congressman sitting on a committee studying the National Security (Unification) bill put the question to an important witness: "I wonder if there is any foundation for the rumors that have come to me to the effect that through this Central Intelligence Agency, they are contemplating operational activities?" [1] In the ten years since its establishment, rumors have continued to circulate regarding the CIA's role. CIA operations have expanded with the years to wide dimensions, as have legends about its nature and functions. Observers returning from overseas continue to generate rumors about CIA's activities. What *are* CIA's functions today?

The main office building housing the Central Intelligence Agency headquarters in Washington in CIA's early years rather clumsily masqueraded behind a sign reading "Department of State Printing Office." In 1958 a modern government office building, capable of housing more than 10,000 persons and expected to cost in excess of $50,000,-000, was under construction in what was formerly Virginia countryside across the Potomac River from the nation's capital. This will be the closely guarded not-very-secret home of the CIA.

The Growing Intelligence Bureaucracy

In its first ten years of existence, the CIA sprawled all over

Washington, occupying some thirty-odd buildings. Like most Washington bureaucracies it spreads its tentacles out into the nation, maintaining more than a score of domestic offices, and also has encircled the globe, where directly or indirectly thousands of agents are on its payroll. The CIA has grown to such size in ten years that its total personnel probably approaches the total of employees of the Department of State. Obviously an agency of this size has more than "co-ordinating" functions.

When the CIA moves its headquarters within the next few years from the "Foggy Bottom" area of Washington out into the District of Columbia's suburbia this move can be counted as symbolic of CIA's growing status and prestige in the Washington community. Although its office wastebaskets will continue to be marked "Classified" and their contents carefully destroyed by security officers, and although carbon paper and typewriter ribbons used by CIA stenographers will be similarly protected, when the CIA takes up housekeeping in its new sparkling and expensive suburban home, the size and importance of this agency will become appreciably more evident.

Though CIA's size and importance in Washington's bureaucratic hierarchy will be evidenced by the shining new building in the Virginia countryside, one notes with some apprehension Parkinson's Law in this regard. Professor Parkinson has suggested, perhaps with as much validity as wit, that organizations tend to achieve architectural magnificence and comfort at a point when symptoms of decline or collapse begin to appear.[2] CIA officials would do well to ponder Parkinson's Law as they pack up their belongings to move from various temporary quarters into the new CIA building.

With all the secrecy surrounding its operations and personnel, the CIA performs functions prescribed generally by Congressional statute and specifically by National Security

Council directives, which are, in turn, interpreted in Director of Central Intelligence directives.

CIA was born of the National Security Act of 1947,[3] which assigned to it responsibility for co-ordinating, evaluating, and disseminating intelligence affecting the national security. Like most other sections of the National Security Act, the central intelligence section was the product of compromise. As previously suggested, the two poles of thought were a loose co-ordinating committee system on the one hand and a fully unified, monolithic intelligence organization on the other.

CIA's Statutory Functions

In the National Security Act, the CIA was given five specific functions, to be performed under the direction of the National Security Council. This somewhat unique status of CIA should be noted. It reports directly to the National Security Council, an advisory agency to the President, who chairs meetings of NSC. Statutory functions of CIA are as follows:

(1) To *advise the National Security Council* on intelligence matters of the government related to national security.

(2) To make recommendations to the National Security Council for *co-ordination of intelligence* activities of departments and agencies of government.

(3) To *correlate and evaluate* intelligence and provide for its appropriate dissemination within the government.

(4) To perform for the benefit of existing intelligence agencies such *additional services* as the NSC determines can be efficiently accomplished centrally.

(5) To perform *other functions* and duties relating to national security intelligence as the National Security Council may direct.

This is what often is called an *organic* act, in that the responsibilities and functions of the agency are defined only in a general way, with more precise assignment of functions left to Presidential and NSC directives.

There are, however, a number of significant *provisos* included in the act, to wit:

(1) The CIA shall have no police, subpoena, law-enforcement powers or internal security functions. Here Congress intended to allay the fears of some Americans that a *Gestapo* or *MVD* would be created in the guise of central intelligence, and, incidentally, perhaps to quiet any FBI concern over the presence of a rival in the internal security field.

(2) It is made especially clear that CIA should not supersede most departmental intelligence functions, for the act states that the several departments shall "continue to collect, evaluate, correlate and disseminate departmental intelligence."

(3) The 1947 Act further gives the Director of Central Intelligence, subject to Presidential and NSC recommendation and approval, the right to inspect the intelligence product of all government security agencies and specifies that these agencies will make their intelligence available to CIA for "correlation, evaluation and dissemination." One exception is the jealously guarded province of the FBI, the vast files of which may be approached only upon "written request."

The CIA is managed by a Director and Deputy Director, both appointed by the President, subject to confirmation by the United States Senate. Commissioned officers of the armed services, either in active or retired status, are eligible for appointment as Director or Deputy Director.* Allen W. Dulles became the first civilian to be named Director when

---

* The two positions, however, may not be occupied simultaneously by officers of the armed services.

appointed early in the first Eisenhower Administration (1953).

A revision of the CIA statute in 1949 by the Central Intelligence Agency Act [4] was designed to improve CIA administration by strengthening the powers of the Director. This new statute gave him virtually free rein to hire and fire personnel without regard for Civil Service regulations.

The 1949 Act exempts CIA from the provisions of any laws requiring publication or disclosure of the "organization, functions, names, official titles, salaries or numbers of personnel employed." The Bureau of the Budget is directed to make no reports to Congress on these matters.

Perhaps even more important, the Director of Central Intelligence can spend money from his multi-million dollar annual appropriations on his personal voucher. This is truly an extraordinary power for the head of an Executive agency with thousands of employees and annual expenditures in the hundreds of millions of dollars.[5]

CIA's Size and Role

It is popular sport for newspaper columnists and others to guess the size and annual expenditures of CIA. A reasonable estimate might put the number of Washington employees at 8,000 to 10,000, with some several thousand additional agents overseas or outside of Washington. Estimates of annual expenditures have been as high as two billions, but this would include all conceivable intelligence activities of the government. CIA direct expenditures probably amount to several hundred millions of dollars annually. The most tangible source for estimating the number of CIA's Washington personnel is the new office building under construction with a theoretical capacity estimated to be at least 10,000 persons.[6]

The general Congressional mandate to the CIA is that it

co-ordinate, evaluate, and disseminate intelligence affecting the national security. But there is also an even broader grant of authority in the assignment to it of "additional services" and "other functions" as the National Security Council may direct. Under these broad grants of authority and the specific administrative latitude given the Director of Central Intelligence in other statutes, the CIA, operating under NSC directives, has expanded into a mammoth governmental institution over the past decade.

The CIA has become at once a central governing authority, a co-ordinator of strategic information, and a correlator of data gathered not only by its own far-flung overseas staff and its thousands of Washington intelligence analysts but also by the dozen or so departmental and agency intelligence units of government. The total number of persons working directly within the intelligence community probably is between 20,000 and 30,000. Tens of thousands of others are less directly involved in intelligence production. Although its inner functions are inevitably shrouded in secrecy, the CIA today is clearly both an extensive "holding company" over this community — a co-ordinator — as well as an intelligence operating agency.

The extent to which CIA should engage in its own intelligence operations was only loosely prescribed in the 1947 and 1949 legislation. A clue to the fact that the extent of its operations may be largely self-determined is the statement that it performs only such activities as directed by the National Security Council. But who is the principal intelligence adviser to NSC? The fact that the Director of Central Intelligence has become *de facto* a constant participant in NSC deliberations seems to answer the question and to suggest that the scope of CIA operations is to a large extent self-determined. Of course the major department heads are *de jure* members of NSC and may be expected to protect the parochial interests of the Defense, State, and other departments, and the Director must also contend with the military service through the Chairman of the Joint Chiefs of Staff. Also an NSC subcommittee exists to oversee CIA Cold War roles and missions. Certainly the Congress has no voice as to how and where CIA is to function, other than prohibiting it to engage in domestic security activities.

As a matter of fact the real operating constitution of the CIA is probably not so much the statutory authority given by Congress in 1947 and 1949, but about a score of super-secret National Security Council Intelligence Directives which probably only a few high government officials have ever seen. It is reasonable to assume that many of these directives were in fact drafted in the Intelligence Advisory Committee, of which the Director of Central Intelligence serves as chairman. So it is very likely that CIA's co-ordinating and operating role is compromised and horse-traded out in the Intelligence Advisory Committee, on which sit high-ranking representatives of the major operating departmental and agency intelligence units.

Although the extent of its co-ordinating function and authority remains somewhat cloudy (for example, how far can the Director actually go in "meddling" in the intelligence process and substance of the various departments?) the CIA today clearly functions in national intelligence policy guidance as a co-ordinator and as a conductor of extensive operations in the field.

The Co-ordinating Function

Sherman Kent has outlined his concept of the basic elements in CIA's co-ordinating function. These include (1) establishment of clear jurisdictions for the several departmental intelligence units, (2) the policing of these jurisdictional boundaries, (3) continuing evaluation of departmental intelligence standards, (4) assistance in raising departmental intelligence standards, (5) management of interdepartmental projects, and (6) setting of government standards for high-quality intelligence personnel.[7]

As for its operating function, CIA Old Hands will say that the agency has no *raison d'être* by and of itself, that it is essentially a gap-filler and "co-ordinator" of the old-line intelligence agencies. Yet the CIA man will add, off the record, of course, an important qualification that there are, however, certain things that can best be done centrally. This latter attitude, along with the pressures of the Cold War and the increasing requirements by decision makers for world-wide information that is well co-ordinated, have nourished the CIA into a major bureaucracy in its own right. Another source of growing power for the CIA over the years is the policy of rotation within the military services and to a certain extent in other departments, with the result that CIA tends to have greater continuity than others in personnel skilled in intelligence evaluation and analysis. As the experience and competence of CIA personnel increase, so do its power and the relative importance of its role. The co-ordinating authority of CIA is exercised according to the shifting winds of personality and issue and inevitably a certain amount of interdepartmental conflict may be expected to be part of the day-to-day life of a government co-ordinating agency in Washington. For, as those who know Washington will confirm, one man's co-ordination is another man's dictatorship; one man's co-ordination may be yet another man's anarchy.

Like the Office of the Secretary of Defense in another sector of the organization for national security, the office of Director of Central Intelligence has gradually increased its operating activities in many areas of the intelligence community. It has assumed not only broad co-ordinating and policy functions but is engaged in extensive operations as well. By means of Director of Central Intelligence directives, details of which are negotiated within the interdepartmental Intelligence Advisory Committee, jurisdictional boundaries in the community have been assigned.

Since the various operating departments and agencies are clearly authorized by statute to continue their own intelligence activities, how and where does CIA come into the operational picture? CIA has assumed responsibility for those common concern functions of the intelligence community which must be centralized for economy and effectiveness. One of the most important of these is world-wide secret operations — the conduct of international "cloak and dagger" functions. This has become a centralized CIA function, taken over from the wartime activities of the OSS and the armed forces, and, in fact, employing a number of OSS veterans as career agents. The armed services conduct such operations only in combat theaters of operation in time of war. It is clear that if each of four or five American government agencies was attempting to run a spy net in and around Cairo, for example, they would, in the intelligence vernacular, quickly "blow each other's cover." Such a system could only lead to compromise or disaster, hence the need for centrally directed covert operations.

In active military theaters during wartime, espionage and related intelligence operations are a legitimate responsibility of the military commanders. However, the question is likely to arise — as it did in World War II with the OSS — as to where military intelligence ends and civilian operations begin. The problem is even more complex when there is a military theater command in certain areas during a time of general peace, as has been the case during the Cold War. The allegations that prior to the Korean War General MacArthur made it difficult for the CIA to operate within the Far East Command, for example, suggest the type of jurisdictional disputes in which CIA and the military can, and have, become involved.[8]

Major issues of conflict today between the military services and CIA are likely to be resolved in Washington within the Intelligence Advisory Committee, the National Security Council, or, if necessary, the President's office. Duplication, overlapping, and interservice conflicts will likely remain a problem nonetheless under the present national security structure, in which the federation concept prevails. Perceptive students of public affairs visiting or working overseas often get the impression that CIA agents, and the intelligence operatives of other government agencies, are operating in unco-ordinated fashion in every dark alley, behind every bush, and apparently often in each other's hair.

Another central function which reasonably has been assumed by CIA is that of monitoring foreign radio broadcasts and other forms of propaganda. Clearly it would be inefficient for various intelligence units of government to attempt to perform this function. Numerous other functions of the intelligence community involving collection, research, and analysis of nonsecret material and the like are best performed by a centralized agency. In its survey of the intelligence activities of government, the 1955 Hoover Commission, for example, recommended that responsibility for procurement and collection of foreign publications and scientific intelligence be shifted from the State Department to CIA. Here, it was felt, was a function that was of common concern to the intelligence community and could best be performed centrally. It would not be unnatural, from a CIA point of view, at least, if more and more functions of foreign intelligence are said to be most efficiently performed by the central organization.

Overseas Political Action

CIA overseas operations apparently are not limited to the clandestine collection of information, as evidenced by this exchange between the CIA Director and a newsman in 1954:

Question. . . . it is often reported in the papers that you send in provocateurs to stir up revolution in satellite countries. What truth is there in that?
Dulles. I only wish we had accomplished all that the Soviets attribute to us. . .
Question. Is that part of your function — to stir up revolution in these countries?
Dulles. . . . We would be foolish if we did not cooperate with our friends abroad to help them to do everything they can to expose and counter this Communist subversive movement.[9]

This colloquy suggests that the "additional services" and "other functions" referred to in the CIA statute now cover a wide range and point to CIA as a major operator in international political maneuvers.

One journalistic account of CIA overseas activities, written when the agency was barely a year old, but apparently based in part upon official sources, contained the following description:

Though little is being said about it, CIA is known to be making wide use of the same spectacular techniques which OSS employed to rally resistance movements against Hitler. Both in front of and behind the Iron Curtain, CIA men are assisting democratic forces to resist Red excesses. Anti-communist political leaders, editors, labor-union chiefs, clergymen and others are getting CIA support in their struggles to retain or regain democracy. CIA men call this "building first columns." [10]

Little reliable information exists about the extent to which CIA has aided foreign rebellions and various resistance movements.

A more recent journalistic description of CIA paints a picture of the CIA undercover operative moving "swiftly through foreign political back rooms, to rescue and revive a friendly government and a friendly people who were on the verge of being choked by Communist pressure." [11] Understandably, only speculation and rumor exist outside the inner sanctum of central intelligence about this kind of CIA function. But if this is a major role of CIA today, its compatibility with the more narrowly defined intelligence function is open to question.

Soviet leaders in recent years have not hesitated to blame CIA agents for fomenting rebellion in East Germany, Poland, and Hungary, and the Chinese Communists have accused CIA of backing Nationalist raids and intelligence operations on the mainland.* Presumably any such CIA activity has been conducted in accord with President Eisenhower's "liberation policy," as reiterated on November 14, 1956, which opposed the fomenting of open rebellion by unarmed people against superior force.

CIA agents reportedly played a part in the overthrow of Premier Mossadegh in Iran in August 1953 after his abortive attempt, in collusion with the Communist Tudeh Party, to exile the Shah. [12]

---

* In late May 1958 the Soviet government newspaper *Izvestia* published a statement by General Ivan Serov, chief of Soviet security forces, in which he reiterated a warning given many times that Western "imperialists" have launched heavy campaigns of "espionage and sabotage" against Russia. "The secret services of the capitalist states," declared Serov, "are trying to smuggle their spies, wreckers and terrorists into the U.S.S.R. and other countries of the Soviet camp."

The Forecasting Function

In the forecasting function CIA has been given credit for producing a forewarning of a Communist attempt to supply the Red-dominated government of Guatemala with arms in May 1954. Foreknowledge allowed this scheme to be thwarted.

But foreknowledge has sometimes been lacking. The CIA was not blamed for failure to anticipate the possibility of the North Korean invasion (the intelligence community thought invasion *improbable*) but, along with General MacArthur, it has come in for considerable criticism for its handling of the Chinese Communist intervention estimates. As for CIA and the over-all intelligence community, this failure appears to lie in an inability to give sufficient weight to Chinese Communist warnings that United Nations crossings of the Thirty-eighth Parallel would compel Chinese intervention. Despite the continuous barrage of propaganda warnings and the carefully monitored movement of troops into Manchuria, intelligence analysts and the policy makers failed to consider seriously such threats and apparently neglected to read history, or they would have recognized the traditional Chinese fear of an enemy north of the narrow Korean waist. President Truman records in his memoirs that "On October 20 [1950] the CIA delivered a memorandum to me which said that they had reports that the Chinese Communists would move in far enough to safeguard the Suiho electric plant and other installations along the Yalu River which provided them with power."[13] Actually the Chinese had begun crossing the Yalu four days earlier with the apparent intention of throwing the United Nations forces out of Korea. Responsibility for the intelligence breakdown in Korea at this stage is shared by the entire intelligence community and also is due apparently to poor liaison between General MacArthur and the Pentagon.

In more recent years, CIA has been criticized for failure to anticipate the speed of certain Soviet technological developments, as well as for an apparent failure to produce adequate forewarning of Soviet economic penetration into the Middle East and Southeast Asia. Intelligence similarly is blamed for failure to predict Egypt's moves in the Middle East crisis in the fall of 1956. Intelligence is credited on the other hand with warning of an Israeli move in the Middle East, which led to the President's abortive warning to the Israeli premier in late October 1956, several days prior to the Sinai invasion, not to launch an attack. These questions will be discussed more fully in the concluding chapter.

The Limits of Co-ordination

The suggestion by one authority in 1949 that CIA should have policing powers over the rest of the intelligence community in order to insure that each department operate effectively within its proper baliwick has already been noted. It was felt that CIA should conduct "a continual survey of departmental intelligence" to see that it was up to standards and then be in a position to "diagnose and help correct the trouble." [14] CIA has not in fact been given this kind of inspector-generalship. It does, however, exercise over-all responsibility for the National Intelligence Surveys, the encyclopedic compendia of intelligence on all major foreign powers, successors to JANIS. And since the Chairman of the Board of National Estimates is from CIA, CIA is in a position to exert influence over other intelligence agencies. The fact that the CIA Director is the only intelligence officer normally to attend NSC meetings and is close to the White House as the President's intelligence advisor, in addition to his position as chairman of the Intelligence Advisory Committee, gives the CIA an advantage of seniority in the intelligence community and, in the person of the Director, a modicum of actual co-ordinating control.

Sherman Kent's fear in 1949, incidentally, was that CIA might not be a co-ordinator but would tend to enter the "substantive" field, that is, would become an active intelligence collector, collator, and evaluator. Kent warned of the danger that CIA might become "little more than a fifth major research and surveillance outfit" — a competitor separated from its consumers.[15] As a matter of fact, as we have seen, CIA has become as much an intelligence operator as a co-ordinator. Roger Hilsman wrote in 1956 that CIA "has undertaken both research and analysis functions and information-collecting functions, setting up a set of research and analysis suboffices for current intelligence and for economic intelligence and another set of information-collecting suboffices for covert collection, for intercepting foreign propaganda broadcasts, and so on."[16] It is still too early to judge whether the fears envisaged by Kent in 1949 will be realized, but certainly CIA today produces a large amount of intelligence "from scratch." Kent has since served as chairman of the Board of Estimates and it is possible that his views have changed since becoming a leader of the intelligence community.

In fulfilling its functions assigned in the National Security Act of 1947, which functions have been broadly interpreted in directives of the National Security Council, and specifically detailed in Director of Central Intelligence directives, the CIA today is thus elaborately institutionalized for (a) *overseas operations,* which include open as well as secret collection of information and backstage, always secret, political action,[17] (b) research, analysis, and other processes involved in strategic *intelligence production* in its domestic headquarters, and (c) *various support functions* for activities noted in (a) and (b). These, then, are the basic operational activities of the Central Intelligence Agency. In addition, the agency performs the vital role of co-ordinating the intelligence activities of other departments and agencies of the intelligence community. These major agencies are described in the following chapter.

The Importance of CIA Directorship

From the foregoing description of CIA's rather vaguely defined functions it is clear that the Office of Director of Central Intelligence requires the best talent the nation can produce. This is not only because of the importance of the intelligence estimate, and the fact that its production and effective communication are an administrative task of the first order. But the existence of a massive institution possessed of secret information and operating invisibly at home and abroad also is a locus of power unchecked by the normal processes of democratic government. Thus the appointment of a Director of Central Intelligence ranks as one of the two or three most important choices a President of the United States may have to make.

A Director of Central Intelligence must be a rare combination of administrative expert, imaginative scholar, courageous master spy, and a person of keen sensitivity to the political ideals of the American Republic. America's master spy also must be a master judge and politician, but not a political partisan, and should be possessed of an inner integrity and common law sense.

It is fair to say, as one observer has noted, that "More than any other individual, Allen Dulles is responsible for CIA as it exists today. In one way or another, he has been involved with the creation of the agency almost from its inception and over the last five years [1953–1958] has put his personal stamp on it." [18] It also seems fair to say that Mr. Dulles has demonstrated that he is possessed, in one degree or another, of most of the aforementioned qualities of an ideal Director. Of the Directorship Allen Dulles has himself simply stated, "If you haven't someone who can be trusted, or who gets results, you'd better throw him out and get somebody else." [19] Given CIA's vital contemporary importance to national security, the qualities required in a Director, and the agency's immunity from popular surveillance and control, the same care that goes into the choice of a Chief Justice of the United States should always attend the choice of a Director of Central Intelligence.

V

THE INTELLIGENCE COMMUNITY:
Other Principal Members

A score of government agencies today are engaged in foreign intelligence work in one form or another.* But the principal members of the national intelligence community are the National Security Council and its staff adjunct, the Central Intelligence Agency; the Department of Defense, whose intelligence functions are performed by the armed services, the Joint Staff, and the National Security Agency; the Department of State; the Atomic Energy Commission; and the Federal Bureau of Investigation.**

As previously indicated, the CIA is today a major collector of foreign intelligence, particularly from secret sources and from the monitoring of foreign radio broadcasts. Even so, the brunt of the responsibility for data collection lies within the three armed services, the Department of State, the Atomic Energy Commission, the FBI, and the National Security

---

* Government organization, particularly for agencies directly involved in national security programs, is fluid. The structure described in the following pages was that found to exist early in 1958, although the description does not reflect fully the many changes consequent to 1955 Hoover Commission recommendations. Most of these changes remain under tight security classification.

** Also participating but without formal representation in the intelligence community are the United States Information Agency and the International Cooperation Administration. Each maintains numerous posts and missions around the globe and each is an intelligence producer and consumer.

Agency. As the 1955 Hoover Commission task force on intelligence activities noted, "Some of these agencies approach or exceed the operations of the CIA in functions and expenditures." [1] Except for the National Security Agency, the nation's ultra-secret, code-making, code-breaking, and communications-security organization, these agencies collect intelligence primarily associated with the nature of their operational role. But this is not to underestimate the value of their efforts to produce national intelligence.

Armed Service Joint Intelligence

To maintain the interservice intelligence co-operation achieved in World War II the armed services established the Joint Intelligence Committee on a permanent basis. Members of this committee are the Deputy Director for Intelligence of the Joint Staff, who serves as JIC chairman; the Army's G–2 (Assistant Chief of Staff, intelligence); the Director of Naval Intelligence;* and the Director of Intelligence, United States Air Force. The chairman of JIC also heads the Joint Intelligence Group, the working level intelligence body within the Joint Staff of the Joint Chiefs of Staff.

Co-ordination with the civilian side of the Department of Defense is maintained through the office of the Assistant to the Secretary of Defense for Special Operations. This assistant (special operations) serves as principal staff assistant to the Secretary and Deputy Secretary on all matters pertaining to the national intelligence effort. He represents the Secretary on special interdepartmental intelligence boards and committees. The Secretary of Defense is a statutory ex-officio member of the National Security Council, for which the CIA works. The Chairman of the Joint Chiefs of Staff also sometimes participates as an adviser in NSC meetings.

* He represents also the United States Marine Corps.

The Office of Special Operations has a director and a small staff. In 1958 this office had an authorized total personnel of nineteen. Its director has the responsibility of advising the Secretary of Defense on national intelligence and counterintelligence. The Director of Special Operations has an Assistant for Intelligence and an Assistant for Operations. The former advises him on policy and monitoring of National Security Agency operations, co-ordination of armed service intelligence and counter-intelligence, and policy for communications security. The latter is charged with monitoring and co-ordinating psychological and "special" warfare planning and activities of the armed forces. He also advises on and co-ordinates Department of Defense relations with CIA, as well as with the National Security Council and its Operations Coordinating Board. The Office of Special Operations also houses the executive secretariat of two permanent National Security Council committees dealing with special operations for which the Department of Defense is executive agent.

Published information on the intelligence organization and function of each of the principal members of the intelligence community is, at best and perhaps inevitably, fragmentary. In the list of numerous histories of each of the armed services, there are no unclassified works dealing in detail with intelligence. And when the armed services submit their annual budgets to Congress, testimony on the intelligence portion, with a few exceptions, has been off the record. For this reason only a very brief and sketchy description of the intelligence structure and function of the major participants in the intelligence community can be given here.

The Army

In Congressional hearings on the Army's 1958 intelligence

budget the Deputy Assistant Chief of Staff, Intelligence —
Maj. Gen. Robert H. Wienecke — was asked whether the
Army could rely entirely upon CIA for information, thus
eliminating the need for the Army's 125 million dollar intelligence apparatus. The General replied to the Senator, "I
think, sir, you will find their mission is a little different from
ours. They get more into the field of political, economic, et
cetera, whereas we try to deal mostly with military hardware." [2]

When asked how closely Army intelligence works with
CIA the General replied "hand in glove." The Army's intelligence system makes major contributions to central intelligence. It is today a giant intelligence bureaucracy in its own
right.

Prior to World War II, Army intelligence, commonly referred to as "G-2," had been largely neglected (as indicated
in an earlier chapter). During the war the Army's intelligence
staff was greatly expanded. By June 30, 1944, Army intelligence maintained in Washington approximately 1,500 persons, including military officers and civilians. Numerous
organizational and administrative problems beset G-2 during
this period. Rivalry and resentment pervaded the wartime
intelligence community, particularly in the relationships between the Army and the Office of Strategic Services and the
growing Army Air Forces, the intelligence staff of which
rivaled in size Army G-2. And the air arm rapidly gained a
status virtually independent from the Army. In this situation,
inefficiency, overlapping of functional authority, and confusion were not uncommon. [3]

A major reorganization of Army Intelligence occurred in
1944, following a study by a civilian-military board, headed
by John J. McCloy, Assistant Secretary of War. The lack of
modern intelligence doctrine in this period is perhaps best

illustrated by the fact that in the survey conducted by this group, members were sent to study the organization and procedures of *The New York Times* and *Time* magazine. So little acquainted was the Army with the requirements of a world-wide intelligence system that leading private news-gathering organizations were asked to help point the way.

The 1944 reorganization of Army intelligence was aimed at eliminating organizational frictions and the administrative and functional hodge-podge. Included among the specific objectives of the new structure were the following: to separate policy activities that were distinctly intelligence from those that were operational; to organize better for specialized information on Germany and Japan, badly needed during the war; to institute better over-all administrative practices in the military intelligence division.[4]

The chief feature of the new organization was the separation of the policy staff of G-2 from the operations staff of the Military Intelligence Service. The aim was to have G-2 restrict itself to intelligence policy and not become involved in the flow of intelligence information. The operating division — the Military Intelligence Service — had three main branches, the first headed by a Director of Information, the second by a Director of Intelligence, and the third under an executive for administration.[5]

In the post-war period, Army intelligence was no longer the neglected step-child of the general staff, although it has not become the career branch of the Army with the most prestige. The rise of the United States to a position of world power and leadership and the nation's extensive collective security and foreign aid programs, however, have brought new importance to Army intelligence and particularly to the attaché program. Nonetheless a Hoover Commission Task Force could report, in 1949, that "G-2 in the Army has had

seven chiefs in 7 years, some of them with no prior intelligence experience whatsover." [6]

Army intelligence since the Korean War, with the importance of intelligence clearly apparent throughout the
military defense community, has been well-supplied with
funds (125 millions for fiscal year 1958) and personnel, and
its status has been elevated. And in the words of the Deputy
Assistant Chief of Staff, G-2, in 1955, Army intelligence was
"attracting some of the best officers in the Army." [7]

Army intelligence activities programmed in the budget for
fiscal year 1958 were broken down into the following categories and planned expenditures: [8]

Army Intelligence Expenditures

	(millions of dollars)
The Army attaché system	2.5
Army centralized intelligence activity	3.0
Secret (classified) activity	27.0
Technical intelligence services	20.0
Continental and overseas field activities	7.0
Army Map Service	44.0
Installation support	15.0
Miscellaneous "small" projects	6.5
	125.0

Army Intelligence Organization

The Assistant Chief of Staff of the Army for Intelligence
(G-2) is responsible for the intelligence function within the
Army. This includes planning, co-ordinating, and super-
vising all Army intelligence activities. The G-2 mission is the
collection, evaluation, and dissemination of information per'

taining to the war potential, topography, and military forces and organization of foreign nations. G-2 also assesses the strategic vulnerability of the United States continent and its outlying possessions.

The domain of Army intelligence includes a world-wide attaché system, a network of training schools and commands, the Army Intelligence Center, the highly specialized Counter Intelligence Corps, and a variety of classified activities and organizations. In addition, each of the seven technical services of the Army — Chemical, Engineers, Ordnance, Quartermaster, Signal, Transportation, and Medical — has a specialized intelligence function, under General Staff supervision. G-2 also utilizes the services of the Army Security Agency, which is responsible for communications security and signal intelligence. Army intelligence personnel are assigned to field and rear echelons both in overseas commands and continental armies.

The Army attaché system, long a traditional source of foreign intelligence, comprises a network of some sixty-nine stations in foreign nations. Attachés serve as official representatives of the Army Chief of Staff to the government of the country in which they are serving. They are also under the direct administrative control of the American ambassador or other chief of diplomatic mission, and act as his adviser on Army matters. Once a prime target of isolationist-minded Congressmen examining Army budgets, the attaché system is now well recognized and is strongly supported.

Army, Navy, and Air Force try to maintain close coordination and liaison both in Washington and overseas in the operation of the attaché system. Unification of policy and function is employed wherever feasible. The communications function, for example, including cryptographic activities, has been assigned to one of the services at each station; Army and Air Force have a unified fiscal and disbursing arrangement; and joint photographic laboratories are maintained in many stations, as are other common use facilities.

A second major functional area of Army intelligence comprises the units of an administratively centralized entity called the Army Intelligence Center. These include the Army Intelligence School, the Central Records Facility, the Army Intelligence Board, and the Photo Interpretation Center, all located at Fort Holabird, Maryland; the Strategic Intelligence School (a joint Army-Navy-Air Force training establishment in Washington primarily for attachés and attachés designate); and the Army Security Center at Fort Meade, Maryland. The Central Records Facility operates largely as a despository for some 5,000,000 personnel security investigation files from all Army commands. The Army Intelligence Board investigates, develops, and tests special devices utilized in intelligence and counter-intelligence operations.

One of G-2's best-known intelligence units is the Counter Intelligence Corps. Its personnel are trained in investigative and security techniques and often in foreign languages. This unit, prior to 1942 called the Corps of Intelligence Police, is concerned with the prevention and detection of attempts at treason, espionage, and sabotage, and the more mundane police problems such as gambling, prostitution, and blackmarkets. A special Counter Intelligence Corps School is operated by the Army. It is the Army counterpart of the civilian FBI and performs overseas many of the functions of the FBI at home.

The CIC is commanded by a Major General, who serves also as Deputy Assistant Chief of Staff for Intelligence. The CIC commander, however, does not exercise true operational control over his personnel. In keeping with the axiom that intelligence and security are functions of command, CIC detachments are generally assigned to field units and are directly responsible to the unit commander.

To illustrate the role of CIC in World War II, a few operations in which CIC participated can be cited. These include the capture of complete records of the Italian Secret Service and the German lists of Axis sympathizers during the North African landings in 1943; the seizure of German radar and wireless transmitter codes and the location of major mine fields during the landing on Sicily; and the responsibility for security of the now-famous Manhattan Project, from its inception to the dropping of the first atomic bomb.

More recently, in areas such as occupied Japan, where the United States Army maintained sizable troop deployments, CIC personnel were stationed in every prefecture and key town, where one of their functions was to monitor all local political, militant, or subversive activity and to keep General MacArthur's headquarters apprised of critical trends and developments. In performing its specialized police mission, the CIC often uncovers positive intelligence data which are fed into the national intelligence system.

Of a 125 million dollar budget for Army intelligence in 1958, 44 millions were allocated to the world-wide Army mapping and military surveys program conducted largely by the Army Map Service, Corps of Engineers, in conjunction with the Department of the Interior. This project, which also includes collecting the intelligence data required by the Corps of Engineers, provides for production and distribution of maps, map auxiliaries, geodetic data, terrain, topographic, and other similar intelligence studies required on a world-wide basis by the Department of Defense and others within the intelligence community. Requirements are established by the Army General Staff in co-ordination with the Air Force, the Navy, and the Joint Chiefs of Staff. This operation is a vital part of the process leading to the production of the National Intelligence Surveys.

National Intelligence Surveys

A good example of the interdependence of agencies within the intelligence community is provided by the process in which these National Intelligence Surveys are produced. As previously indicated, the various technical services of the Army each engage in specialized intelligence operations. Several hundred intelligence specialists, military and civilian, are constantly at work on the technical service level. An important part of their work is to provide basic material for the National Intelligence Surveys.

Let us take as an illustrative, though fictional, example National Intelligence Survey No. 25 which, let us say, deals with the Soviet Union.[9] Its content and format are determined by the National Intelligence Survey Committee, which is an important subcommittee within the Central Intelligence Agency. National Intelligence Survey No. 25 is divided into numerous sections, including, for example, separate sections on highways, telephone communications networks, railroads. Now, who prepares the basic material on Soviet highways? This could conceivably be done by one of the many research branches of the CIA. In the intelligence community as presently constituted, however, the section of NIS No. 25 — section No. 32 — dealing with Russian highways is compiled by the Army's Transportation Corps, the section on telephone networks by the Signal Corps, and so on. Priorities and production schedules for various sections of the NIS come from the NIS Committee, a CIA-chaired committee containing representatives from the various intelligence agencies of government.

As soon as the section on Russian highways is published,

it becomes a "maintenance item" for the intelligence branch of the Army Transportation Corps. The basic material in the section would be the product of the Transportation Corps, with additional information being supplied by other agencies of government — economic data from the CIA, political and cultural data from the Department of State, and so on.

Other technical service functions of Army intelligence include publication of the Army Technical Intelligence Bulletin, published every two months, containing current intelligence, as contrasted with the more general surveys; a "Class B Handbook," containing information on weapons and equipment of potential enemies; and the *Intelligence Review*, a document of current intelligence issued periodically and containing information on latest foreign developments, particularly in the Soviet Russian and satellite military establishments.

Today Army intelligence has progressed greatly since the lean pre-war years when military attachés were chosen only if they had independent means of support, usually a wealthy wife. Army G-2 is no longer an orphan of the Army's general staff system. Its size and prestige reflect the Cold War atmosphere and America's far-flung international commitments. Its role in the national intelligence community is a vital one.

The Deputy Assistant Chief of Staff for Intelligence, Maj. Gen. Robert A. Schow, surprisingly was able to testify in 1956 that G-2 was "getting enough" funds to carry out its mission. Prestige and status of an intelligence career remain a problem, however. Although the situation is greatly improved, an intelligence assignment tends to be a transient one and is not considered a pathway to a successful career in traditional terms. As Representative Daniel J. Flood has noted, G-2 was still only a two-star rank (Major General) while the Chief of Research and Development, for example, was wearing the three stars of a Lieutenant General. General Schow conceded to the Congressman, in fact, that his own assignment to G-2 was, in terms of his future career, "almost the kiss of death. . . ." [10]

It has been proposed that a career "Intelligence Corps" be established within the Army, in order to develop specially trained permanent personnel, to increase the status and prestige of intelligence work and to insure better evaluation and co-ordination of Army intelligence. To date, this proposal has been resisted on the basis that it would fix in G-2 additional operating responsibilities and tend to remove responsibility for intelligence from operational officers. [11]

Overlapping, and considerable and sometimes serious conflict exist between the Army and CIA in the performance of world-wide intelligence operations. The Army's comment on this in 1957 was given by its Deputy Assistant Chief of Staff, Intelligence (G-2). He told an inquisitive senator, "There may be a minor overlapping, sir, but we feel that a lap of small proportion is better than a gap." [12] A fundamental problem of the intelligence community today involves seeing to it that such duplication remains "minor," not only between the Army and the CIA, but among the various other intelligence agencies as well.

The Navy

American strategic design in the decades between the two world wars assigned the United States Navy to the first line of defense. Even so, naval, like army, intelligence was neglected in this period. One convincing bit of evidence was the government's call on the American public, in 1942, for snapshots and motion pictures of recent foreign travel. This was part of a desperate attempt in preparation for the North African (Moroccan) landings to fill the wide gap of information about beaches, sea approaches, and other data needed, particularly for night landings.

Presumably this kind of data is currently provided in the National Intelligence Surveys but it was all too scarce in those days. According to Samuel Eliot Morison, "we dearly wanted, and never were able to obtain, photographs of the Barbary coastline taken from sea level just offshore, in order to enable our forces readily to identify beaches and other landmarks at night." [13]

The frustrations of an able naval intelligence officer in the interwar years are acutely revealed by Captain (later Rear Admiral) Ellis M. Zacharias throughout his book, *Secret Missions*.[14] Even after the advent of the war, in the period 1940–1945, the Office of Naval Intelligence had no less than seven directors. "Of the seven directors," Zacharias wrote, "only one was qualified by previous training, intellectual interest, and personal disposition to fill this particular job." [15] Only once in a while, he recounts, "chance placed an officer at the top who tried, in the predeterminedly limited time at his disposal, to improve the office which was so haphazardly entrusted to his care." [16]

The rather restricted role played by the Office of Naval Intelligence on the eve of America's entry into World War II is revealed in the Pearl Harbor episode. The customary task of ONI was to gather intelligence about the potential enemy, but "it was not allowed to evaluate, much less to disseminate, the information so gathered." [17] Responsibility for evaluating intelligence data and predicting such things as the future movement of the Japanese Navy, and deciding to whom available information should be disclosed, was the assignment of the war plans officer on the staff of the Chief of Naval Operations. This peculiar limitation on the role of the naval intelligence officer reflected, in part, the prevailing attitudes toward the pre-war quality of the intelligence product. If the quality was in fact low, this could be blamed upon official neglect of the intelligence function.

Today the Navy, like the Army and Air Force, recognizes the crucial importance of a high-quality intelligence product. Consequently the Navy now operates a well-staffed, highly trained service-wide intelligence organization. It forms a major cog in the machinery of the national intelligence community. The Navy has been particularly reticent about disclosing in the public record the structure and functions of its intelligence system. The following details were available.

Navy Intelligence Organization

Center of naval intelligence activity is the Office of Naval Intelligence (ONI), within the Office of the Chief of Naval Operations. The Director of Naval Intelligence (DNI) is an Assistant Chief of Naval Operations who reports to the Vice Chief of Naval Operations and also is directly responsible to the Secretary of the Navy.

The mission of ONI is to meet the intelligence and counter-intelligence requirements of the Navy. This includes:

1. informing naval planners and policy makers of the war-making capabilities and intentions of foreign nations;
2. supplying the naval establishment with information needed for plans and operations;
3. warning of threats to the security of the naval establishment;
4. co-ordination of intelligence activities within the naval establishment and providing the naval contributions to the intelligence community of the government; *

* The Marine Corps maintains a small intelligence staff in its Headquarters, and intelligence officers are billeted throughout the Corps. But these are concerned primarily with tactical, or operational, rather than national, intelligence.

5. development and recommendation of policies, to the Secretary of the Navy and the Chief of Naval Operations, on all matters pertinent to naval intelligence and the security of classified material.[18]

One of the major distinctions between ONI and the Army's G-2 is that there is no semi-independent specialized unit such as CIC in the counter-intelligence field, and ONI agents also conduct criminal investigations in the Navy, a task performed by the Provost Marshal's office in the Army.

The field organization for carrying out ONI's missions has three major components: (1) Naval District Intelligence officers, under the management control of ONI and operating in the United States and certain outlying areas; (2) intelligence organizations with the forces afloat, which are directly under unit commanders with over-all ONI supervision; and (3) the Naval Attaché system, functioning under ONI direction as well as State Department supervision.

District intelligence officers operate primarily in counter-intelligence and security fields. The DIO is directly responsible to the Naval District Commandant, with additional duty in some areas on the staff of the commander of the sea frontier of his district. Civilian agents usually are assigned to the district intelligence officers along with naval intelligence officers and the former conduct security and major criminal investigations involving naval personnel or matériel.

With the forces afloat or in overseas bases, flag officers in command of each area, fleet, or task force have staff intelligence sections functioning primarily in the operational or tactical intelligence field. The intelligence officer who heads this staff section works not only for the unit commander, but also performs some collection missions for ONI.

Naval attachés, trained by ONI in intelligence and languages, collect naval intelligence for ONI as well as serve the diplomatic chief at the post to which they are assigned.

ONI not only is responsible for collecting intelligence on the navies of the world, with emphasis today on Soviet submarine capabilities and deployments, but also has major collection responsibilities for beach, port, and harbor information. ONI has continued its World War II program of building up elaborate dossiers on the world's potential amphibious operations targets and these dossiers contribute an important ingredient to the National Intelligence Surveys.

Just as the Army Transportation Corps' intelligence experts supply basic data on Soviet Russian and other foreign highway systems for the NIS, so ONI experts supply data to sections of the surveys dealing with the Russian and other foreign navies, with waterways, ports, and other elements of sea power. Thus naval intelligence serves simultaneously the intelligence community and the specialized planning and operational needs of the Navy.

The achievements of ONI in World War II, particularly in the operational intelligence fields, did much to raise the status of intelligence within the Navy. Under the Military Personnel Act of 1947, provision is made for Intelligence Specialists in the Regular Navy, including flag rank billets in ONI. A feeling remains, however, that intelligence specialization may be a dead end for the ambitious career officer, a sentiment ONI continually works to overcome.

It may be noted, however, that many naval intelligence assignments, particularly with the forces afloat, are closely allied with operational training and experience so that the rotation of line officers with intelligence training, in and out of operational or combat intelligence billets, may in many cases be a desirable system. Yet the need remains for a permanent, professional naval intelligence corps.

The Air Force

Prior to and during World War II the Air Force was a branch of the Army. Air intelligence consequently suffered even more heavily the fate of Army and Navy intelligence — inadequate support in funds, in personnel, and in organizational status. "When the war began," according to air historians, "the AAF probably was more deficient in its provision for intelligence than in any other phase of its activities. . . ." [19]

The sad state of air intelligence in the late 1930's is evidenced by a comment made years later by Gen. Henry H. Arnold, wartime commander of the Army Air Forces. "I know now there were American journalists and ordinary travelers in Germany who knew more about the *Luftwaffe's* preparations than I, the Assistant Chief of the United States Army Air Corps." [20]

When he was appointed Chief of the Air Corps in 1938, General Arnold considered air intelligence as the weakest link in the air organization. This is not to suggest that air intelligence was completely neglected. Military attachés, special foreign trips by Air Corps officers, and other sources produced data on foreign air power. But no formal Air Corps agency existed for the systematic evaluation of information so collected. As an exception, the existence of the Air Corps Board may be cited. This overworked group had many other duties, yet managed to incorporate intelligence data into field and technical manuals and handbooks for aviators. It was not until November 1940, however, that an Intelligence Division was created at the Chief of Air Corps staff level, when the Information Division was redesignated the Intelligence Division. This division became A-2 (Assistant Chief of Staff, Intelligence) within the newly organized Army Air Forces in June 1941, with a responsibility for both assessment and dissemination of intelligence. [21]

Yet air intelligence during the war leaned heavily upon the more experienced British staffs and collection facilities. The air intelligence product in World War II has been judged little better than the product of a "sincere adolescent." [22] When the Army Air Forces gained a semi-independent status, there were constant disagreements between A-2 and G-2, and considerable overlapping of function and jurisdiction. Responsibilities for air intelligence on Japan, for example, were parceled into artificial penny packets to the Navy, the Army, and the Army Air Forces. Thus there was lack of centralized direction, authority, and control, and the quality of the intelligence product suffered.

In his report to the Secretary of War at the conclusion of World War II, General Arnold stated, "Our past concept of Intelligence was insufficient to cover the requirements of modern war." It was clear to the wartime air chief that, particularly for an air force, "Detailed and moment-by-moment knowledge of all aspects of civilian and military activity within the territory of an enemy or a potential enemy is essential to sound planning in times of peace and war." Looking toward the future, Arnold noted that it would be "suicidally dangerous to depend upon reports of military attachés and routine or casual sources of information regarding foreign states." [23] These had been the principal sources of intelligence before the war but clearly were inadequate for the post-war era.

The need for adequate intelligence is particularly urgent today in the United States Air Force, whose wartime mission is to carry the attack far into the enemy's interior on D-day. Knowledge of a potential enemy's air power and of the most profitable targets is absolutely essential to Air Force operations.[24] Furnishing this knowledge is an intelligence function. Thus the Air Force maintains an extensive intelligence organization, reorganized within recent years, and is one of the chief consumers of and contributors to the national intelligence product.

Air Force intelligence activities, under a 1957 reorganization which was stimulated in part by the Hoover Commission study in 1955, are headed by the Assistant Chief of Staff for Intelligence. On the civilian side, a small intelligence staff serves the Secretary of the Air Force, operating under his Special Assistant for Intelligence. This office reviews and evaluates all matters pertaining to Air Force intelligence — policies, plans, and programs.

The Assistant Chief of Staff, Intelligence, under the organization existing in early 1958, has five major subdivisions in his office, grouped along functional lines. A *Policy and Management Group* develops, in conjunction with the Air Force Secretary's Special Assistant, USAF intelligence plans and policies and supervises their implementation. Secondly, an *Electronics Intelligence Coordinating Group* directs and co-ordinates all electronics intelligence activities of the Department of Defense. This group operates the far-flung radar tracking stations which span the globe and from which valuable data — the tracking of Russian missile tests, for example — are obtained. This group works closely with CIA and the Department of State, supplying the required technical data to these and other agencies. The Air Force, in other words, is the intelligence community's principal agent in the highly profitable field, from a data-gathering point of view, of electronics intelligence.

A third subdivision of ACS/Intelligence is the *Directorate of Collection and Dissemination,* which is assigned multiple functions. This division directs the collection of aviation intelligence information; operates the Air Attaché system; determines reconnaissance mapping and charting and geodetic requirements; produces photo intelligence; receives, processes, disseminates, and maintains a document library for all intelligence information; and is the Department of the Air Force point of contact for foreign government representatives in the United States.

The *Directorate of Estimates,* a fourth group, is itself divided into four units. First a topical division supplies topical intelligence as required and daily intelligence reports. It maintains a world-wide surveillance in the aviation field for evidence of possible hostile action or movements. With such responsibility this group contributes important information to the Watch Committee and the Indications Center of CIA. It also publishes the *Air Intelligence Digest.* Secondly, an integration division assembles finished intelligence as required by the Air Staff, by the secretariats of the several armed services and the CIA, and by subordinate Air Force commands. The third and fourth divisions are those estimating military capabilities, east, and military capabilities, west. The former maintains continuing assessment of the Sino-Soviet bloc's present and future aviation capability. The latter keeps a running score of air power within foreign nations outside of the Communist orbit.

Finally, a *Targets Directorate* is engaged in the highly important analysis of potential targets in the event of war and the development of target systems for Air Force operations. To perform this general function, three sub-units exist. The first of these is a target analysis division, which analyzes military, political, and economic strengths as a basis for the development of target systems. This unit compiles all kinds of target information and publishes and maintains the *Bombing Encyclopedia.* Secondly, a physical vulnerability division determines vulnerability of specific targets; estimates weapons requirements in light of knowledge on vulnerability; and calculates the effect of Air Force weapons upon specific targets. Thirdly, a target materials division determines requirements for materials and equipment to be used by air crews and co-ordinates and monitors the world-wide distribution and storage of such materials.

Counter-intelligence in the Air Force, including the investigation of subversive activities and personnel, sabotage and espionage, is divorced from the positive intelligence branch. This function is performed by the Office of Special Investigations (OSI) under the Air Force Inspector General.

The Assistant Chief of Staff, Intelligence, provides the over-all supervision and co-ordination for the intelligence units affiliated with the major Air Force commands, each of which have their own particular intelligence requirements. For example, the Strategic Air Command plans operations upon estimates of Soviet strategic vulnerabilities and Soviet ability to resist strategic air operations. The Air Defense Command is more interested in long-range bomber and missile capabilities of a potential enemy.

Serving the total Air Force intelligence program is the Air Technical Intelligence Center at Wright-Patterson Air Force Base in Ohio, which is directly responsible to the ACS/I in Washington.

A major collection source of Air Force intelligence is the Air Attaché system. The 1955 Hoover Commission Report, *Intelligence Activities*, criticized the Air Force attaché training program, although not indicating whether the deficiencies in this program lay in technical, area, or language training.[25]

The 1955 Hoover Commission explicitly criticized the organizational structure of Air Force intelligence in existence at that time, namely the fact that the Director of Intelligence was subordinate and responsible to the Deputy Chief of Staff,

Operations. The Hoover Commission objected to the "interposing of an echelon" between intelligence and the Chief of Staff and other Deputy Chiefs of Staff, such as the Comptroller, on the grounds that it affected "adversely the efficiency of staff operations." The Commission also stressed the necessity for increasing the "prestige of Intelligence in the Air Force." To raise both efficiency and prestige it recommended that the Air Force Intelligence Director be elevated at least to the level of Deputy Chief of Staff.[26]

Within Air Force intelligence circles there has also been frequent criticism of the organizational structure which lodges the counter-intelligence and security unit (OSI) within the Inspector General's office. The argument is that security information should not go directly to the command but should be channeled through the intelligence officer, where it can be fused with related intelligence data and then presented to the command. The Hoover Commission chose to ignore this controversial topic in its public report.

Intelligence for the Jet-Atomic Age

The Air Force, like the other armed services, faces a crisis in intelligence. The speed and destructiveness of weapons developed since World War II have outrun the institutional arrangements for the rapid and accurate digest of intelligence data. Thus the environment for human control of operational decisions has not kept pace with the time compression which calls for immediate decision and action. The commander of weapons systems that can deliver virtually unlimited destructive power, in a time system in which days have become minutes, must be equipped with the tools for making split-second decisions. He must have the facts — rapidly collected, accurately evaluated, and quickly communicated. The Air Force, and the other armed services as well, thus are faced with a crucial and complex intelligence problem.

Aware of this problem, Air Force intelligence experts speak now of the need for "jet-speed" intelligence and are busily at work devising techniques for high-speed electronic data processing. "Datamation" is a new term introduced into the airman's ever-expanding vocabulary. It refers to "automated" intelligence data processing. Heavy reliance is being placed upon systems for mechanized data reporting, processing, and storage. The ambitious aim is to create for the air commander an environment in which he can regain control over the weapons systems of the jet-atomic age.[27]

National Security Agency

Problems as old as intelligence itself are the secure communicating of secret information and the interception of such information transmitted by foreign governments or their espionage agents. The use of professional code makers and code breakers is perhaps as old as diplomacy and espionage.

Statesmen, diplomats, and soldiers since antiquity have employed various means of "magic" communication. Julius Caesar, for example, employed a regular cipher, consisting of a simple transposition of the alphabet, D standing for A, E for B, and so on. From the fourteenth century onwards cryptography has become an established and highly refined practice, particularly in the diplomacy and espionage so artfully developed during the Renaissance by the Venetians. The Venetian, Soro, who died in 1544, has been called the father of scientific cipher.[28] The cryptogram remains a major factor today in international statecraft, in both intelligence and counter-intelligence operations.

This is the principal business of the National Security Agency. Its structure and specific functions are secrets even more closely guarded than those of CIA. The NSA specializes in communications intelligence. It operates as a semi-autonomous agency of the Department of Defense, under the supervision of the Secretary of Defense's Office of Special Operations.[29]

In addition to maintaining its own professional staff for technical operations, NSA exercises broad supervision over, and co-ordination of, the Army Security Agency and similar communications intelligence groups within the Navy and Air Force.

Little published information is available on NSA structure and functions. One of its chief roles is the making and breaking of codes — the fascinating, challenging, and highly specialized profession of cryptanalysis. Dealing as it does with super-secret "communications security," with codes, ciphers, and electronic devices, NSA is today an almost anonymous agency of government. Only rarely is the agency found listed on the organizational charts of the United States government.

A brief but revealing glimpse into one aspect of the work of NSA was given when the Government prosecuted one of NSA's employees, Joseph S. Petersen, Jr., in November 1954. He was indicted and prosecuted in connection with misuse of government documents dealing with the breaking of the Netherlands government codes, and of North Korean codes. Among other charges, he was accused of keeping in his apartment a document entitled "Chinese Telegraphic Code, SP-D, Second Edition, with Addenda and Errata." [30] It is clear from news accounts of this case that the euphemism "communications intelligence" refers more specifically to the age-old business of code making and code breaking. Obviously, then, NSA plays a major, if unobtrusive, role in the national intelligence community.

Times have changed indeed since the period in the late

1920's when the American cryptographic agency was abolished. Upon becoming Secretary of State in 1929, Henry L. Stimson apparently thought it was immoral at least in times which appeared to be profoundly peaceful that an agency of the United States Government should be reading "other persons' mail."[31] If gentlemen in the late 1920's considered "communications intelligence" as improper, gentlemen of the mid-twentieth century either have changed their standards or have recognized the incompatibility of politeness and Cold War. At any rate, through the National Security Agency and related units, the American government is again engaged in "communications intelligence" on a world-wide scale.

The Department of State

By its very nature and function, the Department of State has always been inextricably entwined in the business of foreign intelligence. Its *raison d'être* has been to bring intelligence to bear upon the nation's foreign affairs. As Professor McCamy has observed,

The practice of intelligence work in the conduct of United States foreign affairs . . . is as old as the practice of American diplomacy. It has not been called intelligence work, but it has been such. From our missions and other sources abroad we have tried to ascertain the effect of actions by other countries upon our own domestic affairs. Putting all the available information together we have decided policies and made plans of our own.[32]

Indeed, the State Department had its birth as a "Committee on Secret Correspondence," to supervise the relations of the American colonies with friendly European countries.

Latter-day State Department officials still regard their department as the center for international information. In the words of Deputy Under Secretary of State Loy Henderson in 1957:

> The Department of State and the Foreign Service represent the framework around which is assembled all of the activities of the U.S. in the foreign field. It is to the Department of State at home and the Foreign Service abroad that all agencies concerned with foreign affairs must turn for information with regard to international developments, for guidance with regard to policies, for advice . . . and for leadership in times of crisis.[33]

State has been specifically assigned, under NSC intelligence directives, the job of collecting, analyzing, and disseminating overt political, economic, cultural, and sociological intelligence for the community. In addition to serving departmental needs, State's intelligence experts make major contributions to the National Intelligence Surveys, to the National Intelligence Estimates, and to almost every major activity of the intelligence community. State's Director of Intelligence and Research is a key member of the Intelligence Advisory Committee, and State's representatives are active members of the Watch Committee and numerous other interdepartmental groups within the community.

A prime function of American diplomats and other foreign service officers has always been to send back information pertinent to the conduct of foreign affairs and the formation of foreign policy. Yet, like the armed services, the Department of State prior to World War II was haphazardly organized for the evaluation, synthesis, and communication of all the information which flowed into Washington from foreign posts. There are those who insist that the department was haphazardly organized for any function. Collection of intelligence data in the field often was inexpertly done. There was, in fact, no separate and distinct intelligence function. One needs only to read the memoirs of pre-war Secretaries of State to see how poorly informed they were on many aspects of foreign affairs. Little information that would meet current standards for intelligence collection and analysis was available, however great was the activity of overseas agents.

The Department of State since World War II serves as a prime producer and consumer within the new national intelligence community. But the intelligence function has been a major and bitterly fought issue of internal department organization in the decade since World War II. The issue has centered upon the question whether research and intelligence should be a function independent of departmental policy offices or amalgamated with them. A parallel issue has been the nature of the relationship between the Department of State and the CIA. The needs and objectives of these two agencies may be the same, but their methods must vary. The CIA can dirty its hands in international espionage; the State Department must strive to keep its hands clean.

On the morrow of victory in World War II, in an atmosphere in which the need for centralized intelligence was widely recognized, it seemed as though the Department of State would become the focal point for co-ordinating national intelligence, and for providing leadership in government-wide intelligence functions. When President Truman abolished the OSS in the fall of 1945 and transferred its experienced intelligence analysts to the State Department, he wrote the Secretary of State on September 20 as follows:

I particularly desire that you take the lead in developing a comprehensive and coordinated foreign intelligence program for all Federal agencies concerned with that type of activity. This should be done through the creation of an interdepartmental group, heading up under the State Department. . . .[34]

The proposal that the State Department should be the agency for co-ordinating interdepartmental intelligence was the advice President Truman had received from the Bureau of the Budget.[35] Accordingly a Special Assistant to the Secretary of State for Research and Intelligence was created. He presided over an office which numbered some 1600 persons in 1945, including a large number of OSS alumni.

Within a few months after the creation of an enlarged intelligence unit within the State Department, the White House under strong pressure from the chiefs of the armed services reversed its opinion that intelligence was to be co-ordinated from the State Department. A major factor in this reversal was the opinion, strongly and widely held, that clandestine foreign operations should not be directed from the State Department but rather from an independent centralized agency. Accordingly the National Intelligence Authority was created in January 1946, in which State served as a co-equal member with War and Navy Departments and the President's military chief of staff. Its operating arm was designated the Central Intelligence Group, the forerunner of CIA, which was established by legislation in the following year. Consequently the number of intelligence personnel in the State Department was reduced to 936 with the transfer out in 1946 of the military segments of the former OSS operation.

State Department Controversy

The new and refurbished State Department intelligence unit's activities were confined within the department. But here it was at once received as an unwelcome guest. After all, veteran State Department personnel seemed to feel, intelligence has been our province for all these years. Why, they asked, these interlopers? Veteran foreign service officers, largely centered in the traditional geographic "desks," greeted the newcomers with "suspicion and hostility," and "were unwilling either to admit the need for the new activity or to accept the new personnel as members of the State Department team." [36]

A bitter struggle ensued between those holding opposite points of view. At issue was the persistent question of the proper status of intelligence personnel. Should the intelligence function be performed by separate and semi-isolated units within the Department? Or should such units be amalgamated with the several policy and operating divisions — the geographic desks, for example? Since World War II, the organizational pendulum has swung widely. In 1957–1958, as a result of revolutionized personnel policies and of new intelligence leadership, new concepts were applied.

In April 1946 the proponents of decentralization temporarily won. Research units were decentralized as "self-contained nonoperating divisions to the four main geographic offices." [37] The intelligence chief, Alfred J. McCormack, resigned in protest. McCormack argued strongly for a "separation of the fact finder from the involvement in policies and objectives." [38] The structure was changed again when General George C. Marshall became Secretary of State in 1947. The intelligence research units were regrouped as a separate staff unit, as advocated by McCormack.

According to Roger Hilsman a feeling persisted among officials of the State Department that professional diplomats, who rely on actual experience, are in a better position to evaluate foreign intelligence and predict future courses of events than research intelligence personnel, considered by some as "too academic." Hilsman, however, reports that on the other hand there is apparent consensus that there should be a branch within State which analyzes and presents "all

the facts" to the policy men, since, if left to their own devices, the latter might only line up facts to fit pre-ordained
policy.[39]

State Department Intelligence Organization

State Department intelligence organization as of mid-1958
embodied new concepts, as earlier suggested, and a new
structure. The new structure is the *Bureau of Intelligence
and Research,* formerly the Office of the Special Assistant,
Intelligence. New concepts were personified in the new
Bureau's Director (1957), Hugh S. Cumming, Jr., a career
foreign service officer whose previous assignment was an
ambassadorial post.

Since reorganization State's intelligence area comprises
two major operating branches under the Director of Intelligence and Research. First, charged with gathering information from all possible sources, is the *Office of Intelligence Resources and Coordination* (IRC), formerly the Office of
Libraries and Intelligence Acquisition (OLI). This unit
comprises various subgroups: a Geographer and a Coordinator of Maps, and divisions for Library, Intelligence Collection and Distribution, and Biographic Information. These
units maintain liaison with CIA, the armed services, and
others.

Secondly, the intelligence production branch is the *Office
of Intelligence Research and Analysis* (IRA), formerly the
Office of Intelligence Research (OIR), headed by a Director
with deputies for "functional" intelligence and for "regional"
intelligence. A Functional Intelligence Division produces
intelligence which transcends specific geographic boundaries. A separate Division of External Research and Publications keeps the Department informed of relevant research
activity outside of the Department. Under the Regional In-

telligence Deputy intelligence is produced on areas corresponding to the geographic desks. Thus there are divisions for Western Europe; American Republics; Near East, South Asia, and Africa; U.S.S.R. and Eastern Europe; and Far East. These divisions and their branches are major contributors to the National Intelligence Surveys.

Past criticism from within State of the departmental intelligence product reflected the feeling that much of it has not been acutely relevant to the policy problems at hand. There was little criticism of State's capability for spot intelligence, such as: What is the average daily tonnage carried by the Suez Canal? Nor was too much fault found with long-range estimates, such as long-range projections on the French economy. Yet on such a question as may have been asked in the spring of 1958 — What are the possible effects upon NATO of De Gaulle's rise to power? — the intelligence capability of State has appeared to be unsatisfactory.

"New concepts" earlier mentioned in State's intelligence organization are partly the result of the influx of foreign service officers into intelligence — "Wristonization" — and partly the result of a redefinition of the intelligence requirements of the Department. Effort is being made to assure that the intelligence produced is attuned to the real needs of State's policy makers and operators. Through various administrative devices closer daily operational contact exists between officials responsible for making and implementing policy and those supplying intelligence.

No longer can it be reported, as it was some years ago, that the intelligence and research divisions "have few customers for their product in the geographic or other traditional parts of the Department." [40] The Secretary of State and his principal deputies receive a daily briefing from State's Director of Intelligence and Research; the geographic desks apparently now are more receptive than previously to the intelligence product; and State's intelligence credit within the national intelligence community clearly is rising.*

State's intelligence organization has suffered somewhat from personnel shortages in the post-war decade. In 1949 some 516 positions were authorized for intelligence activity, compared with some 1600 positions in 1945. For fiscal year 1958, State was allowed to request 406 positions from Congress. The actual number directly on the payroll of the Bureau of Intelligence and Research in mid-1958 was 366. However, a number of persons quite considerably higher than 366 was at work analyzing the various intelligence areas in mid-1958 under inter-agency budgetary arrangements.

CIA and State undoubtedly duplicate each other's coverage in some of these areas. If State is understaffed, CIA may at the same time be abundantly staffed to cover a geographic area. A possible category of duplication is suggested by State's expressed desire for a larger staff to "analyze more in depth evidences on the question how USSR integration of its satellites affects orbit strength, and what actual or potential dissidence or resistance may form a weakness in the orbit." [41]

Such a question undoubtedly receives simultaneous attention from a branch of CIA. State Department intelligence activities do not receive the budgetary support they seem to warrant, in part because of apparent duplication with CIA. At any rate, State must operate its intelligence activity with an annual budget approximating less than 5 per cent of that of CIA. Such a proportionately small sum seems out

* For a detailed and authoritative description of the intelligence process in the State Department, see John W. Evans, "Research and Intelligence: The Part They Play in Foreign Policy," *Foreign Service Journal,* March 1957, pp. 24–25 and ff.

of line with State's vital role in the intelligence community.

The Department of State may now be over its earlier disappointment that it is not to be the leader-co-ordinator of the intelligence community. It is still perhaps a widely held view within the department that State is the principal foreign intelligence agency of the government. There remains the problem of the relationship with the intelligence community leadership agency, the CIA. A basic problem, one that pervades the entire community, is mutual respect for the intelligence product. In the past, CIA tended to regard the product of some of the State Department's research divisions as being "academic research rather than intelligence evaluations." [42]

Maintaining its independent sources of overseas intelligence, CIA today undoubtedly duplicates some of the work of State's foreign service officers. And in a way the two agencies are competitors in this field. But as in the case of other interdepartmental conflicts these may be resolved within the Intelligence Advisory Committee, or, if necessary, the National Security Council. Perhaps in some areas such problems remain unresolved.

The operation by the United States Government of a far-flung secret apparatus for intelligence gathering and political action could have widespread diplomatic ramifications. There may be a basic incompatibility between the maintenance of accredited diplomatic missions in some seventy-eight foreign posts (as of 1958) and the existence of American secret agents in most of these same foreign areas. Greatest care must be exercised in keeping United States diplomacy separated from spying and backstage political maneuvering, at least on the surface, yet the diplomats probably should not be completely in the dark as to the activities of American secret agents.

The observations on this problem of a 1955 Hoover Commission task force are worthy of note:

While all [diplomacy and secret operations] contribute to the end in view, conflicts between them must be resolved, usually on a high level, and always in the national interest. It must be realized that diplomacy is not an end in itself; that, while political ends must be served and unjustifiable risks avoided, the collection of Intelligence is a vital element in the fight to preserve our national welfare and existence. Instances have come to the attention of the task force where too conservative an attitude has prevailed, often to the detriment of vigorous and timely action in the field.[43]

The ticklish issue of what "cover" if any, the State Department or any other agencies operating overseas should provide for CIA's undercover operations is one which inevitably must be resolved behind closed doors. The 1955 Hoover Commission also observed caustically that "among some of those responsible for implementation of our foreign policy by diplomacy and negotiation, there seems to exist an abhorrence to anything that might lead to diplomatic or even protocol complications."

As this is written, the Brothers Dulles are in command of these two sometimes conflicting functions of American government in the Cold War. Of the many delicate problems of government in the Cold War era, this one of accommodating the need for an aggressive program for gathering foreign intelligence with the traditional practices of diplomacy is a most difficult one. No formula for a balanced approach is offered here. Yet wisdom suggests that the right of diplomacy ought to have at least a general notion of what the left hand of espionage and "special operations" is doing.

The FBI

The Federal Bureau of Investigation is a major member

of the national intelligence community, yet its direct role in the production of positive foreign intelligence is limited. This has not always been so. Today, however, the FBI operates largely as an agency for domestic counter-intelligence. Its primary national security jurisdiction is investigating espionage, sabotage, treason, and other facets of internal security.

On the eve of America's entry into World War II there was concern about how the foreign intelligence vacuum would be filled by existing intelligence agencies of government. In subsequent Presidential decisions a major sphere of action was carved out for the FBI. It was assigned responsibility for intelligence and counter-intelligence in the Western Hemisphere, including Mexico, South America, Central America (except Panama), and the Caribbean. Other areas of the globe were the responsibility of the Army and Navy, according to agreements reached in Washington in 1940.[44]

The FBI's responsibility in the Western Hemisphere covered the collection of all "nonmilitary" intelligence, yet after the United States entered the war this assignment appeared somewhat vague. The result was considerable interagency dispute over jurisdiction. The subsequent creation of the Office of Strategic Services led to inevitable friction between the OSS and the FBI. This was reduced somewhat by attempts to define more precisely the FBI's role as that of collecting, primarily, *civilian* intelligence. But this distinction is not always meaningful in a wartime atmosphere.

To perform its new intelligence role, the FBI quickly organized its Special Intelligence Service (SIS). Soon SIS agents were infiltrating south of the border under various guises and cover. One secret agent went to South America as a soap salesman; another to open a stock brokerage business. Other SIS agents were attached to United States embassies or served in liaison posts with national and local police forces when governments involved approved.[45] An SIS school to train such agents was operated during the war by the FBI. In the period of its operations between July 1, 1940, and March 31, 1947, the SIS identified, and in some cases succeeded in having arrested, hundreds of enemy espionage agents and propagandists, located some two dozen clandestine enemy radio stations, assisted in the seizure of huge amounts of contraband, and contributed in countless other ways to Allied security.[46]

In the discussion following World War II on the issue of central intelligence structure, the FBI quickly came forth with its plan to expand the SIS system on a world-wide basis. It would operate as the United States' "civilian" intelligence arm around the globe, leaving "military" intelligence to the armed services. This plan was shelved. As the Central Intelligence Group began to function on a world-wide basis in 1946, the FBI — apparently with some reluctance — withdrew from foreign intelligence operations. The Special Intelligence Service was disbanded. So ended the FBI's direct participation in overseas intelligence operations.

The FBI's World War II operations overseas were essentially counter-intelligence, but then, as now, this function often turns up information of value to positive intelligence. The nature of a foreign nation's espionage or sabotage attempts within one's own country will provide clues as to that nation's foreign policy intentions. The close link between counter-intelligence and positive foreign intelligence necessitates efficient co-ordination between the FBI and the other intelligence and counter-intelligence agencies of government. Co-ordination is provided now at the highest level of the intelligence community, where the FBI has a representative on the Intelligence Advisory Committee — the "Board of Directors" of the intelligence community. In addition the FBI Director is a member of the Interdepartmental Intelligence Conference, which co-ordinates the investigation of all domestic espionage, counter-espionage, sabotage, subversion, and other internal security matters.

Although the FBI relinquished overseas operations in 1946, the bureau still maintains overseas liaison agents with other security and intelligence agencies to insure a link between cases or leads which develop overseas but which come to rest in the continental United States.

Atomic Energy Commission

On February 27, 1958, the Atomic Energy Commission issued the terse announcement that the Soviet Union on that date set off two large nuclear explosions, presumably hydrogen bombs at an Arctic testing site. Such announcements are the product of a world-wide monitoring system established by the Commission for detecting Soviet nuclear explosions.

In the period between 1949, when the first Soviet nuclear test was reported, and the end of February 1958, the AEC announced some thirty-one nuclear explosions as having been detonated by the Soviet Union. Not all Soviet atomic explosions are publicly announced by the commission, nor are full details given. But information about all such tests is quickly communicated within the intelligence community.

Such information is a basic requirement for officials responsible for national security plans and programs. For example, if the Soviets were known to be conducting high-altitude nuclear tests, these might reveal the state of progress of hydrogen warheads for ballistic missiles or progress in developing defensive nuclear missiles.

The Atomic Energy Commission is, therefore, a consumer

and producer of intelligence in the critical national security field of nuclear energy. Accordingly it also is represented on the Intelligence Advisory Committee by its Director, Division of Intelligence. The AEC also conducts liaison with other units on the working intelligence levels. The AEC of course is vitally interested in data on foreign atomic energy or nuclear weapons developments and provides technical guidance to CIA and the intelligence agencies of the armed services in collecting these raw data. The AEC, in turn, becomes a producer of intelligence when it processes information on nuclear energy and develops estimates as to the atomic weapons capabilities of foreign powers. This processed intelligence is disseminated to the National Security Council, the armed forces, and others in the intelligence community.

The Task of CIA

These, then, are the principal members of the intelligence community. They participate jointly in intelligence policy planning through representation on the Intelligence Advisory Committee.[47] Each has its bureaucratic traditions, its unique organizational characteristics, its parochial requirements and outlook. Each is influenced to some extent by its policies, programs, and veteran personnel. It is the task of the CIA, utilizing both its influence in the National Security Council and also the various interdepartmental mechanisms, to create out of these diverse components a truly national estimate, useful to the entire community. This is not an easy task.

VI

INTELLIGENCE END PRODUCT:
The National Estimate

On August 26, 1957, the Soviet Union announced the successful testing of an intercontinental ballistic missile. This was "intelligence" of high order, publicly revealed by a nation known in the past to have used the broad public announcement as a propaganda weapon. What was the significance, the reliability, of this information? Asked about it in a press conference the following day, Secretary of State John Foster Dulles made the strange announcement that the reliability of the Soviet claim was "anybody's guess." He added, "The intelligence community is making a careful study of this statement."[1]

Behind the scenes, the intelligence community for some years had been charting as precisely as possible the course of Soviet missile progress.[2] Using the most advanced methods of electronic detection — radar — and other detection devices and information sources, intelligence analysts working, for example, in CIA's Office of Scientific Intelligence, undoubtedly try to keep a running score of Soviet progress in missiles, as in all other significant developments in world affairs. Presumably, there is a Missiles Panel within CIA's Office of Scientific Intelligence.

The reliability of the missile announcement may have been, in Secretary Dulles' mind, "anybody's guess." But the intelligence community for some time had been producing *national estimates* of Soviet missile capability which were at least well-educated guesses. Undoubtedly a revised estimate was transmitted to the Secretary of State and his fellow members of the National Security Council shortly after the Soviet announcement. Such estimates are the end product of the complex intelligence process and constitute one of the intelligence community's principal contributions to national policy making.

One of the chief criticisms of the intelligence community at the outbreak of the Korean War was that crucial intelligence was available from State, Defense, and CIA, but that these departments merely routed the raw intelligence around to the appropriate agencies without coming up with a joint national estimate. CIA, in particular, was criticized for failing to go far enough in its duty "to correlate and evaluate intelligence relating to national security." [3]

The requirement that decision makers be provided with firm estimates as to future enemy capabilities or actions was recognized by the new Central Intelligence Director, General Walter Bedell Smith, who assumed office in 1950. A hard-driving administrator, General Smith was brought in to "beef up" central intelligence personnel, the process, and its product. He made every effort to use his office as a focal point for the national estimates. The CIA structure today is designed, in part, to produce these vital building blocks of national security policy — the *National Estimates*. It should be noted, parenthetically, that National Estimate refers to an agreed-upon intelligence community estimate and not to a study, such as a National Intelligence Survey, of the characteristics of foreign nations. The National Estimate, a carefully evaluated intelligence report required by the President and NSC, is produced by a complex co-ordinating machinery capped by CIA and representing the entire national intelligence community.

Producing National Estimates

The procedure for the production of national estimates may be roughly described as follows: The President, the Director of Central Intelligence, or some member of the NSC, or — perhaps more likely — the Assistant to the President for National Security Affairs will say, "I'm concerned about the situation in X nation. Let's have a national estimate on X. What's happening in X now, and what can be expected in a year from now?"

The next step in the fulfillment of this request is that terms of reference be defined by the Board of National Estimates. This board, a vital agency in CIA, is composed of nine intelligence experts — soldiers, diplomats, and scholars — who preside as a kind of planning general staff for the intelligence community. This group can initiate a study or, as is usually the case, act in response to a specific request from an intelligence consumer. The problem is defined, broken up into feasible components, and then assigned to appropriate intelligence agencies — that is, military problems going to G-2, ONI, or A-2, and political matters to State, and other components to a CIA research division or some other intelligence organization, perhaps the Atomic Energy Commission's Division of Intelligence.

Resulting staff studies next pour into the Office of National Estimates, which maintains a relatively small staff for integrating material received. The Board may then put together a draft of either a *straight estimate*, one which attempts to assess a foreign nation's intentions or future policies with implicit assumptions as to future United States policy, or, alternatively, *general assessments as to consequences of change in United States policy*. In either case the estimates attempt to consider the intelligence aspects only, staying as far as possible from policy recommendations or from estimates derived from viewing foreign-military affairs through policy-oriented glasses. In the latter alternative — the *general estimate* — the studies are not initiated by CIA or the intelligence community. They are developed only upon request from the decision makers. In this way the estimators try to avoid the danger of meddling with policy. They try to confine their attention only to assessing the consequences of policy changes, either to the United States or to a foreign nation. Where assumptions as to probable or proposed United States policies are involved, these are furnished by persons concerned with policy *per se*, for example, the policy planning staff of the Department of State.

The former type of estimate, the *straight estimate*, must be divided into two categories — the knowable, and the unknowable. An estimate in the knowable category may involve past events or physical facts, such as the existence of an industrial complex, a railroad system, or an atomic reactor. Also in the knowable category may be an estimate of Soviet long-range bomber or missile production by a certain fixed date. In the unknowable category, as previously suggested, are predictions involving human intentions which no one in any government can predict with certainty. These are, of course, relative terms. For even in the "knowable" category, disagreements frequently arise within the intelligence community in the interpretation of the same set of facts by different intelligence units. The system as presently designed attempts to resolve these conflicts so that decision makers will be saved from dilemma.

Intelligence estimates falling into the "unknowable" category are aptly illustrated by a remark by President Eisenhower in 1957 when a newsman inquired about the President's foreknowledge of the sudden demise of Soviet Defense Minister Marshal Zhukov. The following exchange occurred at the President's news conference:

Newsman, (Chicago Daily News). Some weeks ago you expressed a view that Marshal Zhukov's position in the Soviet hierarchy seemed greatly strengthened. In the light of his apparent removal now, I wonder if you could tell us whether you are satisfied whether the intelligence estimates you received about that were adequate.

President Eisenhower. Well, of course, as I have, I think, warned each of you every time I have spoken about this subject, any effort to penetrate the Soviet mind, or at least the mind of the men in the Kremlin to determine their reasons for doing anything, is highly speculative, and that is all it is. I don't think that any intelligence system can give you a complete and positive answer on this. . . . Marshal Zhukov seemed to come up from nowhere, almost, and now we don't know whether he is actually degraded, or whether there is some other move that is contemplated.[4]

A third type of estimate, the ultra-secret *net estimate*,* because of its policy ramifications, is handled by special machinery in the National Security Council system rather than by the Board of Estimates or the Intelligence Advisory Committee. The intelligence community simply supplies the intelligence ingredient to this kind of estimate, the political or policy ingredient being supplied from other sources. A net estimate is the result of a highly classified calculation of a foreign nation's capability and probable intention (usually in the military sphere) with the capability and probable intentions of this nation as part of the equation. An example would be an estimate of this nation's net nuclear-air-missile position vis-à-vis the Soviet Union in 1965. Such an estimate, important to long-range planning, is at once the most difficult and most important kind of estimate to have. Yet significantly it is not handled by the normal CIA estimating system, because it involves important United States

---

* The government has found it necessary in recent years to go outside of existing government institutions for some *net estimates*. Thus the Killian Committee in 1955 and the Gaither Committee in 1957 were called upon to render what, in effect, were net estimates.

policy considerations. Rather, it is "war-gamed" among the major national security agencies — NSC, Office of Defense Mobilization, Federal Civil Defense Administration, Joint Chiefs of Staff, and Atomic Energy Commission.

As the intelligence mass for the *straight* or *general* estimate is evaluated, it may be compressed for example into a fifteen-page document. Such an integrated document is then referred back to the contributing agencies for appraisal and review, at which point dissents can be registered. By this process the product is further refined. How long does such a process take? An estimate on the Soviet aircraft industry may take four months. On the other hand, a new estimate on current Soviet long-range bomber production may take only four days. The machinery can produce either "crash" or long-term estimates. In the fall of 1956, CIA reportedly did "crash" estimates — which, it is claimed, later events proved correct — during the Suez crisis in the total elapsed time of as little as three and one-half hours.

The Intelligence Advisory Committee

The next step in the process is that the estimate, with dissents, amendments, or revisions is submitted to the Intelligence Advisory Committee for final approval. It is within this committee that the last effort is made to reconcile conflicting views. The important Intelligence Advisory Committee serves in effect as a Board of Directors for the intelligence community. Not only is it the final forum for professional intelligence opinion in the construction of the important national estimates but it is within IAC that important managerial problems of the community — jurisdictional disputes, for example — are resolved. Chaired by the Director of Central Intelligence, the IAC is comprised of representatives from the Department of State, the Army, Navy, and Air Force intelligence, the Joint Staff, the Atomic

Energy Commission and the Federal Bureau of Investigation. The latter two representatives confine their contributions to matters relating to atomic energy and internal security.

Recall that the Director of Central Intelligence presides over the IAC. The accompanying chart gives an over-all view of the community in which the Intelligence Advisory Committee is the key group.

As a normal procedure, the Director sits down once a week with the IAC to review finished products. As Allen Dulles has explained, reports to the National Security Council usually take the form of agreed-upon national estimates, designed for use in decision making. But while unanimity is the general rule and the usual goal in producing the estimates, leaders of the intelligence community are quite conscious of criticism for over-processing information. Consequently, split reports are sometimes submitted to the NSC in preference to a watered-down, lowest common denominator agreement. Yet the danger always remains of an overly compromised estimate being submitted.

Sir Winston Churchill offers an example out of recent history of a danger in unanimous estimates. British intelligence, heavily sifted and compromised-down by the various agencies, failed to anticipate the Nazi attack upon Russia in June 1941. Churchill himself had concluded (so he recalls), however, on the basis of raw intelligence, and perhaps intuition, that a German attack was imminent but was being delayed by trouble in the Balkans. He so advised Stalin.[5] Churchill has referred disparagingly to some intelligence estimates. He called them "this form of collective wisdom." One must be alert to the pitfalls in lowest common denominator collective intelligence.

Collective or national intelligence represents nonetheless a great advance over the unco-ordinated, unilateral intelli-

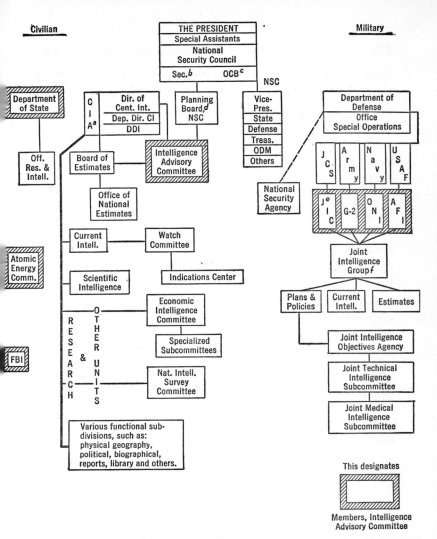

Civilian | THE PRESIDENT | Military

a. CIA has three grand subdivisions: intelligence production, secret operations, and support functions (administration). CIA leadership consists of a Director and a Deputy Director; Deputy Directors for intelligence, secret operations, and administration; and several Assistant Directors for functional subdivisions.

b. The NSC has a small permanent secretariat, operating under the President's Special Assistant for National Security Affairs.

c. Operations Coordinating Board chaired by Under-Secretary of State, and composed of the President's Special Assistant, National Security (vice-chairman), Deputy Defense Secretary, and Directors of CIA, U.S. Information Agency, and International Cooperation Administration.   *d.* Representatives of NSC members and of CIA and JCS.

e. Joint Intelligence Committee, charged with formulating joint military intelligence.

f. Responsible for staff support to JCS and JIC for production of military intelligence.

gence functions performed prior to reorganization of the intelligence community. Among the collateral benefits which are said to have accrued is a dampening of military departments' abilities to budgeteer through their own intelligence, that is, magnifying the Soviet Air Force or Soviet Navy in order to justify a larger United States Air Force or Navy budget.[6]

The Watch Committee and Indications Center

Another vital unit of CIA, one closely associated with the Board of Estimates and the IAC, is the National Indications Center, a warning agency established in 1954. The Indications Center works under the guidance of the Watch Committee, a group subordinate to the IAC. This mechanism, designed to prevent another Pearl Harbor, has been described by Allen Dulles as follows:

It works on a 24-hour basis. Anything coming in would go to our [CIA] watch officers, and to comparable officers in the Pentagon. If these officers felt that this intelligence showed up a critical situation, we would immediately call a meeting of the Intelligence Advisory Committee. . . . At any time of the day or night this Committee would sit down and go over any critical intelligence and make an immediate report to the President and National Security Council. The machinery is there to function, and unless there was a "human" failure, it would function.[7]

There may always be a need for a "crash estimate" which tests the efficacy of the Indications Center, the Board of Estimates, and the Intelligence Advisory Committee. This happened for example on March 3, 1953, when information that Premier Josef Stalin was dead flashed over the wires late in the evening to a teletype in CIA headquarters at 2430 "E" Street, N.W., Washington. Then it soon became known that Georgi Malenkov would succeed Stalin.

What was the precise meaning of this change in the Red

high command? How did Stalin's death affect chances of war or peace? Should the United States leaders be alerted to expect more aggressive moves, or a more conciliatory policy? Was there a chance of revolution in Russia? Informed answers to such questions were vitally needed by the President and National Security Council.

It can be imagined that Allen Dulles, having been given raw intelligence by his CIA associates, quickly disseminated the known facts to key government leaders. His next step was to send orders to CIA agents and undercover operatives around the world. Requests were also sent to other agencies, requesting information on what diplomatic or military moves to expect, information on troop movements, morale behind the Iron Curtain in Russia and her satellites, purges, arms shipments, and other data. The answers poured into the CIA headquarters.

Dulles and his CIA colleagues, in conference with the Board of Estimates and the IAC, probably sifted through the reports, studied the background information on Malenkov and all the other available and relevant data. Finally when Dulles met with the President the next morning, he was prepared to give a summary which possibly read like this: "Russia not prepared for war; an internal revolution unlikely; no immediate foreign policy changes expected," and so forth. On the basis of such intelligence estimates the President was thus able to issue a carefully prepared statement before noon on the day following Stalin's death.[8]

One of the most significant developments in the system for national decision making in the decade since World War II is the National Intelligence Estimate. It is true that such estimates still reflect the innate limitations of any forecast of the actions of human beings or governments, the shortcomings of any product which is the attainable consensus of an interdepartmental committee, and the gap between the real and the ideal in intelligence community spirit. Yet leaders of the intelligence community are perhaps rightly proud of, if not satisfied with, the contemporary estimating mechanism,* and of the closer ties which now exist between policymaking and intelligence estimates.

Leaders of the intelligence community now are assured that a community-produced estimate, granting its limitations, is available as a foundation for national decision, even though the estimate may be disregarded or misinterpreted in the shaping of actual government programs. The intelligence credit with policy makers at least has increased tremendously and continues to grow. Intelligence leaders are encouraged by this growing credit for they feel that for every Churchill there are hundreds of policy makers whose "off the top of the head" guesses prove fatally wrong. And indeed, Mr. Churchill, with all of his self-esteemed intuition, was not always right and his intelligence advisers wrong.

Yet with all the growing intelligence credit within the American governmental system, and with the increasing efficiency of the estimating mechanism, fundamental problems of credibility and receptivity remain. Many responsible officials, in the last analysis, continue to serve as their own intelligence experts. Intelligence-by-committee still tends to suppress what at times may be the vitally significant dissent. Duplication, institutional rivalry, and jurisdictional jealousy continue to deposit sand in the gears. And the irresistible force of the National Intelligence Estimate collides on frequent occasions with the immovable object of budgetary ceilings, or the weighty obstacle of unwillingness to believe. These problems will be discussed in greater detail in later chapters.

---

* For an example of how national estimates are continually revised, see Appendix C.

VII

SURVEILLANCE BY CONGRESS:
The Issue Debated

A dynamic conflict between Congress and the Executive is the inevitable consequence of the American system of government. The existence of a massive and highly secret CIA, expending hundreds of millions of dollars annually with only minimal legislative supervision is expectedly a thorn in the side of a Congress habitually jealous of its prerogatives under the American Constitutional system.

The Inevitable Executive-Legislative Conflict

Delineating precisely the respective roles of Congress and the Executive is a perplexing task under the separation-of-powers concept of American government. Consequently, from the earliest days of the Republic, Congress and the Executive have been in constant struggle as a result of the deliberately imprecise Constitutional division of powers. Usually this conflict has involved a Congressional desire for information which the Executive was unwilling to disclose.

Not only are roles and powers divided between Congress and the Executive. Some of the important functions also are *shared* by both branches. This is particularly true in foreign and military policy determination.

Conflict is heightened when it comes to the question of the status of such a highly secret agency as Central Intelligence.

Congress has by statute in effect given up, in the case of CIA, its normal and traditional controls over agencies of the Executive Branch. Yet the theoretical, Constitutional control of Congress over CIA remains. With the burgeoning of central intelligence in size and importance in recent years, the question has arisen whether Congress should regain some measure of real control over the foreign intelligence activities of the United States government.

This question has come up not only in the legislative halls, where it has taken the form of concrete proposals, but also in a Hoover Commission study (1955), which expressed concern about the absence of Congressional and other outside surveillance of government foreign intelligence activities. To the Hoover Commission, this lack of outside surveillance raises "the possibility of the growth of license and abuses of power where disclosure of costs, organization, personnel, and functions are precluded by law."

Congress and CIA

The issue of closer Congressional surveillance of the intelligence community and particularly of CIA came to a head in Senate action early in 1956. The specific point at issue was whether Congress was to establish a standing Joint Committee on the CIA, similar to the Joint Committee on Atomic Energy, to provide a fuller and continuing look at United States intelligence programs.

The CIA budget, as previously noted, is concealed within the budgets of various government departments. The average member of Congress has no more knowledge than the average citizen of the annual expenditures or of the size and scope of CIA operations. A handful of Congressional members gets occasional briefings on CIA's operations, as members of CIA subcommittees of the Committees on Armed

Services and Appropriations, from the Director of Central Intelligence. As Allen W. Dulles describes the process, "I talk with them and give them a picture of the nature of the work we are doing, tell them about our personnel, and where the money goes." [1] This small group is given what it has apparently considered to be adequate information, but this is not passed along to Congressional colleagues.

CIA officials also present testimony to Congressional committees seeking the latest intelligence estimates from the Executive Branch. In each case this testimony is presented in (secret) Executive Session, normally by the Director of Central Intelligence and his principal deputies. In the published transcript of committee hearings, such testimony is routinely deleted. CIA testimony provides the basis for legislative inquiries into national security, and intelligence estimates received are reflected in the subsequent questioning of other witnesses in open hearings and in the findings and reports of Congressional committees. Although not made public, the testimony of the Director of Central Intelligence was, for example, of basic importance to the Congressional inquiries of the Symington Senate (Armed Forces) Subcommittee's "Study of Airpower" in 1956, and the Johnson Senate (Armed Forces) Preparedness Subcommittee's probe of the defense program in 1957–58. An official description of CIA's normal relationship with Congress is described in Appendix B. But what is the extent of Congressional knowledge of CIA's policy and operations?

A large and vitally important agency of government, approaching in total personnel the size of the Department of State, and spending several hundreds of millions of dollars annually, the CIA operates with only nominal legislative surveillance. Is such secrecy the inevitable impact of the Cold War upon our government system? Is the national intelligence community a proper domain for constant Congressional exploration? Do the existing secrecy and sanctity alter significantly the legislative-executive balance of the American system of government? What are the consequences of such secrecy? What would be the consequences of wider Congressional knowledge of intelligence activities? These and related basic questions were raised in the Senate debate in 1956 over the proposal to set up a Joint Committee on CIA. Therefore this proposal and the arguments surrounding it will be briefly described here.

The Mansfield Resolution

It is not surprising that members of the national legislature, who take seriously the Constitutional provision that no money may be spent from the public treasury without Congressional approval, should become restless about the CIA's privileged position of secrecy. Such unrest has had various manifestations. One was in Senator Joseph McCarthy's characteristic statement in the Senate debate, ". . . I have roughly 100 pages of documentation covering incompetence, inefficiency, waste and Communist infiltration in the CIA, which I am holding in the hope that a committee will be established so that I can turn the information over to it." [2] Another, more temperate, manifestation of unrest was in the Senate resolution to establish a Joint Congressional Committee on Central Intelligence, introduced in the Eighty-fourth Congress (1955) by Senator Mike Mansfield (Dem., Montana), with 34 Republican and Democratic co-sponsors.[3] This was but one, albeit the most important, of a score of bills before Congress in recent years with similar purpose.[4]

The Mansfield Resolution was reported favorably out of the Rules Committee on February 23, 1956, by a vote of 8–1, with Senator Carl Hayden (Dem., Arizona) dissenting.[5] The proposal would establish a joint committee to have legislative oversight of the CIA. It would be composed of six members from each branch of Congress. Core of its membership would be those senators and representatives already serving as CIA subcommittee members from the Appropriations and Armed Services Committees. The Joint Committee was to have the broad mandate to study (1) the activities of CIA, (2) problems relating to the gathering of intelligence affecting national security, and (3) co-ordination and utilization of intelligence by the various departments and agencies of government. All legislative proposals relating primarily to CIA or foreign intelligence would be referred to this committee for consideration.

Senator Mansfield proposed further that the CIA keep the Joint Committee "fully and currently informed with respect to its activities." The committee was to be authorized to hold hearings and to require, by subpoena or otherwise, attendance of witnesses and the production of books, papers, and documents. The committee was also to have a permanent staff. In other words, the proposed committee was to assume the role of a regular Joint Congressional committee, with the power to investigate, advise, and report, and with a budget for its first year set at $250,000.

Proponents of the measure asserted that it followed, in essence, a recommendation made to Congress by the 1955 Hoover Commission. The proposed committee was said to be analogous to the Joint Committee on Atomic Energy and, like it, "dedicated to the promotion of the public and legislative will in a sensitive agency imperative to our country's international survival." [6]

At the same time, the proposal was designed to preserve the continuity of existing Congressional surveillance of CIA by limiting membership on the proposed committee primarily to those senators and representatives already privy to knowledge of CIA's operations. But surveillance was to occur on a more institutionalized scale, with all the trappings and power of a regular Congressional committee, rather than the occasional meeting once or twice a year between CIA officials and members of armed services and appropriations subcommittees.

Arguments for Joint Committee

The Report of the Senate Committee on Rules and Administration on the Mansfield Resolution described the background of the CIA and summarized the various studies and reports made of its operations. It then set forth the major arguments for the adoption of the proposal. These included the following:

(a) The fact that Congressional surveillance has existed, since 1946, in the atomic energy field, an area equally as sensitive as foreign intelligence. Most of the work of the Joint Committee on Atomic Energy, argued the Senate Rules Committee majority, "is of the highest security classification." Discussing its generally successful functioning in a sensitive area, the report concluded: "What is true of the Joint Committee on Atomic Energy can be true of a new joint committee organized to oversee the Central Intelligence Agency." [7]

(b) The suggestion that a specialized joint committee would "promote new confidence between Congress and the CIA." The new committee's staff would maintain "an effective check on the operations of CIA." A Joint Committee would provide a "forum for the registering of congressional doubts and complaints and the initiation of advisory and corrective action with respect to any errors which might be apparent." The effect would be to produce more constant liaison between Congress and CIA. Through all this, the report argues, "No classified or ill-advised revelations would be made."

(c) The belief that studies of CIA by *ad hoc* or temporary groups are not sufficient. The fact that most reports of studies of CIA since its creation in 1947 have been highly secret has excluded Congress from details of CIA operations. The Senate report argues that "It is not enough that CIA be responsible alone to the White House or the National Security Council. Such responsibility should be shared with Congress in a more complete manner." It is argued that in our form of government, a system of checks and balances, it is essential that intelligence operations come under a more thorough Congressional audit. Otherwise, the report states, "there will be no way of knowing what serious flaws in the Central Intelligence Agency may be covered by the curtain of secrecy in which it is shrouded."

(d) An argument that a policy of "secrecy for the mere sake of secrecy" invites abuse and prevents Congress and the nation from "knowing whether we have a fine intelligence service or a very poor one." The report acknowledges the importance of secrecy to any intelligence operation, yet the feeling is expressed that the veil of secrecy has been extended to cover too much from Congressional scrutiny. "Secrecy now beclouds everything about CIA," the report complains, "its cost, its personnel, its efficiency, its failures, its successes. An aura of superiority has been built around it. It is freed from practically every ordinary form of Congressional review. The CIA has unquestionably placed itself above other Government agencies." [8] In sum, the Senate Rules Committee majority felt that while secrecy is vital to certain facets of CIA operations, a wide area of its activities is proper ground for Congressional review.

Sentiments such as these expressed in the Senate report on the Mansfield Resolution were widely held in the Senate, as evidenced by the fact that more than one-third of Senate membership was listed as co-sponsor of the resolution. At the same time some twenty-five similar resolutions had been introduced in the House of Representatives, indicating widespread Congressional conviction that central intelligence needed to be brought under closer surveillance.

Arguments Against Joint Committee

Dimensions of the debate were previewed by the substance of the minority report submitted by Senator Hayden, who set forth the following counter-arguments:

(a) Existing surveillance, by members of the appropriations and armed services committees, is adequate. Testimonial was offered that CIA has demonstrated a willingness to keep these committees fully informed, and CIA officials have "candidly furnished the desired information and have responded to the specific complaints and criticisms that have been voiced in Congress and in the press." [9] Said Senator Hayden, "No information has been denied and all desired information has been candidly supplied." [10]

(b) Functions of the CIA are essentially executive in character, as the agency serves the President, the National Security Council, and other departments in a staff capacity. "If CIA must have a 'watchdog' joint committee, why not have one for the FBI?"

(c) CIA has been intensely, repeatedly, and adequately investigated by various special commissions. Furthermore, the President, following recommendations of the 1955 Hoover Commission, established a Board of Consultants on Foreign Intelligence Activities to advise him regularly and to report its findings at least twice a year. Senator Hayden suggested that Congress therefore let CIA get on with its work "without being watchdogged to death." [11]

(d) The proposal to create a Joint Committee raises a Constitutional issue of separation of powers between executive and legislative branches. It was argued that since CIA undertakes activities only in accordance with National Security Council directives, any Congressional action which seeks to interfere with or pry into this relationship "would tend to impinge upon the constitutional authority and responsibility of the President in the conduct of foreign affairs."

(e) Comparison of CIA with the Atomic Energy Commission, and use of the atomic energy analogy, constitute invalid arguments. In size of operation, in impact upon the domestic economy, and in detailed legislative matters involved in atomic energy affairs, the atomic energy field is not comparable with intelligence. Atomic energy is a subject for general legislative consideration, unlike intelligence activities which were said to be "peculiarly the prerogative of the Executive and intimately associated with the conduct of the foreign relations of the country." [12]

These dissenting views, as presented by Senator Hayden, set the stage for the Senate debate on the issue. A key to the counter-argument was the notion expressed, by quoting Senator Richard Russell, that, "If there is one agency of the Government in which we must take some matters on faith without a constant examination of its methods and sources, I believe this agency is the Central Intelligence Agency." [13] The minority view was that Congress was generally informed, through its designated subcommittees of foreign intelligence activities. What Congress did not know about CIA activities, it was argued, was to be accepted "on faith." For, as Senator Hayden noted, "We must remember that the Central Intelligence Agency carries on its work outside the United States boundaries. Many of its agents are in constant physical danger." [14] About this work a few select members of Congress would be advised on a "need to know" and a "desire to know" basis.

Debate on the Senate Floor

Dimensions of the debate on the Senate floor of the Mansfield Resolution in April 1956 were forecast in the Senate report just described. The arguments pro and con listed above were decorated with the usual Senate oratorical trappings, but few additional basic arguments were made in support of, or in opposition to, the proposal.

A prime mover of the proposal, Senator Mansfield, expressed fear that a creeping secrecy might produce a situation in which Congress would possess a decreasing amount of information about the performance of the intelligence community.[15] Senator Mansfield before and since that time has expressed doubt about the quality of the intelligence product. He felt that closer Congressional surveillance would improve the product; that "Congressional guardians might be able to compel even swifter and surer reform than could an executive committee." [16]

Senator Mansfield made the further point in the debate that the development of CIA under tight Executive control represented "arrogation of power on the part of the Executive and a diminution to that extent of the equality between the executive and the legislative." [17] Through its control of secret information vital to foreign policy making, Senator Mansfield feared that CIA abetted the Executive's increasing domination over this field, to the exclusion of Congress.

On this latter point he was joined by the strongly stated arguments of Senator Wayne Morse, who expressed a suspicion that CIA "determines a great deal of policy. . . . it has great influence in determining foreign policy." [18] Senator Morse's views were the embodiment of traditional American misgivings about maintaining an espionage system. He said that Senators who were opposing the resolution were in effect "supporting a form of American police state system." Referring to an opponent in the debate, Senator Morse declared that "when he defends the present CIA system, he defends a spy system that is based upon a police state procedure." [19] He felt that all members of the Senate Committee on Foreign Relations and Armed Services ought to be informed about "the manner in which the American spy system functions." [20]

Another Senator, Henry Dworshak, although opposing the resolution, spoke up to recount that as a member of a defense appropriations subcommittee he had been unsuccessful in obtaining information from the Director of Central Intelligence. He recounted that he asked questions about number of CIA employees and amount of CIA expenditures and was told, emphatically, "This is classified information." [21] Yet even with thirty-five original supporters of the resolution, only a meager handful joined Mansfield and Morse in debate to support the measure.

Formidable Opposition in the Senate

A bipartisan force of formidable size and prestige spoke out against the measure, with obviously powerful back-stopping from leaders of the Administration. Some of the members of the Senate with most prestige, Democratic as well as Republican, led by Senators Richard Russell and Leverett Saltonstall, echoed the arguments already summed up in the minority report of the Senate Rules Committee. Senator Russell, who like Saltonstall served on CIA subcommittees, declared that "although we have asked him [Allen W. Dulles] very searching questions about some activities which it almost chills the marrow of a man to hear about, he has never failed to answer us forthrightly and frankly in response to any question we have asked him." [22] This view was seconded by Senator Saltonstall and others of the small interlocking group from Armed Services and Appropriations Committees who were the Senate's chosen few to oversee CIA.

Although apparently getting all the information sought from CIA officials, it has been the practice of this select group to exercise self-restraint in asking questions. At least this is the inference from Senator Saltonstall's remark that "it is not a question of reluctance on the part of CIA officials to speak to us. Instead it is a question of our reluctance, if you will, to seek information and knowledge on subjects which I personally, as a Member of Congress and as a citizen, would rather not have. . . ." [23] Meetings with CIA officials (at which such questions went unasked) were held "once a year" in the case of the Appropriations subcommittee; "twice a year" in the case of the Senate Armed Services subcommittee.[24] None of the members of these two CIA subcommittees voted for the Mansfield Resolution.[25]

Most opponents of the measure made the point in the debate that secrecy is vital to intelligence operations and that a Congressional Joint Committee would be incompatible with this required secrecy. As Senator Alben Barkley noted in the debate, "The activities of the CIA cover the entire world, and the CIA makes reports on the entire world situation." [26] As for the need for secrecy, Senator Barkley, who as vice-president sat for four years with the National Security Council, declared: "Some of the information gathered by the Central Intelligence Agency and laid before the National Security Council itself was so confidential and secret that the very portfolios in which it was contained were under lock and key." [27] He added, "I would lose my right arm before I would divulge it to anyone, even to members of my own family." [28]

It soon became clear in the Senate debate that the measure did not have adequate support for passage. Not only did Senator Barkley, former member of the National Security Council, lend weighty oratorical opposition, but he was also joined by a former Secretary of the Air Force, Senator Stuart Symington. Also in opposition were the majority and minority leaders of the Senate, and high-ranking members — both Republican and Democratic — of the Armed Services and Appropriations Committees.

The Senate Vote

At its initiation the proposal had 35 supporters, but it was defeated by a vote of 59 to 27, with 10 Senators not voting.[29] Fourteen of the measure's co-sponsors, all Republicans but one, did an about-face and voted against the measure. It is plausible to suggest that strong Administration opposition to the measure caused this contradictory performance. The 27 members who voted in favor of the resolution fall with a few exceptions into two general categories: liberal Democrats most of whom have lesser seniority on Senate committees, and right-wing Republicans who were generally associated with the McCarthy camp. Support for the measure therefore was a reflection of two general attitudes.

One was the general distaste of liberal Democrats for the "dirty business" of international spying and the existence of a state apparatus for secret intelligence beyond the surveillance of Congress through regular committee procedures. The other group supporting the resolution was composed of the late Senator McCarthy and his associates, who perhaps reflected Midwestern resentment of the size and potential power of CIA, an agency engaged in an essentially intellectual process and led largely by an "Ivy League" assemblage of bright young men. The existence of CIA also was symbolic of America's new internationalism, which left Senators in this group, including, for example, Senator William Langer, of North Dakota, with deep suspicion.

Opposition to the measure was made up of a group of "Eisenhower Republicans" of various degree, and powerful Democratic Senators, mostly Southerners with high committee seniority. These men, some of whom were privy to information about CIA, saw little need for a new Joint Committee. One astute observer of the Senate has concluded that the measure was killed because the "Inner Club" of Senate patriarchs felt it had not been adequately consulted about the measure.[30]

As is often the case in Congressional debate, some of the real and persuasive arguments for or against a measure did not come to the surface. These arguments are the kind that are persuasive in the cloakrooms and corridors, but are not brought out in the public debate for any number of possible reasons. One such argument was the fact that the establishment of wider Congressional surveillance over CIA would be disturbing to the principal allies of the United States. Allied intelligence services work closely though sometimes in an atmosphere of mutual suspicion with United States central intelligence agents in overseas operations, but apparently are wary of supplying the American Congress with details of such operations. Intelligence units in allied nations enjoy immunity from detailed legislative supervision, though parliamentary government gives a direct responsibility to political leaders. Consequently, a more thorough check of CIA operations by the United States Congress, it is held, would tend to inhibit vital and always difficult interallied intelligence co-operation and thus dry up important sources for American government officials. But this was not the kind of argument that would swing great weight in the Senate debate and thus it hardly came to the surface. Apparently it was persuasive in the cloakrooms.

Even more persuasive in the cloakrooms was the realization by senior members of the Senate that creating a Joint Committee on Central Intelligence would have the effect of slicing off a part of their jurisdictional authority. For example, the Committee on Foreign Relations oversees intelligence within the Department of State; the Armed Services Committee looks into intelligence activities in the armed forces; the Joint Committee on Atomic Energy oversees Atomic Energy Commission intelligence activities; and CIA is currently under the purview of a few senior members on Armed Services and Appropriations committees. It is not surprising that senior members of the Senate would oppose alteration in the present fractured structure of Congress, if that change would remove segments of the Executive Branch from their particular domain.

Opposition by Senate patriarchs made possible an effective alliance with the Executive Branch, particularly with the leadership of CIA, to whom the growth of a Congressional committee intelligence staff is an anathema. Such a staff, it is feared, would be a haven for some ex-CIA personnel whose mission in life might be to second-guess National Intelligence Estimates, or generally to harass Executive intelligence agencies.

Whatever their motives, a sizable majority of members of a group traditionally jealous of Congressional prerogative in the continuing Legislative-Executive struggle voted against a measure which seemed to promise at first glance to give them additional power in this struggle. On this issue the Senate exercised restraint. Such restraint has been normal for the national legislature in the past only in wartime, in which large sums of money were blindly granted by Congress. Its wartime motto was said to be: "Trust in God and General Marshall." In the Cold War era of 1956, the attitude seems to have been: "Trust in God and Allen Dulles."

VIII

✳ INTELLIGENCE
and National Policy Making

National decision making involves the acquisition of knowledge and its manipulation within a framework of values and objectives to determine courses of action. Soundness of policy is limited by the quality of information on which it is based. The quality of that segment of information labeled intelligence is itself determined in a complex process involving organization, doctrine, and, most significantly, human beings. Thus it is strategically important to national policy decisions that the nation possess the most effective and efficient organization and personnel for the collection, evaluation, and communication of intelligence. And the product is inextricably related to the process.

The inevitable result of any survey or analysis of the intelligence community, particularly the Central Intelligence Agency, will be a set of recommendations for improving its structure and the quality of its product. It is not surprising that such were the basic recommendations of Hoover Commission task forces in 1949 and 1955.[1*]

It should be understood that the *ideal* intelligence product, that which sets forth with 100 per cent accuracy the capabilities and intentions of foreign nations — allied or enemy — will never be achieved. This is particularly true of attempts to make long-range predictions of what can and may happen two, three, or even five or ten years from now. Certainly a five- or ten-year projection of the strategic capabilities of the Soviet Union is a continuing current requisite for United States national security planning. The Central Intelligence Agency makes such projections, which undoubtedly must be continually revised.* The difficulty of making, and the tentative nature of, such predictions are apparent. For it can be asked: Is it possible to make a fully accurate long-range prediction of our own government's capabilities and intentions?

Yet long-range prediction is an increasingly important intelligence function. It is the goal which challenges the intelligence community, although it inevitably involves speculation. It is a burden added to that of supplying the most accurate current information available. A degree of accuracy in long-range forecasting is essential to the future security of the nation. In such fields as foreign economic policy, weapons development, and information (propaganda) activity, today's plans and programs will affect our international status five to ten years from now. Difficult decisions about major weapons systems made today will determine the characteristics of the American military system five to ten years from now. But the United States also must be able to project its requirements in other fields, such as, for example, the development of enough trained scientists and engineers for future needs. The long-term requirements of other nations must also be predicted in order that the United States may proceed with a coherent program of foreign economic and military aid.

Effective Decision Making

Ideally the first step in the making of important national decisions on plans and programs is a call for all the pertinent

* See, for example, Appendix C.

facts.[2] In the nuclear age, when crucial decisions affecting national security, in spite of all long-range planning, may have to be made within a few hours — or even minutes — there are two basic requisites for making the right decision. First is the availability of all the pertinent data relating to the decision. Second is a recognition on the part of the policy maker that such data are essential to his decision. This recognition, in turn, must be combined with a respect for the intelligence product. The best intelligence product in the world will never be a substitute for human judgment in the final casting of national policy. Yet we have to expect more, in this age, than a reliance by the policy maker upon personal bias, "hunch," or conditioned reflex. Too often in the past public policy seems to have been made either in ignorance of — or disregard for — elementary facts. Yet it is fair to ask whether the basic facts were available, and were in usable form.

A corollary requisite for effective decision making, in addition to all the pertinent data and the policy maker's recognition of the need for it, is a continuing rapport between the producer of intelligence — the leaders of the intelligence community — and the consumers — the responsible decision makers. "All the pertinent data" will not necessarily be forthcoming if there has not been anticipation of what information may be needed. It has been suggested earlier that intelligence, like knowledge, knows no boundaries. Yet clearly some discipline must be brought to the assembling of data. Guidelines must be established for the producer, through anticipation by the producer — the intelligence community — of information which may be required, and through suggestion from the consumer of what he may need to know for policy decisions. Here lies an important distinction between the research and analysis function within the intelligence community and that carried on, say, within a university.

The exacting requirements for an effective intelligence system are not easily filled. There are basic problems of organization, personnel, and attitude which complicate the tremendously demanding burden placed upon the producer of intelligence today. Not only is delicately collected and skilfully evaluated intelligence required about the capabilities of several score foreign nations — friendly, neutral, and not friendly — but this information must be gathered through a score of agencies which are part of the massive, modern American governmental bureaucracy. Their activities must be "co-ordinated" and the intelligence products amalgamated and fused into national estimates, Getting these estimates to the right place at the right time within the massive bureaucracy is no easy task. And, assuming that the intelligence product is of high quality, getting it accepted as reliable and useful remains a basic problem. And finally, as the machinery for central intelligence itself expands into a complex bureaucratic maze, the problem of its supervision and control in keeping with the precepts of popular, representative government remains acute. For if intelligence is to serve popular government, it cannot operate with complete independence from responsible political leaders. Let us now look separately at these and related problems.

The Problem of Organization

The intelligence, like the military, function of government today is performed on an institutional basis, the chief over-all organizational principles of which are confederation and separatism. Most government agencies, whatever their function, have always had their intelligence staffs, whatever they have been called. The need felt after the war for centralized intelligence, like that recognized for military unification, clashed head-on with the fact that well-established organizations already existed for the performance of specialized functions. As earlier indicated, for example, the Department of State has always considered itself to be the principal agency for the gathering of foreign political intelligence. And, in a sense, it always has been. Why then, should the central intelligence function not be centered within the Department of State? A part of the answer is that the production of national estimates transcends the diplomatic province of the State Department. Also, the precarious and dirty business of espionage and political action in foreign lands is not compatible with the protocol requirements of international diplomacy to which foreign officers of the Department of State inevitably must adhere. Further, it would be administratively impracticable for one department of government to attempt to co-ordinate the intelligence activities and products of its co-equal departments and agencies of government.

The result, as earlier described, has been the establishment and growth of the uniquely placed Central Intelligence Agency. Like any agency charged with "co-ordinating" the intelligence activity of the multifarious departments and agencies of the Federal Government, its lot is a hard one. But it has the unique advantage of "working for" the National Security Council. Thus CIA is in an important sense very close to the President and sometimes in a position to utilize his authority and influence to get done the always difficult job of co-ordinating.

The Fusing of Information

A very basic function of the Central Intelligence Agency is to weld conflicting intelligence estimates into a national estimate, not only for the use of the President and the National Security Council, but for all agencies of government operating in the national security field. In the past, a President himself had to perform the last step in the national intelligence process — the fusion of conflicting estimates. Different and conflicting evaluations sometimes came to the presidential desk, prior to the establishment of a system for a co-ordinated national estimate.

Now this impossible burden has been eliminated from presidential shoulders and from those of his principal deputies. One of these, Secretary of Defense Charles E. Wilson, illustrated in 1957 his reliance on the national estimate as follows:

> You see, what I get for my purpose is an agreed-on intelligence estimate, and all the different people in the area, the different services and so on, whatever speculation about it they want to make — and the group comes in with an agreement. . . .

> I have to take that, or I would have to bore through an enormous amount of detail myself to try to say that they were wrong or right, or that if I were making the judgment I would move a little bit. I accept what they say, and I can't go back of that from my time available.[3]

Yet the production of national estimates, with all its advantages, also has its dangers. It has been argued that intelligence estimates are, in the end, a work of art, and who ever heard of a great work of art created by a committee? In compromising out differences of opinion on a difficult question — say, for example, the future capabilities of, and intended use for, the Soviet Navy — it may be that the intelligence estimate will be so watered down by committee as to diminish its validity and usefulness. The intelligence community is apparently aware of this danger arising from its important mission to produce "agreed-on" national estimates. Devices and procedures have been worked out to cope with this danger. These include the use of dissenting footnotes or of language accurately revealing the uncompromised disagreements. This problem, of course, reflects both basic advantages and disadvantages of a federated intelligence system. A national estimate of the future threat of the Soviet Navy, for example, is not the product alone of the Office of Naval Intelligence, but also has traveled the rocky road of sharp questioning by the Air Force, the CIA, and others. This tends to reduce the influence of parochial intelligence estimates and of any tendency that may exist to "budgeteer" by use of narrowly conceived or partisan intelligence. The problems of intelligence-by-committee are discussed in greater detail in the concluding chapter.

Consequences of Federation

The principle of federation underlying the present national intelligence structure fosters not only these beneficial differences of opinion in the process but also a high degree of duplication. The CIA's main activity is in those areas where the intelligence function is best performed by a central organization. It is likely and natural that the central organization will come to believe that more and more of these functions can best be performed centrally, within controlled organizational confines by known and trusted individuals. Thus we are likely to see a steady, if slow, growth of the central organization, as it takes on more and more functions. CIA is unlikely to escape the Washington malady of empire building, although a conscious effort has been made to keep important sections, such as the Office of National Estimates, of manageable size. Meanwhile, the various other departments, to which specialized intelligence will seem increasingly important, and which are spurred on by the activities of the central organization, will increase their intelligence activity.* Duplication is bound to increase, possibly in favor of an improved over-all intelligence product, but not necessarily so. An accelerating technology which bolsters the argument for greater unification of the armed services also will create the need for a more unified intelligence community.

A Separate Function?

The growth to its present size and importance of the Central Intelligence Agency also magnifies the basic organizational question whether intelligence should be an increasingly separate function, divorced from policy making. Central intelligence today is regarded as a separate staff function to be performed by specialists working full-time and separate from policy-making responsibility. It is assumed that the product of these specialists will be fed into policy making at the appropriate time and place. It is further assumed that the over-all intelligence function is logically decentralized into some twenty to thirty separate agencies of government, co-ordinated by a staff agency — the CIA — and the necessary national intelligence processed and produced by an interdepartmental committee, the Intelligence Advisory Committee. It is a very complex administrative structure which, like much government organization, has evolved from organizations existing in the past rather than from a purely rational design. It is a compromise between the needs of centralization and the requirements of institutions with separate and distinct functions. With all its advantages, it is a system difficult to operate. There are plusses and minuses in its performance to date. Let us consider other problems of the intelligence community.

* As an example, the Army's intelligence budget request was 92 million dollars in 1956; 100 million dollars in 1957; and 125 million dollars in 1958.

Intelligence Credibility

One of the most important problems of central intelligence is the acceptability and credibility of the intelligence product. Most of the users of intelligence, whether military commanders or top civilian decision makers, apparently regard intelligence with mixed feelings. They want enough pertinent facts to make the policy choice clear and are thankful for the help intelligence can give them. Yet they know they can never have all the facts. They suspect that somewhere along the line of intelligence production someone has made a guess. They recognize that there is an inevitable element of subjectivity in the selection process at every step. And they know from experience that the intelligence estimate has not always been correct; that, as a product of human judgment, it is fallible. And, usually far removed from the source of data going into the intelligence estimate, there is often lingering suspicion and doubt as to the derivation of the information. For the source, though graded and evaluated, usually remains a mystery.

Intelligence Has Competitors

Since decision making involves essentially the manipulation of information or knowledge within a frame of reference of values and objectives, the element in this process with the label "Intelligence" must compete with the decision maker's bias, experience, and other "pictures in his mind." Each decision maker has various sources of information with which the intelligence product must compete. Let us assume that the final decision maker — the President or the Secretary of State — reads the daily and weekly press, *The Washington Post and Times Herald, The New York Times,* and *U.S. News and World Report.* These sources provide information, albeit with varying degrees of accuracy and bias, which competes in the mind of the decision maker with the papers which come to his desk labeled "Intelligence — TOP SECRET." The decision makers also encounter daily large numbers of advisers, ambassadors, and military officers from the field, foreign visitors, and others, all bearing information of various kinds, and most all of them attempting to influence the shape and color of their minds' pictures.

The growing band of professional intelligence experts in Washington, increasingly confident of their product, not unnaturally want to manage the intellectual process by which decisions are made. They see their role to be the procurement of facts out of which enlightened policies evolve. They undoubtedly regard as half-baked much of the advice that reaches the ears of decision makers from other sources. They recognize these outside threats. Thus the modern corps of intelligence experts can be heard speaking of the problems of "selling their product."

Intelligence operators, incidentally, have sometimes been more successful in leading the enemy — in time of war — to believe fabricated intelligence than they have been in selling their legitimate product in the home office. During World War II, the British by an artfully devised and minutely planned scheme managed deliberately to mislead the Germans in a *ruse de guerre* of spectacular success. After the battle for Tunisia, the Allies decided that the next step would be the invasion of Italy via Sicily. By causing to be washed ashore in Spain the body of a fictitious Royal Marine carrying letters containing "secret" military planning information, the Allies tricked the Germans (who were promptly informed by the Spanish) into spreading their defense across Europe, even to the extent of removing warships from the

Sicily area. This ruse paved the way for a relatively easy invasion of Sicily.[4]

Suspicion of the Intelligence Product

Although the intelligence credit has probably risen gradually in the ten years of CIA existence, the debit side of the ledger is not empty. Popular sentiment about intelligence, and the feeling in some policy making circles, still reveal considerable doubt and suspicion about the reliability of the intelligence product.

A striking bit of evidence of this is seen in Admiral Arthur W. Radford's off-hand comment, while serving as Chairman of the Joint Chiefs of Staff in 1956. "In general in the intelligence field they tend to err on the safe side," he told a Senate committee. The Admiral admittedly based this view upon his experience in World War II, which apparently left him with a deep-seated suspicion of intelligence estimates. Even with an increasingly efficient CIA, the Admiral was willing to suggest that "There is good reason to believe that we normally overestimate Communist capabilities in almost every respect. . . . there has been an almost hysterical assumption of great capabilities on the part of the Communists, some of which, in my opinion, do not exist." [5] These remarks were made to a committee very much concerned with the other side of this coin of Soviet vis-à-vis United States air power. Admiral Radford's implication was that such concern was based upon exaggerated intelligence.[6] We can infer that he sensed that some intelligence was being used to increase the money appropriations for one or another of the armed services.

General cynicism and skepticism are sometimes displayed in the press about some intelligence estimates. A *New*

York Times dispatch from Washington on July 6, 1957, stated, "The United States Army suggested today that the Soviet Army was better equipped than itself to fight any type of war under any conceivable conditions." A few paragraphs later the article stated, "It has been recognized here that a good deal of the emphasis on Soviet capability is motivated by the United States military leaders' efforts to gain support for their own estimated requirements." [7] If such were the motives, this does little to help build up the credit side of the intelligence ledger. If not, this news account demonstrates the skepticism with which seasoned newsmen view some intelligence estimates.

Intelligence blunders or failures often become public knowledge. Intelligence successes usually go unnoticed. In either case, the leaders of the intelligence community can say little, for either defense or bragging may have the effect of disclosing secret sources of information. It may be that too much is expected of intelligence, yet the debit side of the ledger provides the basis for lingering skepticism in the face of those who would "sell the product" as always first-quality material.

Mistaken Estimates of Potential Enemies

Allen Dulles once commented that "Events which seem to defy analysis happen somewhere in the world every day. Few trends seem to follow a predictable course." [8] Mr. Dulles could have added that regrettably many important events of the first ten years of CIA's existence have succeeded often in defying analysis. Our policy planners have not always been armed with adequate foreknowledge.

One of the major intelligence tasks today is keeping abreast of the Soviet Union. Little comfort can be found in the Hoover Commission's expression of deep concern over "lack of adequate Intelligence data from behind the Iron Curtain." [9] This concern was sharply reflected in a colloquy on Air Force research and development in 1956 between Senator Allen Ellender (D., La.) and Lyle S. Garlock, Assistant Secretary of the Air Force (Financial Management).

Senator Ellender. Why are we so far behind? Have you any idea?
Mr. Garlock. . . . there was too much of a letdown in the postwar period. We get a little behind that way.

This matter of being ahead or behind depends on how fast the other fellow is running and our finding is that he is apparently going much faster than we thought he would go.

Senator Ellender. Do you charge that to faulty intelligence, or what?

Mr. Garlock. I would say inadequate intelligence. It is fairly obvious that the development was faster than we anticipated and he [Soviet Russia] got quite a ways down the line before we apparently knew about it. [10]

Mr. Garlock's critique of intelligence on the Soviet Union is shared, if not by Admiral Radford, by the Brothers Alsop, although they lean more to the "faulty" rather than "inadequate" intelligence thesis. The Alsops wrote in January 1956: "In every case where there has been a test to date, the official American intelligence forecast indicated that the Soviets could not do the job so soon, or that they could not do it really well. And in every case where there has been a test to date the result has shown, alas, that Soviet capability has been sadly underestimated." [11] This is a view obviously contrary to that expressed by Admiral Radford. At any rate the nation is slow to get over its tendency to view the Soviets as clumsy blacksmiths, capable only of copying our technological achievements.

While there seems to be fairly general agreement in Washington that intelligence effort should be intensified, it remains a moot question as to whether we underestimate or over-estimate the military resources of the Soviets. The Chairman of the Joint Chiefs of Staff, as already indicated, believed, in 1956, that we tend to overestimate.

The Secretary of Defense, Charles E. Wilson, shared Admiral Radford's position that Soviet power has been over-estimated. Wilson has the opinion that Americans have an unfortunate proclivity for thinking that the Soviets are all ten feet tall. Yet since everyone presumably has been looking at the same fact or set of facts, why is there no consistency on our intelligence opinions vis-à-vis the Soviet Union? More specifically, for example, General Twining's view of Soviet air strength relative to the United States differed sharply in 1957 from that held by Mr. Wilson. Was it because they each have a different estimate of United States strength? Mr. Wilson testified in July 1956 that while both he and General Twining had the same intelligence estimates, "he [Twining] might interpret them differently." Added the Secretary, "I think that General Twining might have been speaking more for the Air Force itself, forgetting the Navy and our allies and some other things." [12]

Allen Dulles, incidentally, apparently feels that intelligence analysts should avoid becoming involved in interpretations of United States power. In a television interview with Representative Harold Ostertag in June 1956, Mr. Dulles maintained that he was "not an expert on the American position" and "am not really in the job of making comparisons." He then proceeded, perhaps inadvertently, to compare Soviet missile progress with our own, stating, "I have no evidence that they are ahead of us." [13] Senator Symington later claimed that Dulles' comparison was misleading, thereby confusing an already clouded intelligence picture.[14]

The relationship between intelligence on the resources of

a potential enemy and estimates of our own capabilities or intentions must be finely balanced. President Truman, for example, in his *Memoirs* rebukes General MacArthur for "estimating" in October 1950 that the Chinese would not intervene in Korea. This estimate, which proved totally wrong, was not based on poor intelligence as to Chinese capabilities — these were well known.[15] The poor guess was made with regard to Chinese *intentions* and MacArthur has maintained that his misinterpretation of Chinese intentions was largely due to his misreading of our own. MacArthur has stated that his estimate was based on an assumption that *we* would "massively retaliate." He reasoned that the Communists would be working on the same assumption regarding United States' intentions, and thus would not intervene. MacArthur's assumption and the Washington war plan, however, were not the same. If nothing else, this incident points up the fact that intelligence estimates of this sort cannot be made in a vacuum. There must be a closer link between national intelligence and United States policy, but the ultimate fusion of all factors — including value judgments as well as pure intelligence — should take place beyond the boundaries of the intelligence community.

Another episode often cited as an intelligence failure was the German counter-attack on the Western Front in December 1944, commonly called the "Battle of the Bulge." In this case Allied commanders were surprised; they lacked foreknowledge of the attack. Here a basic intelligence problem is well illustrated in one observer's analysis of this episode:

The function of an Intelligence Officer is first to collect, then to evaluate, and finally to disseminate to other levels of command, information of the enemy. Through a process of over-specialization, which often seems to pervade our life, Intelligence Officers seemed to operate in a vacuum, charged with describing enemy intentions without consideration to our plans. Because our actions so directly affect theirs, it is difficult to say what the Germans may do if we do not first say what we intend to do, but this is exactly what our Intelligence Officers were doing throughout their combat career. For example, to discuss German intentions in the Ardennes without analyzing the weakness of our positions there, our present and pending attacks elsewhere, is to overlook the true situation.[16]

Intelligence analysts, clearly, cannot be blind to our own policy and intentions in constructing their estimates, whether they work at the tactical, or the highest strategic, level. Yet the parallel danger remains that policy preferences may color the intelligence estimate. A finely balanced mechanism for relating policy and intelligence will help in meeting this dilemma.

The initial phases of the Korean conflict also presented an interesting intelligence problem. Mr. Truman claims that "we knew that this was one of the places where the Soviet-controlled Communist world might choose to attack," but that this was true of many other places on the periphery and we couldn't be strong everywhere.[17] The failure was not so much due to faulty intelligence as to an inability of the policy planners to prepare for the eventuality of a limited war in Korea. Having ruled Korea outside of the defensive perimeter in the event of all-out war with Russia, there had been no consideration given in Washington or Tokyo to providing for defense of Korea against limited war or satellite aggression. Intelligence, in a sense, was thus falling on deaf ears. Again, intelligence must finally be related to policy and, if the policy guidance to intelligence analysts is absent, the intelligence may be aimless.

Great Expectations

Often too much is expected of intelligence. As Allen Dulles has suggested, many decisions and events in the world occur on an *ad hoc* basis without direct relation to patterns of enemy capability or intention. This is an intelligence problem even more frequently faced by the Communists, who fail to anticipate a United States move because we ourselves often act at the eleventh hour with little regard for capabilities or previously avowed intentions. Witness the American intervention in Korea.

The existence of an effective collection network capped by a co-ordinated and efficient estimating mechanism provides no guarantee that the right policies will automatically emerge. In fact, many of our national policies are made with a seemingly willful disregard for intelligence. Domestic considerations often seem to be given more attention than the most careful intelligence estimates. The best intelligence estimate, moreover, can never be a substitute for responsible political judgment. Even the most efficient intelligence community cannot compensate for military weakness, or leadership failure, or lack of national will to take necessary action. What it can do is attempt to insure that policy blunders are not made because of a lack of evaluation and dissemination of known information.

Most critics agree that for all its lingering deficiencies, the intelligence community has taken giant steps since 1948, when Hanson Baldwin wrote that intelligence, our "first line of defense . . . is today one of the weakest links in our national security." [18] In today's nervous jet-nuclear-missile world of two great rival nations and a host of insecure and anxious lesser powers, there is little room for intelligence error. If being the first line of defense seems to be a great expectation for central intelligence, it must be remembered that the price of failure may be national survival.

The Personnel Problem

The growing recognition of the importance of accurate

intelligence tends to decrease the problem of securing well-qualified personnel for the various operations and tasks of the intelligence community. This problem within the military services has already been discussed. It seems almost unnecessary to say, as did the 1955 Hoover Commission, that "The effectiveness of our national intelligence effort is measured to a large degree by the character and ability of the personnel, both military and civilian, engaged in this work." [19]

Nonetheless, serious problems remain in the procurement and maintenance of the highly qualified persons needed to staff the multifarious functions of central intelligence. First there is the problem of the "career" secret agent, serving overseas. With the nation's global interests and commitments, it is necessary to have secret agents operating, or trying to operate, in every corner of the globe. These persons must possess a unique combination of skills and be unusually motivated. They must be willing to serve the country in this anonymous and often dangerous capacity — in what Harold Nicholson has called "the most boring and dangerous of all human occupations." They must possess a keen intellect and sensitive judgment. They often must have, in addition, special language skills, sometimes in the most remote languages or special dialects. The CIA maintains a well-developed assessment and training program for its overseas operatives, who require special indoctrination, area knowledge, language and communications skills, and the special paraphernalia of the international spy. This whole program, like the activities of American secret agents overseas, is inevitably shrouded in secrecy.[20] But presumably a nation as large as the United States can supply the required number of individuals willing to become members of what is now a well-developed career service of overseas secret agents.

A second problem is the procurement, training, and retaining of qualified intelligence analysts for the domestic activities of CIA, largely centered in Washington. Even on the domestic front, service with CIA requires special motivations and qualifications. The 1955 Hoover Commission referred to some of CIA's problems in the personnel management field. Reference was made to the need for improving the prestige of the civilian analyst, developing career incentives, and for providing greater flexibility in recruitment of specially qualified individuals.[21] In the early days of CIA's existence, employment with that agency was not highly regarded in many of the academic faculties training Ph.D.'s. A standard quip, when employment opportunities were being discussed, was the sarcastic comment: "Well, there's always the CIA." In some circles prejudice remains.

There have been periods of CIA's development when large numbers of employees were hired without adequate attention to their real qualifications for the exacting work required. Many of these were persons retiring from the armed services. Under the Directorship of Gen. Walter B. Smith between 1950–1953, a vigorous weeding out of unqualified personnel took place.

An additional personnel problem exists, threatening the future effectiveness of the agency. Since CIA is essentially an organization of specialists, the problem has arisen of providing administrators from within the organization. Those who tend to rise to the top via the ladder of promotion usually are the area or technical specialists, often with little administrative bent or talent. Since there is an innate tendency for the agency as it is to be compartmented into isolated groups of specialists, this problem is compounded when specialists without administrative or co-ordinating talent are promoted to the top positions in their section or division of CIA. This is a common problem on the Washington administrative scene, but it is particularly acute within CIA.

Another serious problem is that persons needed for much

of the work of intelligence analysis, such as the trained economist, historian, or political scientist, still regard work with CIA as too inhibiting to be attractive as a career. Security restrictions and the requirement of almost complete anonymity in CIA work continue to be major obstacles to the recruitment of the best personnel. Undoubtedly many loyal and otherwise qualified persons just do not care to work for an agency where lie detector tests are routine. To be willing to work for CIA, one must follow a career in which much of his work cannot be discussed even at home with his wife, let alone with colleagues in other branches of his agency, or in other sectors of government. This problem will always be difficult to surmount.

The Problem of Overseeing the Intelligence Community

The burgeoning of the national intelligence community, in size and importance of function, has left unresolved the question of who should oversee the intelligence community, particularly the far-flung operations of CIA. Its freedom from Congressional and other outside surveillance led a Hoover Commission task force in 1955 to express a sentiment others have felt, that "There is always a danger that such freedom from restraints could inspire laxity and abuses which might prove costly to the American people." [22] This apprehension led to the move in Congress, still unsuccessful as of this writing, to establish a Joint Congressional Committee on Intelligence. (This move was described in Chapter VII.)

As a neophyte agency engaged in a highly controversial activity, CIA has not, however, been left to enjoy merely the limited scrutiny of the National Security Council, the Bureau of the Budget, and a handful of Congressmen. Two broad investigations were made in 1949 and 1955 by Hoover Commission task forces. In 1951 and again in 1954, additional surveys were conducted at Presidential request. Detailed findings were reported confidentially to the President.

The 1949 Hoover Commission's Committee on National Security Organization made an assessment of CIA after it had been operating less than two years. It found that unsatisfactory relationships existed between CIA and other intelligence agencies of the Government — particularly Army Intelligence, the Federal Bureau of Investigation, and the Atomic Energy Commission. It found also that:

> Too many disparate intelligence estimates have been made by the individual departmental intelligence services; that these separate estimates have often been subjective and biased, that the capabilities of potential enemies have frequently been interpreted as their intentions, and that a more comprehensive collection system, better coordination and more mature and experienced evaluation are imperative.[23]

A number of recommendations were made for change, notably the suggestion that a top-level evaluation board be established to produce national estimates.

This latter deficiency had become painfully evident during the period of the Berlin Blockade in 1948. It persisted throughout the earlier stages of the Korean War and effective corrective steps were not taken until 1950 when General Walter Bedell Smith set up the formal estimating mechanism.* Today there is a well-established Board of National Estimates, composed of full-time, well-paid, long-tenure members with no present agency or service affiliations.

In 1955 the Hoover Commission Task Force on Intelligence Activities, headed by General Mark W. Clark (U.S.A.,

---

* William L. Langer, Professor of History at Harvard and chief of Research and Analysis in OSS during World War II, returned to Washington during this period as General Smith's deputy for establishing an efficient Office of National Estimates.

Ret.), conducted an extensive survey of the community and produced two reports; one, dealing with organizational aspects, was made public and the other, dealing with operations, stamped TOP SECRET. The published report recommended more intensive linguistic training (a long-time glaring weakness in the community); that CIA assume from the Department of State responsibility for procurement of foreign publications and scientific intelligence (thus giving CIA more operational tasks); utilization of more retired military officers in CIA; salary increases and funds for new CIA headquarters. Also, the CIA Director was reminded of "certain administrative flaws which have developed in the CIA" and was mildly rebuked for having "taken upon himself too many burdensome duties and responsibilities on the operational side of CIA's activities." [24]

The Clark Task Force took special note of the relative freedom from surveillance enjoyed by CIA and commented that liaison between Congress and CIA through the Armed Services committees' channel lacked the essential "wide scope of service and continuity." To fill this surveillance void, the Hoover Commission recommended creation of a civilian watchdog board and a "Joint Congressional Committee on Foreign Intelligence, similar to the Joint Committee on Atomic Energy." [25]

Based on the first of these recommendations, monitoring by the Executive Branch was established on February 6, 1956, when President Eisenhower appointed an eight-man civilian watchdog group, the President's Board of Consultants on Foreign Intelligence Activities. This board, chaired until February 1958, by President James R. Killian, Jr., of the Massachusetts Institute of Technology, is a part-time survey group charged with conducting periodically "an objective review of the foreign intelligence activities of the

Government and of the performance of . . . the Central Intelligence Agency." [26] In February 1958, the chairmanship of this board was assumed by General John E. Hull, a retired Army officer.

The Survey by Allen Dulles

The survey which reported to the President in 1951 was conducted by a three-man group headed by Allen W. Dulles, later to become Director of Central Intelligence in 1953, after serving two years as Deputy Director.[27] The findings of this group were never made public, but its study apparently spanned several years, "watchdogging" the intelligence community at the request of President Truman and the National Security Council. The Dulles group apparently helped to straighten out organizational and administrative difficulties which beset the institution of a new centralized intelligence system. It also attempted to referee some of the bitter interdepartmental battles over the intelligence function in the period when jurisdictional lines were not clearly drawn.[28]

The second special survey was conducted by a four-man board headed by retired Air Force Lt. Gen. James H. Doolittle.[29] This study came at a time when Senator Joseph McCarthy was threatening an investigation of CIA. It also followed closely upon the defection to the Communists of Dr. Otto John, former Western German security chief, who had been in a position to know of detailed operations of Western intelligence agencies. Just before his defection in the spring of 1954, Dr. John had spent some time in the United States on a semi-official visit. At that time he was reportedly the guest of honor at a dinner given by the Director of Central Intelligence. He also met with officials of the State and Defense Departments and the Federal Bureau of

Investigation.[30] These and other events motivated the appointment of a special group to look into CIA operations for the President.

The Doolittle group reported to the President in October 1954. Through the White House a brief report was issued by General Doolittle stating that the CIA was doing a "creditable job," but that there were "important areas in which the CIA organization, administration and operations can and should be improved." Specific recommendations made by the Board to the President were not disclosed.[31] As *The New York Times* commented at the time of the Doolittle report: "For Congress, which must appropriate funds for C.I.A., and for the general public, the verdict would have to be accepted pretty much on faith." [32] To date, then, CIA surveillance has come largely from specially appointed Presidential groups, plus the few Congressmen serving on the two Hoover Commissions and the handful of members of Congress on the CIA subcommittees of Armed Services and Appropriations Committees. Surveillance, at best, has been part-time and sporadic.

Public Relations

Proposals for closer auditing of CIA and the intelligence community have not always been directed at establishing outside surveillance over intelligence activities. The Hoover Commission insisted that one of the aims of its watchdog groups was to assure the public of the "essential and trustworthy accomplishments of our Intelligence forces, and to enlist public support and participation in the Intelligence effort." [33]

The Hoover Commission was justifiably concerned about the lack of prestige the intelligence community held in the minds of both policy makers and public. Representative

Daniel Flood also pointed up this problem at the 1957 House hearings on Army appropriations when he remarked: "The average American thinks . . . that our intelligence is a laughing stock, . . . that the British are the finest intelligence people in the world, that the Germans are great, but that we do not have anybody on this intelligence business. . . ." [34] Congressman Flood, expressing his own confidence in United States intelligence, inquired about what might be done to change this attitude without compromising intelligence techniques and sources. The Army G-2 representative squirmed at this suggestion and replied that he was in no position "to start a television program or a radio program publicizing United States intelligence activities." It might be noted that the presidential Board of Consultants also had not revealed any plans to educate the public about the American central intelligence system. Nor had any report to the President of its surveillance of foreign intelligence operations been publicly indicated by early 1958. It is unlikely that such reports will be publicly disclosed. Whether the intelligence services will ever even approach the public esteem generated for the FBI seems open to question. As it stands, the intelligence function continues to provide fodder only for dramatized TV thrillers.

CIA's public relations problem was described as follows by its Director in 1957:

I am the head of the silent service and cannot advertise my wares. Sometimes, I admit, this is a bit irksome. Often we know a bit more about what is going on in the world than we are credited with, and we realize a little advertisement might improve our public relations. For major reasons of policy, however, public relations must be sacrificed to the security of our operations.[35]

Public relations aside, central intelligence inevitably must remain in essence a silent service. This is so because, in part, it is a *staff arm* of the presidency; in part, because it deals in the shadowy realm of espionage and backstage foreign political action. Yet this secrecy must somehow be made compatible with democratic self-government. An invisible branch of government possessed of superior knowledge is a source of great potential power. American political liberties are theoretically safeguarded by the checks and balances of constitutional government. The central intelligence apparatus must not be allowed to operate completely free, as it is inclined to do, from the checkreins of the American system.

IX

INTELLIGENCE AND SECURITY:
Retrospect and Prospect

Allen W. Dulles wrote in 1947 that "intelligence work in time of peace differs fundamentally from that in time of war." * Since that time, Americans in the era of Cold War have become increasingly aware that distinctions between war and peace have tended to become blurred. Now it is widely recognized that national security depends in part upon a nation's willingness to maintain indefinitely a war preparedness and forces-in-being, including intelligence forces previously marshaled only in war. Only in this way can a flexible, viable strategy for peace be effectively waged.

In order to maintain such preparedness, to develop and sustain a national strategy, decisions must be made in an environment featuring carefully developed forecasts of what will happen, or what possibly can be made to happen, in future years. Not only is knowledge required of foreign strategic capabilities some years hence, but decisions also must rest upon predictions of future international political behavior. Thus the demands upon central intelligence have never been greater than today, nor has intelligence ever been more influential in governmental affairs. Not only must the nation's central intelligence apparatus sustain the constant sentinel-on-duty in anticipation of future Pearl Harbors, it

* See Appendix A.

185

must also provide the equally important fundamental information on which a positive foreign policy may be based. Additionally it has been given the burden, wisely or not, of overseas espionage and political action.

Perhaps the outstanding feature of America's national security organization following World War II was the creation of governmental machinery for integrating various components of national policy. Of the various parts of the new decision-making machinery created for fulfillment of the post-war unification concept, none plays a more significant role than the Central Intelligence Agency. As the right arm of the National Security Council, CIA is charged with coordinating the government-wide intelligence effort, and with giving spirit and life to a national intelligence community. If reason and a scientific approach are to guide the formation of national policy, a heavy burden in so doing has fallen upon central intelligence.

Impact of Post-war Decade

America's new role of Free World leadership, an accelerating technology which has shattered traditional time-space relationships, the new reality of warfare fought not on the battlefield but by means of espionage, propaganda, and economics, all combine to require a kind of intelligence preparedness which in the past has only been mobilized in time of shooting war. Another reason for the growing importance of central intelligence in the United States is the Soviet strategy of deliberate ambiguity [1] coupled with the Soviet's own world-wide espionage network.

No government in modern times has placed greater emphasis upon foreign political, economic, and military intelligence than that of the Soviet Union. To Soviet Communist leaders, *razvedka* (a Russian term meaning the intelligence institution as well as the process) provides the life blood for world-wide political, economic, and military operations. The existence of the Iron Curtain itself is a cold, hard intelligence fact. Much of the foreign and military policy of the United States since World War II has been developed in reaction to aggressive Soviet politics. So the growth of America's massive central intelligence bureaucracy has been a response, in part, to the Soviet challenge and to Russia's pervasive and ceaseless world espionage and political action. The far-flung Soviet intelligence agencies function as arms of Soviet foreign and military policy in pursuit of the goals of the international communist movement. A central intelligence system would be required in the United States without the East-West conflict. But the bi-polarization of world power, and modern technology, obviously have accentuated the urgency and scope of the intelligence required, and the secret operations thought to be necessary.

Providing unvarnished facts and foreknowledge to government leaders and military commanders is at once the oldest and most difficult of all staff functions. In performing the intelligence function the basic elements in the process are, too, age-old and simple: collection and communication of information; its evaluation and interpretation; and its dissemination to the right person at the right place and time. Yet the task of bringing to the attention of government policy makers, particularly those who meet each Thursday in Washington as the National Security Council, *all the facts they need to know* is not a simple assignment. Even partial fulfillment of such an assignment involves fundamental problems in organization, doctrine, and personnel.

Lessons since Pearl Harbor

The Japanese surprise at Pearl Harbor signified the lack of

a national intelligence community in the United States in 1941. Pearl Harbor provided the stimulus for the first step in creating a central intelligence system, a vital element in the "unification" of national security organization. But more Pearl Harbors were to come. The Communist invasion of South Korea in 1950 and Red China's subsequent intervention, both of which events were a surprise in Washington, indicated that the great expectations of 1947 were not ready for fullfillment. After three years under the 1947 Unification Act, unsolved problems of central intelligence remained. Questions were still unanswered as to who was to collect what kind of intelligence; how information was to be transmitted and to whom; and how and by whom intelligence estimates were to be co-ordinated, evaluated, and utilized. At the time of the Korean War an even more fundamental question remained: what can be expected from intelligence — how great shall the expectations be? Such problems, indeed, have not been resolved to this day.

The Korean War provided the first great intelligence lessons since Pearl Harbor. One lesson was that co-ordinating and integrating national intelligence estimates would have to become a reality. Truly national intelligence estimates which would effectively override and supersede narrow departmental or service estimates would have to be developed. Intramural conflicts among intelligence agencies were the rule rather than the exception at the beginning of the Korean War. An intelligence *community* was only a theoretical design.

A second lesson was that expectations were too great as to what intelligence, in fact, can do. When General MacArthur was asked by senators in 1951 about the alleged breakdown of intelligence on the North Korean invasion, he gave this significant reply:

I don't see how it would have been humanly possible for any men or group of men to predict such an attack as that, any more than you could predict such an attack as took place at Pearl Harbor.

There is nothing, no means or methods, except the accidental spy methods — if you can get somebody to betray the enemy's higher circles, that can get such information as that. It is guarded with a secrecy that you cannot overestimate. Not even, probably, the commanding officers of the units, military units, concerned knew what was going on until they got the order to march.[2]

General MacArthur prefaced those words with this observation: "There has to be an evaluation made in the highest governmental level of all the information that flows in from the chancelleries of the world to make the predictions."[3] In other words, in order for intelligence to attain its maximum capability in the performance of its warning function, there must be a government-wide amalgamation of all available information. The concept of an intelligence *community* had to become, then, a functioning reality. If such were not the case in 1949–1950, giant steps have been made in this direction in intervening years. Today's national estimates — which go, as they should, far beyond the predictive or warning function — available to those who must make the hard decisions of foreign and military policy, are indeed more of an intelligence community composite than ever before.

Recent Intelligence "Failures"

Even so, more recent events again have underscored limitations in what intelligence can do. It is commonplace to speak from hindsight of intelligence "failures." Typical is the comment by a United States Senator: "We were caught by surprise in Poland, caught by surprise in Hungary, caught by surprise in the Middle East." Reference was to the events in these areas in 1956.[4] Of the 1956 events in the Middle

East, the Eisenhower Administration seems from the record to confess that it had no certain foreknowledge. Secretary of State John Foster Dulles, for example, later testified: "We had no advance information of any kind," on the Israeli attack against Egypt in 1956. "The British-French participation also came as a complete surprise to us." [5]

Leaders of the intelligence community would be quick to point out that when Secretary Dulles testifies about no "information" he refers to being informed through diplomatic channels. Prior intelligence estimates and reports existed which pointed undoubtedly to the possibility of the kind of action taken subsequently by the Israelis, French, and British. Yet because an "unknowable" element existed prior to such action, the intelligence community in retrospect can be accused, superficially, of failure. Central intelligence leaders cannot reveal in self-defense the estimates transmitted to policy makers. They must remain silent, as on most other occasions, in the face of allegations of intelligence "failure."

It is a moot question as to whether the performance of the intelligence community could have been been better in providing foreknowledge of these events. After the seizure of the Suez Canal Company in 1956 by Nasser of Egypt — which act itself seemed to surprise official Washington — intelligence did reveal to our policy makers that military action was being considered in the cabinets of Israel, France, and Great Britain. In each of these governments, Washington officials were informed by intelligence digests that there were advocates of military action. But apparently the intelligence experts did not predict such action. This may, in fact, have been an intelligence "failure," but on the other hand it may have been no more than another illustration of the limitations of any intelligence system. Intelligence will always be fallible when it comes to forecasting the future. The unknowable element, the incalculable human variable, will always plague the intelligence forecaster.

Yet, as earlier suggested, the timely availability of accurate and detailed foreknowledge does not eliminate the need for the exercise of human judgment by officials ultimately responsible for decision. This fundamental problem was graphically illustrated by Vice President Nixon's tour of South America in May 1958. When Mr. Nixon encountered stone-throwing, expectorating — indeed, assassination-minded — crowds during what were planned as good-neighbor visits to Peru and Venezuela, immediately the age-old question was raised: "O, where hath our intelligence slept?" Congressmen tossed their own stones at CIA and the State Department. Capitol Hill reverberated with demands for Congressional investigations of "intelligence failure."

When the furor subsided, public statements by the President, the Secretary of State, and Mr. Nixon himself made clear the existence of intelligence forewarnings about anti-American demonstrations. Indeed, obtaining and communicating such information should not have taxed any intelligence system possessing even a modicum of cultural understanding. The probability of anti-American demonstrations, including violent attack upon the Vice President, was discussed and the decision made to proceed with the Nixon tour as planned. Secretary of State Dulles later conceded that "if we had all known what was going to happen there [Caracas] and had been able to foresee the events, probably he [Nixon] would not have gone." This was admittedly hindsight.

Central intelligence obviously failed to supply officials with information sufficiently precise to deter the Nixon tour.

Even more precise forewarning, however, would not have eliminated the responsibility for decision *before* the events. The fallible human judgment of the politically responsible official is, finally, as crucial a factor in decision making as the quality of the intelligence estimate. Both the inherent limitations of any intelligence system and the equal importance of each step in the collection-evaluation-interpretation-utilization cycle of the intelligence process are acutely demonstrated in the Nixon Latin American episode.

Predicting Russian Progress

Reference was made earlier to another field in which American intelligence has seemed to fail badly in the decade since World War II: predicting the rate of Russian progress in science and technology. Here is illustrated a problem fundamental to all intelligence systems, that of a receptivity by decision makers of unvarnished facts or of an objective interpretation of available facts.

Events in 1957 illustrate this problem. The first was the announcement in late August that the Soviets had tested an intercontinental ballistic missile. This was followed within a few weeks by a successful launching by the Russians of the first so-called earth satellite. From published information available, it is apparent that in each case there was considerable surprise, even skepticism, in official Washington. These examples are only the more recent in a long list of what seemed to be mistaken estimates of Russian scientific capabilities over the past decade.

Some government officials were clearly surprised by the speed with which Russia produced its first atomic bomb. They were amazed at the quality of Soviet jet fighter planes (MIG-15) in the Korean War, were astonished by the early detonation of the first Russian thermonuclear (hydrogen) bomb, were taken by surprise by a public display of long-range jet bombing planes in Moscow in May, 1955, and were startled by the speed and quality of Soviet missile and rocket developments in 1957. These were either not forecast accurately by the intelligence community, or if so, and more likely, such forecasts fell upon the unbelieving ears of government leaders. Certainly the American public was not forewarned of these potential developments.

What are the reasons behind such an apparently poor showing in this regard? A basic difficulty is, of course, the inaccessibility of data from behind the Iron Curtain. To this is added the fact that technological breakthroughs are, by their nature, not always predictable. Thus there is the problem of producing accurate forecasts, of intelligence production.

But there are other problems, less tangible, but also serious. Remedies may exist for them if the government community is aware of their nature. These problems are more pertinent to those who receive, than to those who produce, national intelligence estimates.

First, there seems to have been an ingrown American stereotype of the Russian as the dumb peasant, tyrannized by a power-hungry Communist elite and living in a primitive economy in which there are too few flush toilets, in which the office building elevators do not work, and in which the want of free enterprise dooms them to a second-rate economy.

Secondly, a feeling has been widespread that the United States has, or can have, the biggest and best of all things. This has been described as a sort of national superiority complex leading to a belief that if a product were Not Invented Here, it is somehow of second quality.[6]

Thirdly, America's deep-felt antipathy to, and abhorrence

of, communism often result in the substitution of wishes for facts. One may hear a leading government official or businessman react to an intelligence estimate: "No regime as amoral, as vicious as that [Russia or Communist China] could possibly produce that much steel." Recognition that the tenets of communism are the antithesis of basic democratic values has probably colored the American viewpoint of what the Soviet system can produce in modern hardware. Indeed, not too many years ago even leading American intellectuals were questioning whether Soviet science could thrive at all under totalitarian, party-line control.

Soviet society may eventually be fractured internally and dissolve because of inherent contradictions within the Soviet system. Yet clearly it would be unwise in planning for national security to allow our aspirations, or faith in the long-range superiority of the democratic system, to interfere with a clear-headed interpretation of the facts of life about current and future Soviet capabilities.

This problem centers more largely upon responsible political leaders than upon the intelligence experts. To these government leaders the words of Winston Churchill, speaking to the House of Commons in the somber days of 1939, are worthy of recall:

It seems to me that Ministers run the most tremendous risks if they allow the information collected by the Intelligence Department and sent to them, I am sure, in good time, to be shifted and coloured and reduced in consequence and importance, and if they ever get themselves into a mood of attaching weight only to those pieces of information which accord with their earnest and honourable desire that the peace of the world should remain unbroken.[7]

The intelligence community has publicly disclaimed responsibility for the degree of surprise visited upon the nation by Soviet technological achievements in the fall of 1957. Speaking, in February 1958, of Soviet satellite and ballistic missile achievements, the Director of Central Intelligence stated that "contrary to what may be the generally accepted view, these happenings have not caused us to make any basic changes in our earlier estimates of the Soviet challenge. It was serious before. It appears to be slightly more so today." [8] The problem here involved the receptivity of policy makers and leaders of public opinion to unvarnished intelligence estimates, submitted apparently about a year in advance of the world-shaking events of the fall of 1957.

Accepting the Central Intelligence Director's testimony at face value, it becomes all too clear that governmental leaders disregarded the available and reasonably accurate estimate and fashioned their own picture of Soviet capability. At least in shaping United States goals, priorities and specific programs, it is clear that an obsolescent estimate of the power, stability, and future growth of the Soviet Union served in recent years as a basis for American policy and programs.

But why obsolescent? Perhaps, and leaders of the intelligence community may readily admit this, intelligence estimates are so produced as to lend themselves to various interpretations. In part this may be due to the *unknowable* factor in forecasts of the future. But a more significant reason may be that intelligence estimates are the product of compromise-by-committee, which tends to diminish their impact. At any rate it has been common practice for political leaders, in the shaping of future policies and plans, to redraw and reduce estimates of Soviet capability, so as to conform with preconceived assumptions about domestic economic and political requirements and so as not to disturb previously developed programs. As James A. Perkins has observed in this regard, "The capacity of the human race for self-deception is more considerable than we care to admit." [9] As a consequence, every fact that increases the Russian capability must swim upstream against the current of American acceptance and every possible indication of reduced Russian strength, or of instability within the Communist orbit, tends to be accepted eagerly.

Until the announced testing of a Soviet Intercontinental Ballistic Missile and the launching of the first two Sputniks in the fall of 1957, the ranks of Americans even at the highest level of government were filled with those persons who could not believe in the high technological capability of the Russians, and its implications for future American security. Perhaps, as Allen Dulles has stated it, "No intelligence appraisal could have had the impact of a Sputnik." [10] Yet an ideally functioning intelligence system has its own built-in Sputniks.

Problems of Intelligence by Committee

Intelligence estimates, as previously suggested, are produced by committee. [11] Recognizing the dangers and possible defects of any multi-agency effort, of any paper written by committee, the intelligence community has tried to take precautions to protect the integrity and utility of the composite product, the important national estimates. One danger comes from the adjectival form of expression of a quantitative estimate. For example: "There is a serious possibility that the Communists will intervene." This expression can be accepted by both the State and Defense Departments, the former believing that the chances are three-to-one, the latter one-to-three. This may turn up as an agreed-upon estimate that dangerously conceals the existence of disagreement, a constant threat to the integrity of information upon which national security policy makers must reach decisions. The decision maker, therefore, must know the precise nature of the agreement *and* the extent of disagreement. But he should know this without having to involve himself in the intelligence process.

Serious dissenting views on national estimates should be brought to the attention of the policy maker. A national estimate would be of little use to policy making officials, however, if it contained merely a series of split views on big and little issues alike. In highly disciplined organizations, which military services are, and civilian departments tend to be, affirmative steps are necessary to assure that when a staff paper — or national estimate — is presented to higher authority serious areas of dispute are identified and discussed. To achieve the happy medium between a series of split opinions and a unified paper suppressing dissenting views, convocation of the Intelligence Advisory Committee is used in order that differences may be argued out and compromised while preserving the integrity of information. If compromise cannot be reached, the various armed services or departments represented on the IAC then have the right to "take a footnote" expressing dissent.

The question arises here of the adequacy of representation on the Intelligence Advisory Committee. Recall that the three armed services, the Pentagon's Joint Staff, the Department of State, the Atomic Energy Commission, and the FBI, comprise the IAC, under the chairmanship of the Director of Central Intelligence. Rather obviously missing from the group, however, are representatives of the United States Information Agency and the International Cooperation Administration. The former group — USIA — is engaged in propaganda activity around the globe in behalf of the United States, and thus not only requires the best possible intelligence estimate for its operations, but also can serve as a valuable instrument for intelligence collection. The latter agency — ICA — with its responsibilty for policy planning for, and supervision of, United States foreign aid programs, also is in a position to be heavily involved in strategic intelligence production and consumption. Although some argue that it would be unwise to have these agencies associated with the central intelligence system, the advantages of having USIA and ICA represented on the Intelligence Advisory Committee outweigh the assumed disadvantages.

Papers for the National Security Council are presumably drafted today so as to reflect dissents of major substance while stating minor disputes in order-of-magnitude terms. Yet the decision maker must be sensitive to the possibility, as in any multi-agency negotiation, of horse-trading and log-rolling. He must try to make sure that important dissents are not squeezed out in the elaborate process below him of producing an attainable consensus. On the most important of questions is likely to be found the greatest variety of dissenting views. And one suspects that the pressure is great to dissolve dissents into what sometimes is watered-down consensus.

A third danger against which precautions should be taken by the intelligence community is that of viewing intelligence through the colored glasses of policy bias or vested interest. The danger exists always that in each step of the intelligence process, from the first collection of raw data to its final evaluation and utilization at the highest levels of government, a commitment to an armed service, fiscal or particular foreign policy will pollute or dilute the intelligence product. It is impossible to screen out this tendency completely. Yet the organization for, and administration of, the intelligence function must be such as to minimize this tendency.

One method has been an attempt to create a morale or *esprit* that makes colored-glasses techniques easily identifiable and disreputable in a closely knit group. A specific intelligence community device is the Board of National Estimates, composed of full-time, long-tenure scholars, men experienced in statecraft, and soldiers, with no present agency or service affiliation. It will be recalled that the Board of National Estimates is, in a sense, subordinate to the Intelligence Advisory Committee, where the final fusion of government-wide intelligence takes place. But the Board of National Estimates, performing a sort of independent audit of the estimating function of various members of the intelligence community, is bound to have a dampening effect upon any tendency to introduce nonintelligence ingredients into intelligence estimates.

Another threat to the effectiveness of an agency of CIA's nature is the easy acceptance of past demonstrated error. It is clear from international events of the past few years that our government officials on occasion have been in the dark about impending events in various parts of the world — events of great import to the national interests of the United States.

As earlier suggested, government officials may be in the dark about world events either because they are uninformed by daily intelligence digests or because they are unwilling to believe, to accept, intelligence estimates of the situation. Little can be done in this latter case, which may be the result of human stubbornness or healthy skepticism. Yet it behooves intelligence producers to create intelligence digests in such a form that their true meaning and significance will have the proper impact upon the receptive government official.

Even the best of scholarship is in one sense a failure if

not transmitted to others in understandable prose. So, too, with the daily intelligence digests, weekly summaries, and National Intelligence Estimates. If they are to have impact, estimates must be presented in a way that will arrest the mind of a busy President eager to get on with the endless paperwork and out to the golf links, or will flag the attention of a harassed Secretary of State, beset by numerous position papers, crowded for time before flying off to the next international conference.

What are needed perhaps are intelligence papers drafted with a particular official in mind: one kind of intelligence report for the President; another format for the Secretary of State; still another form and language for the Secretary of Defense. Leaders of the intelligence community might admit, in private, the need for a strategy of intelligence salesmanship. Recognizing such a need, however, must not blind them to the hazards of combining attempts to influence policy makers with their basic role of furnishing unvarnished intelligence appraisals.

Certainly all the information available is not today obtained for policy makers. And even more certainly, policy makers do not use properly all information at hand. Any agency will make mistakes. In the intelligence business it is relatively easy to shrug off such errors by alluding to the "unknowable" nature of some intelligence. The fact that even the best intelligence system cannot always fathom the motives and predict the actions of an Egyptian dictator, a Syrian general, a Red Chinese leader, a crowd of Hungarian youths, or even the Prime Minister of one of our closest allies, can lead to a kind of complacency about inadequate or inaccurate intelligence predictions. Each mistake must not be shrugged off, however, as "just one of those things." Rather it should produce a vigorous effort to analyze past errors of fact or judgment in order to revise procedures so that recurrence of error is made less likely. If such post-mortems now are in fact a part of CIA routine, this would indicate a healthy sign of industrious self-evaluation. Central intelligence's relative immunity from outside surveillance, such as by a Congressional committee, makes rigorous self-evaluation all the more important.

Intelligence and Policy

Granted that procedures exist to help avoid some of the pitfalls of intelligence by interdepartmental committee and granted that progress has been made toward creating an intelligence community in form and spirit, the question remains as to the proper relationship today between intelligence and foreign-military policy. Allen W. Dulles has stated, "CIA is not a policy-making agency: we furnish intelligence to assist in the formulation of policy." [12] Certainly the CIA has no policy-making responsibilty. Yet policy making is not a simple static action. Rather it is a dynamic process. A key element in this process is the information available to policy makers. The man, or group, controlling the information available to policy makers does in fact play a major if indirect role in policy making. If one assumes, as seems to be the case, that the intelligence credit — decision makers' respect for the intelligence product — is rising, then the intelligence agency and its leaders come closer to a degree of control over policy.

Is the product of the intelligence community used in policy making today? The answer seems to be "more and more so." [13] The Director of Central Intelligence asserted early in 1958 that "There never has been a time in history to my knowledge when intelligence has had as clear an opportunity to get its views over as it has had in this country in recent years...." [14] Yet it is important to ask what views are possessed by intelligence. If one says that intelligence estimates of Soviet progress in intercontinental ballistic missile development have been disregarded in recent years, what does this mean? Presumably it means that a certain policy or program has not been adopted by the government in spite of a certain set of intelligence estimates. Yet it is not the function of intelligence estimators to recommend policy or program. To do so would be to step over the line drawn by central intelligence doctrine separating objective intelligence analysis from program recommendation.

Even assuming a perfect intelligence product, the success or failure of a national security program will depend heavily upon, to again use the words of Allen Dulles, "the goals and priorities set, the promptness and the correctness of the decisions reached, and the energy applied in terms of man hours with the proper tools and equipment." [15] In the final analysis, therefore, the intelligence estimate can be only a contributive factor to, but not an absolute determinant of, successful national security policies.

A fine line, indeed, separates an intelligence estimate explaining the significance of certain developments in foreign affairs and a policy paper calling for a specific course of action. In excited enthusiasm for intelligence salesmanship, leaders of the intelligence community could easily find themselves well across this line.

The principal security policy documents of the United States are the highly secret National Security Council papers, accepted and approved by the President. Those who supply the facts upon which these NSC papers are written cannot be said to be divorced from policy making, even though they hold no responsibility for policies adopted and in fact try to refrain from making what can be identified as policy recommendations. National Security Council papers are the outgrowth of meticulously prepared policy documents drafted and energetically debated by its Planning Board. Planning Board drafts lean heavily upon the National Intelligence Estimates, which usually serve as the foundation for the Planning Board's policy recommendations. But in the selection of information from world-wide sources, in its processing, and in its melding into a national estimate, alternate choices are made which cannot be divorced from policy bias and which are not in fact outside of the decision-making process.

Representatives of the Central Intelligence Agency on the National Security Council, on its Planning Board, and on the Operations Coordinating Board are not expected to take positions on issues of foreign-military policy. Though they sit with these groups they sit as advisers. Yet they are always at hand with the intelligence ingredient and perhaps with a more thorough knowledge than most other representatives. And the fact that CIA representatives in these top-level decision-making institutions tend to be long-tenure personnel while others are more transient strengthens their real influence. The opinions of CIA representatives, even though they advise "from the purely intelligence point of view," presumably have great influence. It would be unrealistic to suggest that the bright young men of CIA, by training, talent, and personality, do not hold strong views on controversial issues of national security policy. If it is granted that knowledge is indeed power, it will be recognized that in reality the CIA, through an increasing efficiency — and consequently rising credit with responsible decision makers — has come to play a major role in creating national security policy.

The CIA: A Third Force?

Quite possibly the ascendancy of CIA to prominence and power in national policy making represents the growth of a third force within the Executive Branch in the production of foreign-military policy. The CIA conceivably could come to have its own implicit foreign-military policy in the event that a vacuum exists by an *impasse* on a major issue between the Department of Defense and the Department of State, or between the Executive Branch and Congress. While it is true that the CIA is an adjunct to the National Security Council, on which sit the Secretaries of State and Defense, and while it is a fact that the creation of national estimates comes from the interdepartmental Intelligence Advisory Committee, the CIA's representatives on these groups are likely to achieve increasing power.

CIA influence increases not only within the Executive Branch but upon Capitol Hill as well. In the post-Sputnik fall of 1957 and in the early months of 1958, for example, the Director of Central Intelligence and his principal deputies were in greater demand than ever before by Congressional committees. Congressmen were stirred up by Soviet technological successes and the apparent threat that Russia would soon overtake the United States in military power. Testimony by CIA officials on this subject is given, as always, in secret session. Certainly these officials are in a position of great potential power in such a circumstance to influence Congressional attitudes, since the national security crises of 1957–1958 were in part crises arising out of conflicting information on Soviet Russian strategic capability. Intelligence agents possessing, or believed to possess, superior, authoritative knowledge, have a kind of power in a crisis which must be exercised with keen discretion.

The building blocks of national intelligence in the nuclear age transcend the functional interests of the various component parts of the intelligence community. Thus the CIA very likely will find itself engaged in an increasing amount of strategic intelligence production from scratch. Starting its existence as primarily a co-ordinating body, it has inevitably become necessary for CIA to engage in extensive operations. These involve not only the covert collection of secret information from all corners of the globe, but also what amounts to underground political action. The latter is done always, in theory at least, under directive and supervision from the National Security Council. But the nature of the Council and its ex-officio membership may tend to make this *pro forma* supervision. So the CIA must be regarded not only as a staff arm of the Executive Branch but also as a "line" agency for potentially explosive overseas political action.

A much debated issue is raised by the amalgamation into the same general organization of the distinct functions of intelligence research, analysis, and production and international espionage and political action. To mix the two functions involves the danger that foreign agents collecting facts and trying at the same time to bolster or cause the overthrow of a foreign government in America's apparent interest may develop a less than objective sense for distinguishing between fact and aspiration. But to separate completely these two functions creates the danger of competition, duplication, even outright conflict. Within the Central Intelligence Agency as presently organized, the functions of strategic intelligence production and overseas secret operations are kept administratively separate. Yet under the Director and Deputy Director are maintained devices for co-ordinating over-all central intelligence operations, so that the left hand of espionage and "special operations" is at least guided by those possessing the knowledge of what the right hand of intelligence production knows, or what it needs to know.

Secrecy and Public Surveillance

CIA's increasing power in the governmental policy-making process and its extensive overseas operations raise the troublesome question of the compatibility of the requirements of a huge and vitally important secret bureaucracy and the requirements of popular, representative government. Although the secret operations of any intelligence system are incompatible with publicity, nonetheless, legitimate reasons may be advanced for the establishment of a Joint Congressional "watchdog" committee on Foreign Intelligence Operations. Many functions of government carry a TOP SECRET label and yet are under surveillance by Congressional committees. This, Congress must do, if it is to perform its constitutional role. Such committees include armed services, atomic energy, foreign relations, and even those dealing with information about agricultural commodities. And, viewed only from the Executive Branch, any agency of government requires within the legislative halls support for its projects and defense against unfounded attack.

It is common experience for security policy makers, military and civilian, to find their fear of Congressional interference changed into gratitude for Congressional support, frequently more effective support than has been accorded on the executive side of government. No executive agency today reveals everything to Congressional committees with jurisdiction over its operations. Officials of central intelligence may be expected to reveal even less. But more advantages are to be gained than lost from establishing a more institutionalized system for Congressional surveillance.

Secrecy, particularly in an information-gathering field, allows the operation of unidentified power. Citizens require knowledge of the operations of government in order to participate meaningfully in representative government. For this knowledge they depend heavily upon Congress and upon the free press. As for the press, one widely respected Washington journalist has testified that the "whole area of CIA . . .is a growing problem for the press. . . ." [16] Thoughts expressed by the late James V. Forrestal are worthy of recall in this regard:

> . . . in a democracy in which we live, and which we certainly intend to keep, intelligence activity is a difficult task. By the nature of its objectives it ought not to have publicity, yet that is one of our difficult problems — just as during the war, one of our greatest problems was the making available of the news that should be available, and yet denying to the enemy the things that could lend him not only comfort but substantial and effective help; and the same is true of intelligence.[17]

Problems of access to governmental information are, in turn, problems for an electorate in a democracy. The growth of a great secret service requires within reason some of the checks and balances of our democratic system.

Secrecy, while a prime requisite for certain kinds of intelligence operations, can become merely a convenience to an agency of the Executive Branch. That agency will be inclined to extend this secrecy to cover as many of its operations as possible. Congressional surveillance, as any Washington bureaucrat will admit, is sometimes an inconvenience; indeed, often a nuisance. Yet the very nature of democratic government is appreciably altered by abuse of secrecy. Abuse comes when secrecy is used for administrative convenience rather than for national security. Allen W. Dulles has himself noted from his experience with the German underground in the second World War, that "An intelligence service is the ideal vehicle for a conspiracy." [18]

Nazi Germany's chief of wartime foreign intelligence, if we accept the authenticity of his memoirs, was by his own account engaged in behind-the-scenes political maneuvering, both at home and aboard.[19] The power he held was largely the outgrowth of the secret information he possessed. He used intelligence in attempts to alter policy. Certainly there is little to compare between the internecine intrigues of the Nazi regime and today's American governmental process. But the point is that secrecy allows for invisible government and provides a breeding ground for conspiracy both of which are incompatible with representative government.

Walter Millis has observed that all secret intelligence operators naturally are inclined "to use their secret information as a weapon to influence policies; on the proven principle that 'knowledge is power' those who possess (or imagine they possess) superior knowledge are almost compulsively driven to employ it to enhance their own power and importance." [20] Policy makers, on the other hand, as Mr. Millis has also pointed out, often are prone to resist the power drives of secret intelligence experts. History is replete with examples of politicians who, for one reason or another, refused to believe intelligence estimates, which, in many cases, turned out to be accurate. There are instances, whether it be in Hitler's Chancellery or more recently the United States National Security Council, where the acceptance of hard and accurate intelligence has been impossible because of skeptical recipients. Secrecy, nonetheless, provides the environment for invisible government. And by the testimony of the intelligence community's own leaders, the intelligence opportunity is greater within the contemporary American government than in any other government in history.

Toward the Future

In any federal system, power tends to accrete to the central unit. This occurs usually during times of stress in which unified direction is essential. The intelligence community is founded on the concept of federation. But the power and functions of the central unit, the CIA, have tended to grow. The function of co-ordination has had the natural tendency to become one of centralized direction. An accelerating technology continues to exert pressure further to unify the foreign-military policy of the United States government. A revamping of our governmental machinery, including the armed forces, seems in order so that the challenges of the nuclear age may be met effectively.[21] The federation concept which underlies not only the intelligence community but the national defense establishment as well will have to be modified in the direction of greater centralization. The requirement for central intelligence, like the need for more closely unified strategy and forces, seems to compel changes in the direction of greater organizational unification.

Such unification must come about in such a form that does not do too much violence to the chief advantage of the federation principle — keeping the intelligence producers in rapport with the users of intelligence. A certain amount of duplication is inevitable and can be beneficial. Failure to accommodate national security organization to the requirements of the modern age may result, however, in harmful duplication and ineffective national strategy and forces.

The scope and size of separate departmental intelligence operations should be reduced and carefully circumscribed, with a reassignment of functions on the basis of a rational allocation both of armed service and other departmental intelligence requirements and also with reallocation of national intelligence functions which can best be fulfilled centrally. Necessary changes perhaps will be effected when agreement is reached, as it must be in the not too distant future, on the rearrangement of our armed forces for rationally determined nuclear-age functions rather than along traditional or sentimental lines of the age of flintlocks and horses.

The intelligence requirements of the future are quite different from those of the Pearl Harbor or Korean War era. Lessons have been learned from those tragic events and our structure for national security altered accordingly. But looking to the future, strategic intelligence can be seen assuming a role more important than ever before. Serious lags in institutions and doctrines for national security must be avoided in order to preserve security. Yet one should not lose sight of the fact that even a perfect intelligence system cannot itself insure the creation and maintenance of sound national policy, nor of national security. These can only be a product of the national will. Organized intelligence can serve merely as a necessary, if sometimes fallible, guide.

No less than the entire world today, its geography, its economics and politics, its personalities and social forces, are under the surveillance and scrutiny of American central intelligence. Research operations required to establish meaningful patterns from such ambitious observation are as impressive in their breadth, as breathtaking in their scope as America's far-flung collection network. If results have been disappointing, it is because goals set have been so high, and methods so crudely fashioned. But perhaps it is also because too little attention has been given by the intelligence community to the discovery of factors by which the United States may influence the future.

The Need for Basic Research

This, of course, is by no means the job alone of the intelligence community. The Free World map is dotted with research centers, usually operated by universities or private research foundations, where work proceeds in the direction of better understanding of national and international political behavior. For example, Russian Research centers such as those at Columbia and Harvard and elsewhere, with their outpourings of research reports, are of incalculable value to national intelligence work. Centers for study of international affairs which adorn the contemporary academic landscape, and area study programs, such as those for the Middle East, Far East, Africa, and other areas, provide basic material for national intelligence estimates. Basic research is required for strategic intelligence just as it is a vital need for progress in the natural sciences. The root purpose of central intelligence is to apply scientific analysis to the fundamental questions about the world around us for which answers are required to guide national decision.

Take for example the expanding academic field of area studies — scholarly exploration in depth into the basic characteristics of, for example, the Soviet Union, the Middle East, or the Far East — and one will find, as many knowledgeable observers have commented, an "enormous disjunction between the scholarly output from our universities and the understanding of these areas on the part of government officials and the general public." [22]

If United States security policy is ever to develop into a positive attempt to shape future events in the nation's interest instead of a somewhat negative containment or a sterile, anxiety-ridden co-existence, the foundation for such development must be a constantly improving central intelligence product.

To perfect the analysis of the current and future capabilities and intentions requires precise calculations of alternate choices and inherent limitations in the environment of foreign nations. Here indeed is a challenge to academic social scientists as well as to Washington strategic intelligence practitioners. The practitioner has a formidable task alone in keeping up to date on what social scientists already have discovered. One needs only to examine, for example, the bibliography, *International Communication and Political Opinion*, by Bruce L. and Chitra M. Smith,[23] to realize the massive amount of research done in a number of fields of great pertinence to national intelligence. Even so, whether one's primary aim is to reduce international conflict and confusion or to apply strategic pressure skillfully in the national interest, basic research toward this end will be found to be merely in its infancy.

Neither practitioner nor scholar should lose sight of this truth as expressed by Pendleton Herring that, "in matching our social science potentials against the magnitude and complexity of the human problems that surround us, we realize our kinship to builders of a fire with wet wood on a stormy mountainside." [24]

Yet all the scientifically determined intelligence estimates in the world cannot provide the values or other products of human judgment which must finally be melded into national decision. The day may come, though not soon, when the social sciences have reached such an advanced state of development that decisions at the highest level of government may be made by the purely scientific approach. Such a day cannot be seen even on the horizon. Meanwhile, even the best possible intelligence product can serve as but one of the elements going into national decision.

Concern within the intelligence community with current information and with "indicators" of current events tends to overshadow the development of methods for long-range research and analysis. Basic research always tends to get short shrift in any staff agency involved with pressing problems of contemporary decision. The sentinel-on-duty concept of intelligence is indispensable in the modern world, but it should be regarded as only one important function.

The Problem of Intelligence Doctrine

In meeting the requirements for information on which long-range security planning can confidently be based, the intelligence community faces some fundamental questions. How, for example, are to be determined the really important problems toward which the massive intelligence bureaucracy and its agents should devote primary attention? Even more important, perhaps, is the question of how intelligence work may aid the creation, for consideration by decision makers, of alternate foreign policies by which the United States can favorably influence future events in the world. The point to be made here is that an ideal intelligence system maintains a proper balance between policy-oriented activity — applied research — and theoretical considerations — which may be termed basic research.

This raises the question of contemporary intelligence doctrine. It has been the purpose in this book neither to analyze existing doctrine, nor to propose a new one. Such an analysis has been done by others, particularly Roger Hilsman.[25] Yet what Mr. Hilsman and other critics have found is not encouraging.[26]

In surveying the prevailing basic philosophy of intelligence work, Mr. Hilsman discovered attitudes which can be described only as outmoded. Contemporary intelligence doctrine tends to put too much emphasis on accumulation, *per se*, of descriptive facts. A tendency also exists to separate various steps in the process of decision making into narrow compartments, such as problem-solving, estimating, warning, or integrating the various products of the intelligence community. As the size of the operation grows, and as the specialization of its compartments deepens, as has been the case in the dozen years since World War II, it becomes a Herculean task to fit together into a coherent pattern the information so independently developed.

The whole intelligence enterprise tends to focus upon the filling of a vast warehouse of encyclopedic data. The endless compartmented accumulation of facts tends to be identified as the essence of knowledge. Present or past American foreign policy serves as principal guidance at best for this activity. Too little regard is shown, generally, to theory, reasoning, or the inductive method. Heavy dependence rests upon empirical observation guided by narrowly defined, or vaguely defined, hypotheses. Thus, with all the intelligence activity on a global scale, too little attention is given the purposeful accumulation of data which can support a broader theoretical approach to foreign policy problems.

This tendency to define knowledge as the orderly accumulation of facts or the stringing together of endless footnotes is, of course, not a characteristic of the intelligence community alone. It is in keeping with the American style in intellectual activity, derived in part indirectly from American attitudes toward knowledge and more directly from the mores of much American graduate school training. Certainly there are profound differences within the social sciences as to what constitutes meaningful research. Differing schools of thought abound, yet the empirical method tends to predominate.

The intelligence community, too, appears to be heavily oriented toward the narrow empirical approach. There is preoccupation with making current situation estimates, with predicting what will happen under existing conditions, or simply with the accumulation of data on a specialized subject as an end in itself.

This is not to question the utility and necessity to a central intelligence system of building authoritative and extensive encyclopedias of world-wide information. A vast library of accurate and up-to-date information must be maintained continuously. But, given the prevailing doctrine, much of the activity toward maintaining such a library may be, in effect, wasted effort. This may be so because much of the effort is not related to questions for which it is important to develop answers, or because it is not productive of data for creating theoretical alternatives to existing foreign policy.

Certainly the ethics and conditions of government-sponsored research differ from private intellectual endeavor. The CIA and other members of the intelligence community inevitably must primarily provide staff assistance to responsible political leaders, faced with concrete immediate — indeed often urgent — problems of decision. Yet in the last analysis political leaders and those in command of the intelligence system should be acutely aware of any deficiency in doctrine which results in an imbalance between massive accumulation of information to aid the resolution of immediate policy problems, and creative theoretical considerations.

Much work remains to be done in developing methods and techniques and in utilizing scientific assets for more precise predictions and interpretations of national power and of political communication and behavior. Until this homework is more adequately tended to — and it needs multi-type experiments and varied approaches — it seems likely that the intelligence community will continue to exhibit the obvious shortcomings of the kind shown in the dozen years since the end of World War II.

The Limits of Intelligence

Was it not Socrates who expressed the doctrine that knowledge, not accidental desires or opinions, makes conduct rational and right? The knowledge required for rational policy and action may indeed be beyond mankind's reach. Certainly the President and his advisers, the Congress and its staff, the American public and its leaders will never have all the knowledge required to guarantee national security.

To comprehend or predict the future capability or action of nations requires an understanding of the behavior of human beings who create national will, and of the forces which produce certain behavior patterns. To use available knowledge to influence the future course of events toward a predetermined goal requires infinitely greater knowledge and skill. This knowledge and skill we must strive to develop as best we know how, aided by the best possible institutions and methods. Such knowledge and skill will always be elusive, as will reliable guidance for its use.

If, as the Director of Central Intelligence has asserted, the intelligence estimate has a more influential place in contemporary American government than it enjoys in any other government of the world, this is cause for rejoicing. Yet it also calls for a reminder of the humility required in the face of all that American government leaders need to know but which even the best of intelligence services today cannot tell them.

Central Intelligence
The 1947 Views of Allen W. Dulles,
Director of Central Intelligence, 1953 ——

(Note: Officials of the CIA are expectedly reticent in discussing its structure and functions. The memorandum which follows was prepared in 1947 when Congress was considering the National Security (Unification) Act. It does not necessarily contain Mr. Dulles' present views on intelligence doctrine and organization, yet it indicates his general approach to the problems of central intelligence, and his general view of the requirements for a Central Intelligence Agency. The memorandum was contained in Hearings, *"National Defense Establishment," Senate Committee on Armed Services, 80th Congress, 1st Session, on S. 758, Washington, 1947, pp. 525–528. For a more recent discussion of the views of the present (1958) Director of Central Intelligence, see an interview with him, "We Tell Russia Too Much,"* U.S. News and World Report, *March 19, 1954, pp. 62–68.)*

MEMORANDUM RESPECTING SECTION 202 (CENTRAL INTELLIGENCE AGENCY) OF THE BILL TO PROVIDE FOR A NATIONAL DEFENSE ESTABLISHMENT, SUBMITTED BY ALLEN W. DULLES, APRIL 25, 1947

I

To create an effective Central Intelligence Agency we must have in the key positions men who are prepared to make this a life work, not a mere casual occupation. Service in the Agency should not be viewed merely as a stepping stone to promotion in one of the armed services or other branches of the Government. The Agency should be directed by a relatively small but elite corps of men with a passion for anonymity and a willingness to stick at that particular job. They must find their reward primarily in the work itself, and in the service they render their Government, rather than in public acclaim.

Intelligence work in time of peace differs fundamentally from that in time of war. In time of war military channels and military facilities, and consequently military personnel, can effectively be employed in far greater measure than in peacetime. In time of peace intelligence with respect to foreign countries must come largely through civilian channels.

Because of its glamour and mystery overemphasis is generally placed on what is called secret intelligence, namely the intelligence that is obtained by secret means and by secret agents. During war this form of intelligence takes on added importance but in time of peace the bulk of intelligence can be obtained through overt channels, through our diplomatic and consular missions, and our military, naval, and air attachés in the normal and proper course of their work. It can also be obtained through the world press, the radio, and through the many thousands of Americans, business and professional men and American residents of foreign countries, who are naturally and normally brought in touch with what is going on in those countries. A proper analysis of the intelligence obtainable by these overt, normal, and aboveboard means would supply us with over 80 percent, I should estimate, of the information required for the guidance of our national policy. An important balance must be supplied by secret intelligence which includes what we now often refer to as "Magic."

Mr. Dulles, brother of John Foster Dulles, has had extensive experience as a diplomat, lawyer, and "master spy." For his exploits as an Office of Strategic Services (OSS) leader in Europe, 1942–1946, he was awarded the Government Medal of Merit. Born in 1893, he has a B.A. from Princeton, an LL.B. from George Washington University. He headed a three-man team which surveyed the CIA in its formative years, 1948–1951. He became Deputy Director of Central Intelligence in 1951; Director in 1953. See his *Germany's Underground*, New York, Macmillan, 1947.

II

I believe that the agency which is to be entrusted with assembling and analyzing intelligence should be predominantly civilian rather than military and under civilian leadership.

Whoever takes the post of Director of Central Intelligence should make that his life work. If previously a military man, he should not look forward to resuming a position in one of the armed services. The same should be true of his top staff. Whatever may have been their previous professions, whether military or civilian, once they take high position in the central intelligence organization they should, if military, divest themselves of their rank as soldiers, sailors, or airmen and, as it were, "take the cloth" of the intelligence service.

The success of the FBI has been due not only to the ability of the director and the high qualities of his chief assistants, but to the fact that that director has been on that particular job for a sufficient period of years to build up public confidence, and esprit de corps in his organization, and a high prestige. We should seek the same result for our intelligence service, which will operate in the foreign field, and on items of foreign information.

I do not suggest that the legislation should lay down a hard and fast rule that the chief of the Intelligence Agency must come from civilian life. Certainly there are many men of military training who are competent to hold that job. But if a military man takes the job, he should operate from that time on as a civilian. Further, he must be assured, subject to good performance, a specified term of duty, which should be subject to extension as long as he carried out his task efficiently. Appointment as Chief of Central Intelligence should be somewhat comparable to appointment to high judicial office, and should be equally free from interference due to political changes. In fact, the duties the Chief will have to perform will call for the judicial temperament in high degree. An appointee must gain that critical faculty which can only come of long experience and profound knowledge to enable him to separate the wheat from the chaff in the volume of information which will pass through his office.

Of course, the Central Intelligence Agency should also have attached to it a substantial number of men from the armed forces as well as from civilian life, many of whom will not make it a life career but who can perform useful functions for a term of years.

Much of our thinking relating to an intelligence agency is colored by our recent dramatic war experiences. Intelligence work in time of peace will require other techniques, other personnel, and will have rather different objectives. The prime objectives today are not solely strategic or military, important as these may be. They are scientific — in the field of atomic energy, guided missiles, supersonic aircraft, and the like. They are political and social. We must deal with the problem of conflicting ideologies as democracy faces communism, not only in the relations between Soviet Russia and the countries of the west, but in the internal political conflicts within the countries of Europe, Asia, and South America. For example, it may well be more important to know the trend of Russian communism and the views of individual members of the Polit Bureau than it would be to have information as to the locations of particular Russian divisions.

Having this conception of the task of a central intelligence agency, I am skeptical as to the wisdom or adequacy of the provisions in the bill to provide for a national defense establishment with respect to central intelligence. These provisions seem to me to set up what, in effect, is likely to become merely a coordinating agency for the military intelligence services, G-2, A-2, ONI. This is useful, and this function should be performed by the agency, but it is not enough.

The constant changes in the chiefs of the military intelligence services has crippled their efficiency and lessened their prestige. As these services are a part of a professional career, of which intelligence is only one segment (and too often it has been a stepchild), such changes are somewhat inevitable. But this precedent should not be carried over to the new Central Intelligence Agency. There provision must be made for permanence and continuity. And yet the Central Intelligence Authority, heretofore based on Presidential order, will have had three heads in the space of 1 short year. The two men who up to now have been the heads of that agency were both extremely able, devoted, and competent men, but no man can do much in this most difficult field in a few months. Constant change destroys the morale and prevents the long-range planning which must be the task of a properly functioning intelligence agency.

Hence I would recommend that any legislation provide long-term tenure for the Chief of the Agency, with the establishment of a precedent that his chief subordinates should also have that degree of permanence which is necessary to insure team play between the Chief and his immediate assistants. The Chief should not have men imposed upon him for political or other like reasons. He should have the right to pass upon his assistants. The legislation should provide that the Chief and his immediate assistants, so long as they are attached to the Central Intelligence Agency, should act in a civilian and not in a military capacity.

III

Under the legislation as proposed, the Central Intelligence Agency is to operate under the National Security Council, the stated purpose of which is "to advise the President with respect to the integration of foreign and military policies, and to enable the military services and other agencies of the Government to cooperate more effectively in matters involving national security." This Council will have at least six members, and possibly more, subject to Presidential appointment. From its composition it will be largely military, although the Secretary of State will be a member. If precedent is any guide, it seems unlikely, in view of the burden of work upon all the members of this Council, that it will prove to be an effective working body which will meet frequently, or which could give much supervisory attention to a central intelligence agency. It would seem preferable that the Chief of Central Intelligence should report, as at present, to a smaller body, of which the Secretary of State would be the chairman, and which would include the Secretary of National Defense, and a representative of the President, with the right reserved to the Secretaries of State and of National Defense to be represented on this small board by deputies, who should have at least the rank of Assistant Secretary. And this board must really meet and assume the responsibility for advising and counseling the Director of Intelligence, and assure the proper liaison between the Agency and these two Departments and the Executive.

IV

In time of peace intelligence will probably be of more importance in the day-by-day operations of the Department of State than any other agency of the Government, even the Department of National Defense. Further, in time of peace, intelligence can only be properly collected if there are the closest working arrangements with the Department of State, as the bulk of the intelligence collected abroad will come through the facilities of that Department.

The proposed intelligence set-up in the draft legislation is over-weighted on the side of the military department of the Government, as contrasted with the State Department. This is natural because it appears in a bill for our National Defense Establishment. This fact, however, should not blind us to the realities of the situation.

The State Department, irrespective of the form in which the Central Intelligence Agency is cast, will collect and process its own information as a basis for the day-by-day conduct of its work. The armed services intelligence agencies will do likewise. But for the proper judging of the situation in any foreign country it is important that information should be processed by an agency whose duty it is to weigh facts, and to draw conclusions from those facts, without having either the facts or the conclusions warped by the inevitable and even proper prejudices of the men whose duty it is to determine policy and who, having once determined a policy, are too likely to be blind to any facts which might tend to prove the policy to be faulty. The Central Intelligence Agency should have nothing to do with policy. It should try to get at the hard facts on which others must determine policy. The warnings which might well have pointed to the attack on Pearl Harbor were largely discounted by those who had already concluded that the Japanese must inevitably strike elsewhere. The warnings which reportedly came to Hitler of our invasion of North Africa were laughed aside. Hitler thought he knew we didn't have the ships to do it. It is impossible to provide any system which will be proof against the human frailty of intellectual stubbornness. Every individual suffers from that. All we can do is to see that we have created the best possible mechanism to get the unvarnished facts before the policy makers, and to get it there in time. [*Sic*]

V

Any Central Intelligence Agency (in addition to having access to the intelligence collected by the State Department and the armed services, to intelligence gained through intercepted messages, open and deciphered alike, and from the results of its own secret and overt intelligence operations) must have a corps of the most competent men which this country can produce to evaluate and correlate the intelligence obtained, and to present it, in proper form, to the interested Government departments, in most cases to the State Department, in many cases to the Department of National Defense, or to both.

It is important to avoid splitting up and dissipating the personnel available for this work through having over-all specialized intelligence evaluating agencies in both the State Department and the Central Intelligence Agency. If close working relations are established between the Central Intelligence Agency and the State Department — as is essential if the Agency is to function properly — it would seem desirable, for reasons of economy and efficiency, that the task of evaluation should be delegated to the Central Intelligence Agency without, of course, affecting the work in the geographical and other divisions of the State Department. This would mean that the specialized intelligence agency within the State Department should be coordinated with, or amalgamated into, the branch of the Central Intelligence Agency devoted to the analysis and evaluation of intelligence.

VI

In addition to these basic considerations, the Central Intelligence Agency should have the following powers and attributes:

1. Control its own personnel but with the right to co-opt personnel from other departments of the Government, with the consent of the head of the department in question but without affecting the rank, civil-service status, or pay of the employee assigned for temporary duty.

2. Have its own appropriations but with the possibility of

supplementing these appropriations from available funds of the
Department of State or the Department of National Defense
under conditions to be provided by law, in order to carry on
certain special operations which may, from time to time, be
deemed necessary by the President, the Secretary of State, or the
Secretary of National Defense.

3. Have exclusive jurisdiction to carry out secret intelligence
operations.

4. Have access to all intelligence information relating to foreign
countries received by all departments of the Government, including "Magic."

5. Be the recognized agency for dealing with the central intelligence agencies of other countries.

6. Have its operations and personnel protected by "official
secrets" legislation which would provide adequate penalties for
breach of security.

VII

It has truthfully been said that intelligence is our first line of
defense. The European countries more immediately exposed to
danger in the past have realized this, and have spared no pains
to develop adequate intelligence services. Among them the British have had signal success, and this success, in no small part, has
been responsible for pulling them through periods of the direst
danger. The British system has behind it a long history of quiet
effective performance, based on a highly trained personnel with
years of service and great technical ability. In this country we
have the raw material for building the greatest intelligence service in the world. But to accomplish this we must make it a
respectable, continuing, and adequately remunerated career. The
personnel need not be very numerous. The operation of the
service must be neither flamboyant nor overshrouded with the
mystery and abracadabra which the amateur detective likes to
assume.

With the proper legislative backing, a correct technical set-up,
and adequate leadership, all that is required for success is hard
work, discriminating judgment, and common sense. Americans
can be found who are not lacking in these qualities.

APPENDIX B

Relations Between Congress and the Central Intelligence Agency — Exchange of Letters, Senator Mike Mansfield and Director, CIA

(Note: The following two letters were reprinted in Congressional Record, *daily edition, March 10, 1954, p. 281.)*

August 25, 1953

HON. ALLEN W. DULLES,
    Director of Central Intelligence,
      Washington, D.C.

DEAR MR. DULLES:

As you know, I have introduced a bill to establish a joint congressional committee, along the lines of the Joint Committee on Atomic Energy, for the CIA. I would appreciate receiving an answer from you on the questions listed below:

1. What is the present relationship between Congress and CIA?

(a) Before what committees, other than Appropriations, have CIA representatives appeared on agency business? Is there any regular survey of CIA's activities by any committee? What is CIA's procedure for getting desired legislation? How many Members of Congress know CIA's annual appropriation?

(b) In what instances do Members of Congress receive intelligence reports from CIA? Is it only when some other executive agency recommends it to support their position?

2. Does the Central Intelligence Agency feel that the present ties with Congress are adequate? What is its opinion of a Joint

Committee on Central Intelligence similar to the Joint Committee
on Atomic Energy?

3. What action was taken on the Hoover Commission recommendation that vigorous efforts be made to improve the internal
structure of the CIA and the quality of its product?

Must close now but hoping to hear from you soon, and with
best personal wishes, I am,

Sincerely yours,

MIKE MANSFIELD.

CENTRAL INTELLIGENCE AGENCY,
OFFICE OF THE DIRECTOR,
Washington, D.C., September 4, 1953.

THE HONORABLE MIKE MANSFIELD,
  United States Senate,
  Washington, D.C.

DEAR SENATOR MANSFIELD:

In Mr. Dulles' absence from the country, I am taking the liberty
of replying to your letter of August 25, 1953, regarding CIA relations with the Congress. The answers below are numbered in
accordance with the numbers of the questions in your letter.

1. (a) CIA representatives have appeared on Agency business
before the following Senate committees: Armed Services, Government Operations (permanent Subcommittee on Investigations),
Judiciary (Immigration Subcommittee), (Internal Security Subcommittee).

Agency representatives have appeared before the following
House committees: Armed Services, Foreign Affairs, Government
Operations, Un-American Activities.

Agency representatives also have appeared before the Joint
Committee on Atomic Energy and liaison is maintained with the
Joint Committee on Printing.

Concerning regular surveys of CIA's activities by congressional
committees, it should be noted that special subcommittees of the
House and Senate Appropriations Committees receive a detailed
briefing on the various aspects of CIA work in the course of the

annual review of CIA's budget requirements. The Armed Services Committees also receive briefings on CIA, particularly in connection with CIA legislation. In addition, in connection with atomic energy, the joint committee is regularly advised of CIA's activities in this field.

CIA legislation is handled by the Armed Services Committee in both Houses.

The CIA appropriation figure is very tightly held and is known to not more than 5 or 6 Members in each House.

1. (b) The only committee which receives intelligence reports from CIA on a regular basis is the Joint Committee on Atomic Energy. The Agency also makes certain information available to the Immigration Subcommittees of the Judiciary Committees of both Houses, and has also been of some assistance to the Internal Security Subcommittee of the Senate Committee on the Judiciary.

CIA intelligence reports are not made available merely to support the position of another executive agency, in fact there would probably be many instances in which CIA could give intelligence reports to certain other committees if requested.

2. It is our opinion that, from our point of view, the present ties with Congress are adequate. As far as we are able to determine, these ties are stronger than those which exist between any other nation's intelligence service and its legislative body.

In view of the fact that a decision to establish a joint congressional Committee on Central Intelligence involves many factors, some of which are not within the knowledge of CIA, it would not appear appropriate for CIA to express an opinion on the establishment of such a group.

3. At about the same time as the Hoover Commission subcommittee was making its study of intelligence in 1949, a special group appointed by the President, consisting of Mr. Allen Dulles, Mr. William H. Jackson, and Mr. Matthias [sic] F. Correa, was requested to make a detailed survey of CIA. At the time of the survey, these men were all in private life. Many of their recommendations, as well as those of the Hoover Commission, were carried into effect and were largely implemented upon the advent of General Smith as Director in October 1950 and Mr. Jackson as Deputy Director. This implementation has been carried forward by Mr. Dulles, who succeeded Mr. Jackson as Deputy Director,

and subsequently succeeded General Smith as Director. While it is safe to say that no intelligence organization is ever completely satisfied with the quality of its end product, nevertheless, we feel, and have been informed by impartial observers, that the organization and the end product have been continuously and vigorously improved.

I know that Mr. Dulles would be happy to discuss this entire problem with you in greater detail at your convenience upon his return.

Sincerely,

C. P. CABELL,
Lieutenant General, USAF, Acting
Director.

APPENDIX C

Revising National Intelligence Estimates: the Case of Soviet Airpower

(Note: The following letter, from Allen W. Dulles, Director of Central Intelligence, to Senator Stuart Symington illustrates the nature of national intelligence estimates and the role of CIA. It was reprinted in Congressional Record, *daily edition, April 4, 1957, pp. 4611–4612.)*

CENTRAL INTELLIGENCE AGENCY,
OFFICE OF THE DIRECTOR,
Washington, D.C., March 18, 1957.

THE HONORABLE STUART SYMINGTON,
United States Senate,
Washington, D.C.

DEAR SENATOR SYMINGTON:

Yesterday, in your telephone call, you asked me for a memorandum with respect to the change in the national intelligence estimate on Soviet heavy-bomber strength which differed from that given in the testimony before your subcommittee last April. You also called my attention to certain newspaper publicity which appeared recently with respect to this matter.

The facts are as follows:

The intelligence community is continually reviewing its current and projected estimates of Soviet strengths against the best evidence obtainable. Production difficulties, modifications of design, change in emphasis, and other factors mean that actual production here, in the U.S.S.R. and, in fact, anywhere, does not necessarily coincide with predictions.

The estimate of Soviet heavy-bomber strength as of April 1,

1956, which was given in my testimony before your subcommittee, was based largely on an estimated buildup rate which rested upon earlier evidence.

Subsequent to my testimony before your subcommittee in April 1956, the intelligence community acquired new and better evidence on Soviet heavy-bomber production and strength in operational units and we undertook a complete review of our estimates on this subject. Our revised estimate was not completed until after the conclusion of hearings before your subcommittee and after the adjournment of the Congress. It was based on new evidence and not on any extraneous considerations. This new agreed national estimate revised downward the estimated total production of BISONS as of July 1, 1956, but did not change the estimated number of modern bombers which the U.S.S.R. could and, in the opinion of competent experts, probably would provide in its long-range force in the time period beyond the next 2 years, as submitted to your subcommittee in April. Obviously, this estimate of future Soviet heavy-bomber strength will be subject to constant review in the light of new intelligence.

As you will recall, an insert for your subcommittee's record of my testimony, including the revised BISON estimate for July 1, 1956, was delivered to the staff director of your subcommittee on November 5, 1956.

As Director of the Central Intelligence Agency my responsibility with respect to national intelligence estimates is set forth in section 102 (d) (3) of the National Security Act of 1947, which provides that —

"(d) For the purpose of coordinating the intelligence activities of the several Government departments and agencies in the interest of national security, it shall be the duty of the Agency, under the direction of the National Security Council . . .

"(3) to correlate and evaluate intelligence relating to the national security, and provide for the appropriate dissemination of such intelligence within the Government, etc."

In exercising this responsibility, I am assisted by those members of the intelligence community who have competence in the particular field involved.

Sincerely,

ALLEN W. DULLES,
Director.

BIBLIOGRAPHY

NOTES

INDEX

A SELECTED BIBLIOGRAPHY

This bibliography contains items concerned primarily with United States central intelligence or providing pertinent background information on this subject. No attempt has been made to include materials dealing primarily with military (combat) intelligence except insofar as these seem to be an integral part of strategic intelligence. Nor is there full coverage here of the vast and highly uneven mass of published work on espionage and counter-espionage. A selected number of items has been included on various foreign intelligence systems. Under this latter category, however, no claim is made for comprehensiveness. On certain specific subjects, some items have been cited in the notes but are not included in this bibliography.

1. UNITED STATES

A. Books

Alsop, Stewart and Thomas Braden, *Sub Rosa*, New York, Reynal and Hitchcock, 1946.

A somewhat overly dramatic account of Office of Strategic Services operations during World War II, but full of details and accounts of episodes and personalities of the OSS.

Baker, Lafayette, *History of the United States Secret Service*, Philadelphia, King and Baird, 1868.

An autobiographical account of the Federal Government's secret service activities during the Civil War, by the officer who became chief of intelligence for the Federal Government.

Baldwin, Hanson W., *The Price of Power*, New York, Harper and Bros., 1948, Chap. IX, pp. 203–219.

Baldwin's chapter on intelligence reviews critically American intelligence from 1939 to 1947 and contains recommendations on how CIA should function.

Bradley, General Omar Nelson, *A Soldier's Story*, New York, Henry Holt, 1951, pp. 33, 449–464.
Useful for commentary on intelligence role and alleged failures during "Battle of the Bulge."

Dulles, Allen Welsh, *Germany's Underground*, New York, The Macmillan Co., 1947.
Written by a man sometimes described as America's "master spy," this book deals indirectly with operations of the Office of Strategic Services in Europe in World War II and directly with events leading up to the unsuccessful attempt to assassinate Hitler in 1944. The author became Director of Central Intelligence in 1953.

Farago, Ladislas, *War of Wits, The Anatomy of Espionage and Intelligence*, New York, Funk and Wagnalls, 1954.
Journalistic opus on intelligence doctrines and operations written by a newspaperman and wartime reserve officer in the Office of Naval Intelligence.

Ford, Corey and Alastair MacBain, *Cloak and Dagger: The Secret Story of the OSS*, New York, Random House, 1946.
A somewhat melodramatic account of the activities during World War II of the Office of Strategic Services.

Goudsmit, Samuel A., *Alsos*, New York, Henry Schuman, 1947.
The *Alsos* mission, of which the author of this book was the scientific head, was to follow Allied armies in the invasion of Europe to determine precisely how much the Germans knew about the atomic bomb and how much progress the Germans had made. This is the story of one important aspect of scientific intelligence by American forces in World War II.

Glass, Lt. Col. Robert R. and Lt. Col. Philip B. Davidson, *Intelligence Is For Commanders*, Harrisburg, Penn., Military Service Publishing Company, 1948.
Concise manual on combat intelligence doctrine.

Hall, Roger, *You're Stepping on My Cloak and Dagger*, New York, Norton, 1957.
As the title suggests, this book is designed as a humorous account of one man's experiences in the Office of Strategic Services during World War II. It contains much implicit information about the training and activities of OSS agents during the war.

Hilsman, Roger, Jr., *Strategic Intelligence and National Decisions,* Glencoe, Illinois, The Free Press, 1956.

> Dr. Hilsman, now with the Legislative Reference Service, Library of Congress, has served with OSS and CIA. His book is based in part on interviews with State Department, CIA, and other officials. This is a valuable treatise on relationship between intelligence and the decisional process. Hilsman develops at some length a "working model" of the relationship between knowledge and action.

Industrial College of the Armed Forces, Emergency Management of the National Economy, Vol. XV, "Economic Intelligence and Economic Warfare," Washington, Industrial College of the Armed Forces, 1954.

> Study by Professor Benjamin Williams prepared for the Industrial College on economic intelligence techniques and problems.

Kent, Sherman, *Strategic Intelligence for American World Policy,* Princeton, Princeton University Press, 1949, 1951.

> The classic primer on strategic intelligence written by a former Yale history professor, one-time OSS and State Department intelligence official, and now chairman of the Board of National Estimates, of CIA. Book is somewhat outdated but remains a practical professional analysis of intelligence problems and techniques on the national strategic level and a good appraisal of what can and should be expected of intelligence community.

Kintner, William R., with others, *Forging a New Sword,* New York, Harper and Bros., 1958.

> A well-informed analysis of Department of Defense and national security organizations which are prime consumers and producers of national intelligence. Contains proposals for Pentagon reorganization. A valuable supplement to the book by Timothy W. Stanley listed below.

Klein, Alexander, *The Counterfeit Traitor,* New York, Henry Holt, 1958.

> One of World War II's most bizarre true stories of succesful espionage. An account of the activities of Eric Erickson, American-born Swedish oilman who posed as a pro-Nazi and was able to supply the Allied high command with intelligence

data vital for methodical strategic bombing of German oil refineries. The book offers excellent insight into both Allied and Nazi wartime espionage organizations.

MacDonald, Elizabeth P., *Undercover Girl*, New York, The Macmillan Co., 1947.

A somewhat dramatized personal account of the experiences of an OSS agent in India and China, 1943–1945.

⟶ Marshall, S. L. A., *The River and the Gauntlet*, New York, Morrow, 1953.

Although this book deals primarily with the Chinese intervention in the Korean War and subsequent battles, its first chapter contains one of the most incisive commentaries on intelligence ever written.

Mashbir, Sidney Forrester, *I Was An American Spy*, New York, Vantage Press, 1953.

Personalized account of an Army G-2 officer's experiences, with emphasis on Army psychological warfare campaign against the Japanese.

⟶ McCamy, James L., *The Administration of American Foreign Affairs*, New York, Alfred A. Knopf, 1952.

See especially chapter XIII, "Intelligence and Foreign Affairs," pp. 281–307. A thoughtful treatise on administration, broadly construed, of foreign affairs and the role of the intelligence element therein.

Millis, Walter, ed., *The Forrestal Diaries*, New York, The Viking Press, 1951.

Comments by the late Secretary of Defense on post-war effort to establish a centralized intelligence body.

————, *This is Pearl!*, New York, Wm. Morrow, 1947. Esp. Chap. 6.

Detailed, smoothly written analysis of events leading up to Pearl Harbor attack with frequent reference to intelligence role. One of the best books available on the Pearl Harbor attack.

Morgan, William J., *The O.S.S. and I*, New York, Norton, 1957.

Memoirs of a professional psychologist who served in the Office of Strategic Services during World War II. He attended the British school for spies and counter-spies — "Pemberly" — and later parachuted into France to help in organizing the French anti-Nazi underground, the *Maquis.*

Morgenstern, George, *Pearl Harbor, The Story of the Secret War,* New York, Devin-Adair Co., 1947. Esp. Chap. 17.

Critical analysis of Congressional hearings on Pearl Harbor with suggestion that Washington withheld intelligence from commanders at Pearl Harbor. A polemic with important information on intelligence at Pearl Harbor.

Nelson, Otto L. Jr., *National Security and the General Staff,* Washington, Infantry Journal Press, 1946. Esp. pp. 521–534. One of the few accounts available, and the best informed, of intelligence organization and re-organization in the United States Army in World War II.

Office of Strategic Services, assessment staff (Henry A. Murray and others), *Assessment of Men,* New York, Rinehart and Co., 1947, 1950.

A detailed report by psychologists and psychiatrists who worked at the various stations established during World War II for testing and assessing the qualifications of men and women recruited for a variety of tasks performed by OSS during the war. The book offers valuable insight into OSS and various concepts of the tasks of secret intelligence and special operations and the personal qualities required for such assignments.

Padover, Saul K., *Experiment in Germany: The Story of An American Intelligence Officer,* New York, Duell, Sloan and Pearce, 1946.

An account of the effort to analyze the attitudes of German civilians in the Rhineland during World War II.

Pettee, George S., *The Future of American Secret Intelligence,* Washington, Infantry Journal Press, 1946.

Pettee's book, by a World War II intelligence specialist, contains more critical opinions of specific intelligence substantive and organizational problems than either Kent's or Hilsman's. Although outdated somewhat, this book remains of great value.

Pinkerton, Allan, *The Spy of the Rebellion,* New York, G. W. Carleton, 1886.

An autobiographical account by the famous detective who was, for a time and under the *nom-de-guerre* of Maj. E. J.

Allen, Chief of General McClellan's Union Army intelligence service. This book reveals some of the ineptness with which this job was handled by Pinkerton, who had no experience qualifying him to lead a military intelligence service. See especially pp. 151 ff.

Platt, Washington, *Strategic Intelligence Production: Basic Principles*, New York, Frederick A. Praeger, 1957.

An attempt to establish basic principles of strategic intelligence production, written by an Army reserve officer experienced in military intelligence. The specific structure and role of the contemporary intelligence community are not discussed.

Price, Don K., *Government and Science*, New York, New York University Press, 1954.

Primarily an analysis of the impact of scientists upon the American governmental system, this book is highly relevant to some of the problems of central intelligence, particularly chapter V, "The Machinery of Advice."

Smith, Nicol and Blake Clark, *Into Siam, Underground Kingdom*, Indianapolis and New York, Bobbs-Merrill, 1946.

An account of OSS field men in Siam during World War II.

Stanley, Timothy W., *American Defense and National Security*, Washington, D.C., Public Affairs Press, 1956, pp. 20–22, 35, 54.

Provides background on position of intelligence in the national security mechanism. The best general description of the organization for national security since World War II.

Stratton, Roy O., *SACO, The Rice Paddy Navy*, Pleasantville, New York, C. S. Palmer, 1950.

The story of intelligence activities of the United States Naval group — the "Sino-American Cooperative Organization" which operated in and around China in World War II.

Sweeney, Lt. Col. Walter C., *Military Intelligence, A New Weapon in War*, New York, Stokes, 1924.

Contains an account of military intelligence in World War I and reveals the general state of intelligence doctrine of the early 1920's.

Theobald, Rear Adm. Robert A., *The Final Secret of Pearl Harbor*, New York, The Devin-Adair Co., 1954.

An apology for the commanders at Pearl Harbor and a bitter condemnation of Washington's role in pre-attack intelligence dissemination. Argues that Roosevelt deliberately left Pearl open to attack as device for rallying Americans to World War II cause. Even though a diatribe, it contains important information on the Pearl Harbor intelligence failure.

Townsend, Elias Carter, *Risks, The Key to Combat Intelligence*, Harrisburg, Penn., The Military Service Publishing Company, 1955.
Analysis of combat intelligence and relationship to the commander. Stresses theory that it is responsibility of commander to take calculated risks on basis of intelligence.

Truman, Harry S., *Memoirs*, Vol. I, Year of Decisions; Vol. II, Years of Trail and Hope, Garden City, Doubleday & Co., 1956. Vol. I, pp. 98–99, 226. Vol. II, 51–60, 277, 284, 306, 331, 341, 372, 376, 378, 381, 390–91.
The former president's personal recollections of events leading to CIA's establishment and some comments on intelligence in the Korean conflict.

Vagts, Alfred, *Defense and Diplomacy*, New York, King's Crown Press, 1956, Chap. 3, "Diplomacy, Military Intelligence, and Espionage," pp. 61–77.
Vagts traces the historical experience of intelligence concluding with a section on "American Intelligence in the 'Cold War.'"

Whitehead, Don, *The FBI Story*, New York, Random House, 1956.
A sympathetic history of the Federal Bureau of Investigation. The sections on "World War II" (pp. 181–242) and "The Cold War" (pp. 265–320) are of particular interest to those interested in counter-intelligence. Here is found one of the few accounts of the operations of the FBI's Special Intelligence Service, which during the period 1940–1946 had responsibility for foreign intelligence in the Western Hemisphere. For details of SIS's activities, see pp. 210–230.

Willoughby, Charles A. and John Chamberlain, *MacArthur, 1941–1951*, New York, McGraw-Hill, 1954, Esp. pp. 350–425.
Controversial account of MacArthur's exploits told by his G-2. Especially valuable for background on intelligence preceding and during the Korean War.

Yardley, Herbert O., *The American Black Chamber,* Indianapolis, Bobbs-Merrill, 1931.

> The "Black Chamber" was the American Cryptographic Bureau, which operated out of the Department of State in the decade after the first World War. It monitored the secret correspondence of foreign nations and was abolished as a "dirty business" early in 1929 by a new Secretary of State, Henry L. Stimson. This book's author was its director. He presents a somewhat melodramatic although apparently authentic account of some of the "Black Chamber's" operations.

Zacharias, Ellis M., *Secret Missions,* New York, G. P. Putnam's Sons, 1946.

> Personalized account by a senior naval intelligence officer of ONI operations before and during World War II with considerable background on Navy's psychological warfare campaign waged against Japan. One of the best and most revealing books available.

————, *Behind Closed Doors, The Secret History of the Cold War,* New York, G. P. Putnam's Sons, 1950.

> An account of intelligence activities from 1945 to 1950 coupled with a foray into American foreign policy problems.

B. Articles

Anonymous, "Have We An Intelligence Service?" *The Atlantic,* April 1948, pp. 66–70.

> Sharp criticism of intelligence weaknesses in immediate postwar era and comment on the future of CIA.

Alsop, Joseph and Stewart, "The National Estimates," *New York Herald Tribune,* January 8, 1956.

> Description of National Estimates Board and Intelligence Advisory Committee; critical of estimates on Russian capabilities.

Ayer, Frederick W., Jr., "The Intelligence Services," *Vital Speeches of the Day,* February 1, 1958, pp. 247–251.

> A general description of Cold War intelligence requirements, by the Special Assistant for Intelligence to the Secretary of the United States Air Force.

Baker, Russell, "The Other Mr. Dulles—Of the C.I.A.," *The*

New York Times Magazine, March 16, 1958, pp. 17, 96–97.
A journalist's evaluation of the work of CIA under the leadership of Allen W. Dulles. The writer, a staff member of *The New York Times* Washington bureau, gives the agency and Mr. Dulles high marks on the basis of its personnel, intelligence reporting, and intelligence evaluation.

Baldwin, Hanson W., Series of five articles in *The New York Times* on intelligence:

> July 20, 1948, p. 6: "Intelligence — One of the Weakest Links in our Security Survey Shows — Omissions, Duplications."
> July 22, 1948, p. 2: "Older Agencies Resent a Successor and Try to Restrict Scope of Action."
> July 23, 1948, p. 5: "Intelligence III: Errors in Collecting Data Held Exceeded by Evaluation Weakness."
> July 24, 1948, p. 5: "Competent Personnel Held Key to Success — Reforms Suggested."
> July 25, 1948, p. 15: "Broader Control Set-Up is Held Need With a 'Watch-Dog' Committee for Congress."

———, "Myopia on Intelligence," *The New York Times,* June 3, 1954.
Baldwin's support of Joint Congressional Committee. See also *NYT* article of October 14, 1954.

Bingham, Woodbridge, "Historical Training and Military Intelligence," *Pacific Historical Review,* June 1946, pp. 201–206.
A description of the types of military intelligence work in which scholarly training proved of value in World War II.

Bowie, Robert R., "Analysis of Our Policy Machine," *The New York Times Magazine,* March 9, 1958, pp. 16, 68–71.
This article is of particular interest as it points to the significant role the intelligence estimate plays in the formation of national policy. The author is a former director of the policy planning staff in the Department of State.

Chamberlain, John, "OSS," *Life,* November 19, 1945, pp. 119–130.
Capsule history of OSS and General William J. Donovan's role in its wartime activities.

Donovan, William J., "Intelligence: Key to Defense," *Life,* September 30, 1946, pp. 108–120.
Critique of pre-war intelligence and of wartime OSS by its

founder and director together with suggestions for post-war organization. See also *New York Herald Tribune,* April 10, 1946, for Donovan's criticism of the post-war National Intelligence Authority.

————, "Foreign Policy Must Be Based on the Facts," *Vital Speeches,* May 1, 1946, pp. 446–448.

Largely an account of OSS work during World War II.

————, "Intelligence" *Encyclopedia Britannica,* 1956.

A general discussion of the history and process of national intelligence.

Dulles, Allen W., "Russia's Growing Strength Could Be a Weakness," *U. S. News and World Report,* May 11, 1956, pp. 124–127.

Analysis of growing Soviet technology and a long-range estimate that the new economy may make the Russians less tolerant of "the present type of dictatorship."

————, "Reds Plan 'To Use Freedom to Destroy the Free,'" *U. S. News and World Report,* May 25, 1956, pp. 132–140.

Text of a Dulles public address discussing Soviet techniques for infiltrating Free World Parliaments and labor unions.

————, "Memorandum Respecting . . . Central Intelligence Agency. . . ." submitted to Senate Committee on Armed Services, April 25, 1947. Printed in *Hearings,* "National Defense Establishment," 80th Congress, 1st Session, on S. 758, Washington, 1947, pp. 525–528.

A concise statement of Mr. Dulles' views on a central intelligence organization as of 1947, reprinted in Appendix A of this book.

Eliot, George Fielding, "Is Our Intelligence System Reliable?" *USA,* June 1952, pp. 26–33.

A critical evaluation of central intelligence after its first five years, stressing some of the intelligence "failures."

Falkner, Leonard, "A Spy for Washington," *American Heritage,* August 1957, pp. 58–64.

An account of John Honeyman's activities as a double-agent during the American revolution. Illustrating that American espionage is at least as old as the Republic, Honeyman's intelligence operations for George Washington may have made the surprise and significant victory at Trenton possible.

"A Good Man is Hard to Find," *Fortune*, March 1946, pp. 92–95, 217–223.

Recollections of the OSS estate in Virginia where psychologists tested and screened intelligence personnel for clandestine work.

Green, Murray, "Intelligence For Sale," *Air Force*, November 1955, pp. 82–86.

Citation of the wealth of security information available to the Soviets in technical journals and Congressional hearings. General comment on the over-all value of overt intelligence collection to us as well as to our enemies. Author raises question whether we "give away" too much military information.

Gunther, John, "Inside CIA," *Look*, August 12, 1952, pp. 25–29.

An incisive reporter gives a lively description of CIA, with emphasis upon the agency's principal administrators in 1952. Contains some of the first published details of CIA's executive organization.

Harkness, Richard and Gladys, "The Mysterious Doings of CIA," *Saturday Evening Post*, October 30, November 6 and 13, 1954.

A journalistic but impressively detailed three-part account of CIA activities and organization. Security regulations prevent confirmation or denial of article, but tone indicates CIA may have "assisted" in compiling this publicity *tour de force*.

Hillenkoetter, Rear Admiral R. H., "Using the World's Information Sources," *Army Information Digest*, November 1948, pp. 3–6.

A generalized description of intelligence sources, written by an early Director of Central Intelligence.

Hilsman, Roger, "Intelligence and Policy Making in Foreign Affairs," *World Politics*, October 1952, pp. 1–45.

A detailed argument about the role of intelligence in policy making. A forerunner of Hilsman's book, *Strategic Intelligence and National Decisions*.

Hobbing, Enno, "CIA: Hottest Role in the Cold War," *Esquire*, September 1957, pp. 31–34.

A journalistic account of CIA organization and activities, with some interesting detail on how CIA recruits and uses defectors from behind the Iron Curtain.

Kendall, Willmoore, "The Function of Intelligence," *World Politics,* July 1949, pp. 542–552.

A critical analysis of Sherman Kent's book, *Strategic Intelligence.* Professor Kendall's arguments here are well worth examining, as they challenge the prevalent view of the function, organization, and role of intelligence and intelligence specialists.

Kent, Sherman, "How Effective Is Our Intelligence?" *The Reporter,* September 12, 1950.

An informed discussion of the potentialities and limitations of national intelligence, with particular reference to the performance of CIA in its early years, including the first several months of the Korean War.

———, "Prospects for the National Intelligence Service," *Yale Review,* September 1946, pp. 116–130.

A well-informed, thoughtful account of the first two postwar years of the American government's evolving central intelligence system.

Langer, William L., "Scholarship and the Intelligence Problem," *Proceedings of the American Philosophical Society,* March 1948, pp. 43–45.

A discussion of the role of scholarly research in intelligence production by a Harvard professor of history who headed the Research and Analysis Section of the Office of Strategic Services during World War II and subsequently was chief of the Research and Intelligence section in the Department of State.

Leviero, Anthony, "CIA Now Operating A Far-Flung Network," *The New York Times,* June 20, 1954.

Highlights of CIA operations and organization and Congressional pressure for investigation. A journalistic review.

Newsweek, "Warning Pigeonholed," April 26, 1948, pp. 22–23.

Report on House subcommittee investigation of alleged intelligence failure to warn of Bogota revolution during 1948 International Conference of American States. CIA Director attributes failure to State Department suppression of CIA warning, and demonstrates that some warning was in fact given by the intelligence agency.

Pratt, Fletcher, "How Not to Run a Spy System," *Harper's*, September 1947, pp. 241–246.
Best known as a naval historian, Pratt argues in support of departmental intelligence as opposed to a strong centralized agency.

Richardson, Seth W., "Why Were We Caught Napping at Pearl Harbor?" *Saturday Evening Post*, May 24, 1947.
The Joint Congressional Committee's General Counsel backs committee's findings on Pearl Harbor attack, especially the conclusion that Hawaiian commanders failed to exchange all significant intelligence or to appreciate its significance.

Robinson, Donald, "They Fight the Cold War Under Cover," *Saturday Evening Post*, November 20, 1948, pp. 30 ff.
Written within the first year of CIA's existence and apparently with help from inside government sources, this article reveals the extensive overseas operations and political maneuvering of CIA agents as early as 1948.

Ruggles, Richard and Henry Brodie, "An Empirical Approach to Economic Intelligence in World War II," *Journal of the American Statistical Association*, March 1947, pp. 72–91.
An account of the technique developed by the Economic Warfare Division of the American Embassy in London to analyze markings and serial numbers from captured German equipment in order to obtain estimates of German war production and strength. This was sometimes useful in the selection of air targets in World War II; at other times it gave indication of German tank and rocket strength.

U. S. News and World Report, " 'Beedle' Smith: An Accidental Glimpse Into a Supersecret Agency," October 10, 1952, pp. 47–49.
Survey of CIA, with emphasis on personnel and security procedures, prompted by Smith's testimony that there might be Communists in CIA.

———, "Better Spies for the U. S. Needed," July 8, 1955, pp. 34–36.

———, "Spy Business Keeps on Booming," May 25, 1956, pp. 51–54.

Brief review of some mid-1956 intelligence incidents and comment on importance of intelligence in Cold War.

——, "U. S. Intelligence Blamed for Surprise in Korean Conflict," July 21, 1950, pp. 26–27.

Assumes premise intelligence failed to warn of North Korean capabilities and attack, fails to find the answer why, and discusses mechanics and key personalities of intelligence community.

——, "We Tell Russia Too Much," Interview with Allen Dulles, March 19, 1954, pp. 62–68.

Some reasonably candid comments by the CIA Director on Soviet intelligence and the operations and goals of his own agency.

Unna, Warren, "CIA: Who Watches the Watchman?" *Harper's*, April 1958, pp. 46–53.

A well-informed journalistic account of CIA's role in the contemporary Washington decision-making process. Emphasis is placed upon the question of Congressional surveillance of CIA.

C. Government Documents

(a) U. S. Congress

House, Committee on Military Affairs, Investigations of the National War Effort, "A Report on the System Currently Employed in the Collection, Evaluation, and Dissemination of Intelligence Affecting the War Potential of the United States," House Report No. 2734, 79th Congress, 2nd Session, December 17, 1946.

Joint Committee on the Investigation of the Pearl Harbor Attack, 79th Congress, 2nd Session, 1946.

Report on the "Investigation of the Pearl Harbor Attack."

Senate Committees on Armed Services and Foreign Relations, *Hearings,* "The Military Situation in the Far East," 82nd Congress, 1st Session, 1951, pp. 18, 84, 86, 122, 157, 239, 241, 350, 436, 545, 639, 758, 1035, 1190, 1429, 1463, 1778, 1832, 1859, 1990, 2113, 2267, 2273, 2583, 2629, 2914, 3581.

Some background on intelligence before and during Korean

conflict as seen from Washington and Tokyo; the "MacArthur Hearings."

Senate Committee on Armed Services, *Hearings*, "National Defense Establishment," 80th Congress, 1st Session, on S.758, 3 parts, Washington, 1947.
Part 3 contains testimony on central intelligence.

Senate Committee on Armed Services, Subcommittee on the Air Force, *Hearings* (23 Parts) and *Report*, "Study of Airpower," 84th Congress, 2nd Session, and 85th Congress, 1st Session, Washington, 1956, 1957.
Frequent references were made to United States intelligence in these hearings by the Symington Committee. See *Index* of these hearings, under "Intelligence," for various page references.

Senate Judiciary Internal Security Subcommittee, *Hearing*, "Interlocking Subversion in Government Departments," 83rd Congress, 1st Session, Washington, June 25, 1953, Part 13.
This part contains testimony and important documents and memoranda relating to intelligence organization within the Department of State, 1945–1947. See especially pages 854–882.

Senate Committee on Naval Affairs, *Report* to the Secretary of the Navy, "Unification of the War and Navy Departments and Postwar Organization for National Security" (Eberstadt Report), 79th Congress, 1st Session, 1945, pp. 12–13, 159–163.
Brief account of World War II intelligence organization and Navy proposals for post-war reorganization.

Senate Committee on Rules and Administration, *Report*, "Joint Committee on Central Intelligence Agency," Senate Report No. 1570, 84th Congress, 2nd Session, Washington, February 23, 1956.
The Committee supports, by an eight-to-one vote, the proposal to establish a Joint Congressional Committee on CIA. This document contains the outlines of the argument in favor of such a move as well as the dissenting argument.

(b) Other Documents

Commission on Organization of the Executive Branch of the

Government (Hoover Commission), "Intelligence Activities," *A Report to the Congress* (containing the Commission and Clark Task Force Reports), June 1955.

Commission on Organization of the Executive Branch of the Government (Hoover Commission), 1949: *Task Force Report on Foreign Affairs* (Appendix H), January 1949, p. 95; *Foreign Affairs, A Report to Congress*, February 1949, pp. 15, 16, 56, 57; *Task Force Report,* National Security Organization, Appendix G, January 1949, pp. 4, 32, 76–78.

Department of State:
"Coordination of Foreign Intelligence Activities," *Department of State Bulletin,* February 3, 1946, pp. 174–175.
"Intelligence Objectives," *Bulletin,* May 12, 1946.
Intelligence, *A Bibliography of Its Functions, Methods and Techniques, Part I, Bibliography No. 33,* December 20, 1948 (mimeographed). Part II (Periodical and Newspaper Articles), *Bibliography No. 33.1,* April 11, 1949 (mimeographed), Office of Intelligence Research.

U. S. Bureau of the Budget, "Intelligence and Security Activities of the Government," A Report to the President, Washington, September 20, 1945 (mimeographed).

(c) Statutes

National Security Act of 1947 (Public Law 253, July 26, 1947, 80th Congress, 1947, 61 Stat. 495, 50 U. S. C. Supp. 403).
Section 102 contains provisions establishing CIA. This is CIA's basic charter.

Act to Provide for the Administration of the CIA . . . And for Other Purposes (Public Law 110, 81st Congress, 1st Session, June 20, 1949, 63 Stat. 208).
This act was designed to strengthen the administration of CIA. It gave additional powers to the Director, both in the realm of protecting the secrecy of CIA operations and in the unvouchered expenditure of money.

2. GENERAL

"Battle Order of World Espionage," *United Nations World,* Vol. 3 (June 1949), pp. 31–33.

A general description, with considerable detail, of the intelligence systems of the United States, Great Britain, and Russia as of 1949.

Cookridge, Edward H., *Secrets of the British Secret Service,* London, Sampson Low, Marston & Co., 1947.

A behind-the-scenes account of British intelligence, particularly counter-intelligence, operations against German espionage activities during World War II. In effect the book extols the British Secret Service, but in the process reveals a great deal of apparently authentic information about German espionage in World War II.

Daugherty, William E. with Morris Janowitz, *A Psychological Warfare Casebook,* Baltimore, The Johns Hopkins Press, for Operations Research Office, 1958.

Chapter 7 deals with the "Role of Intelligence, Research, and Analysis in Psychological Warfare," pp. 425–549. This section contains selected writings by scholars on the subject. The premise is that "psychological warfare depends on intelligence for all aspects of its operation."

Galland, Joseph S., *An Historical and Analytical Bibliography of the Literature of Cryptology,* Evanston, Illinois, Northwestern University, 1945.

Knorr, Klaus, *The War Potential of Nations,* Princeton, Princeton University Press, 1956.

This treatise presents valuable background information on the question of a nation's strategic capabilities, which in turn have their impact upon the alternatives open to the leaders of a given nation.

Newman, Bernard, *Epics of Espionage,* New York, Philosophical Library, 1951.

An episodic semi-popular account of the history of espionage.

Possony, Stephen T., "Organized Intelligence: The Problem of the French General Staff," *Social Research,* Vol. 8 (May 1941), pp. 213–237.

An analysis of the French military collapse in 1940, said to be the result of "the failure of organized intelligence." Intelligence here is considered in a broad sense. The article deals largely with the sociology of French military institutions, particularly the General Staff.

Rowan, Richard W., *Spy and Counterspy: The Development of Modern Espionage*, New York, Viking, 1928.

A general account of espionage up until the late nineteen-twenties by a noted writer on espionage.

————, *The Story of Secret Service*, Garden City, New York, Doubleday, Doran and Co., 1937.

An eighty-eight chapter survey of espionage covering "thirty-three centuries." This is a popular survey of the activities of spies and counter-spies in all major periods of world history. A useful general survey prior to the beginning of World War II.

Seth, Ronald, *Spies at Work*, New York, Philosophical Library, 1954.

A general semi-scholarly history of espionage, covering most of the major world powers, with selected bibliography.

Sprout, Harold and Margaret, *Man-Milieu Relationship in the Context of International Politics*, Princeton University, Center of International Studies, Princeton, 1956.

Professor and Mrs. Sprout explore in this essay the general subject of geographic and other environmental factors in international politics. Since one of the basic functions of central intelligence is to forecast the political behavior of foreign nations, the hypotheses set forth by the Sprouts are of considerable interest.

3. GERMANY

Colvin, Ian, *Chief of Intelligence*, London, Victor Gollancz, Ltd., 1951.

A biography of Admiral Canaris, Chief of the *Abwehr*, the German covert intelligence agency. (Published in the United States as *Master Spy*.)

Felstead, Sidney T., *Intelligence: An Indictment of a Colossal Failure*, London, Hutchinson, 1941.

An account of German intelligence and implicit criticism of British intelligence organizations, published in the early years of World War II.

Giskes, H. J., *London Calling North Pole*, London, Kimber, 1953.

Authoritative study of *Abwehr's* utilization of captured British agents to disseminate misleading reports on Lowlands operations.

Hagen, Walter, *Die Geheime Front: Organisation, Personen und Aktionen Des Deutschen Geheimdienstes,* Zurich: Europa-Verlag, 1950.

Book said to be based upon author's experiences. It contains an account of the organization and evolution of the Nazi secret service, emphasizing its work in Czechoslovakia, Yugoslavia, Rumania, Bulgaria, Hungary through World War II.

Hoettl, Wilhelm, *The Secret Front,* New York, Praeger, 1954.

Some intelligence footnotes to German operations in Balkans theater.

International Military Tribunal, *Trial of the Major War Criminals* (42 vols., Nuremberg, Germany, 1947–1949).

See especially testimony of Colonel Lahousen, of the *Abwehr,* Vol. II, pp. 440 ff; IV, pp. 231–238; XXII, 378, 456–464, and *passim.* Also see, Index (Vol. XXIII), under "Abwehr" and "SS Reich Security Main Office" for a listing of other pertinent testimony.

Joesten, Joachim, "Mysterious Herr Gehlen," *The New Republic,* October 4, 1954, pp. 11–14.

A short review of post-war West German intelligence including allegations of United States financing.

Leverkuen, Paul, *German Military Intelligence,* New York, Praeger, 1954.

Detailed study of organization and inner-workings of the *Abwehr* with a discounting of the popular thesis that *Abwehr* leadership committed "treason" against the wartime government.

Liddell Hart, Basil H., *The Other Side of the Hill,* London, Cassell, 1951.

Based upon interviews with German generals, Hart suggests that strategic intelligence deficiencies contributed greatly to Germany's defeat in World War II.

Moyzisch, L. S., *Operation "Cicero,"* London, Wingate Press, 1950.

German version of the story of the valet to the British Ambassador to Turkey. Known as "Cicero," this valet worked for German intelligence to steal important documents.

Nicolai, Walter, *The German Secret Service,* London, S. Paul and Co., 1924.

An account of German intelligence and counter-intelligence

in World War I by the Chief of the German Secret Service during that war.

Schellenberg, Walter, *The Labyrinth*, New York, Harper and Bros., 1956.

Memoirs of an important Nazi intelligence official. One of the most revealing accounts of the Nazi espionage system and the complex of Nazi internecine intrigue.

Sheen, Col. Henry G., "The Disintegration of the German Intelligence Services," *Military Review*, Vol. 29 (June 1949), pp. 38–41.

A brief account of German wartime organization for intelligence operations, revealing the internecine struggle of various intelligence agencies and analyzing reasons for their inefficiency and eventual breakdown.

Shulman, Milton, *Defeat in the West*, New York, E. P. Dutton and Co., 1948.

The author has interrogated high-ranking German officers. The book includes a discussion of the efficiency of German intelligence services.

Singer, Kurt D., *Spies and Traitors in World War II*. New York, Prentice-Hall, 1945.

Stories of German espionage all over the world.

Trefousse, H. L., "Failure of German Intelligence in the United States, 1935–1945," *Mississippi Valley Historical Review*, June 1955, pp. 84–100.

A detailed account of Nazi attempts at espionage and sabotage in the United States. The author concludes: "Despite the time, money, and effort expended on its activities, the German intelligence service in America neither contributed materially to Hitler's power nor seriously impaired the contribution made by the United States in bringing about his destruction."

Von Papen, Franz, *Memoirs*, London, Andre Deutsch, 1952, pp. 509–519.

Further illumination on the "Cicero" incident with an account of the intelligence product's evaluation by various German leaders which points up the dangers inherent in mutiple and independent evaluation by intelligence consumers.

4. GREAT BRITAIN

Babington-Smith, Constance, *Air Spy: The Story of Photo Intelligence in World War II,* New York, Harper and Bros., 1957.
A detailed personal narrative of British photo reconnaissance and interpretation, so vital to the intelligence on which Allied bombing operations were planned in World War II.

Jones, R. V., "Scientific Intelligence," *Journal of the Royal United Service Institution,* August 1947, pp. 352–369.
A brilliant and revealing account of a scientist's experience with British intelligence in World War II. The author was particularily concerned with air and scientific intelligence.

Landau, Capt. Henry, *All's Fair: The Story of the British Secret Service Behind the German Lines,* New York, Putnam, 1934.
A personal account of British secret intelligence in the first World War.

Marshall, Bruce, *The White Rabbit, The Story of Secret Agent Yeo-Thomas,* Boston, Houghton Mifflin Co., 1953.
A factual account of the operational and political problems encountered in organizing and controlling an underground movement based upon British collaboration with French Resistance.

Montagu, Ewen, *The Man Who Never Was,* Philadelphia and New York, J. B. Lippincott Co., 1954.
Brief story of the famed British deception operation for Sicilian invasion involving faked body and papers of an English officer.

Newman, Bernard, *They Saved London,* London, Werner Laurie, 1952.
An account of espionage that revealed to the British the work of German scientists on the V-1 missile at Peenemunde in World War II.

Owen, Frank, *The Eddie Chapman Story,* New York, Julian Messner, 1954.
Tale of an Englishman recruited by German intelligence who "doubled" to the British while winning an Iron Cross.

Read, Conyers, *Mr. Secretary Walsingham and the Policy of Queen Elizabeth,* Cambridge, Harvard University Press, 1925, 3 vols.

A detailed three-volume biography of Sir Francis Walsingham, Queen Bess's principal State Secretary who operated
an extensive intelligence network.

Richings, M. G., *Espionage: The Story of the Secret Service of
the English Crown*, London, Hutchinson and Co., 1934.
An historical account of government secret service operations
in England from the fourteenth to the twentieth century,
from the Plantagenet kings to the period of the first World
War.

Tickell, Jerrard, *Odette*, London, Chapman and Hall, 1949.
Adventures of a female British agent in Occupied France
— one of the better stories of its type.

5. JAPAN

Henry, Fred, "Japanese Espionage and Our Psychology for
Failure," *U.S. Naval Institute Proceedings*, Vol. 69 (May
1943), pp. 639–641.
A brief description of Japanese espionage before World War
II. Attributes early military successes of the Japanese to
pre-war intelligence work.

Seth, Ronald, *Secret Servants: A History of Japanese Espionage*.
New York, Farrar, Straus and Cudahy, 1957.
A general history of Japanese intelligence operations by a
well-known British writer on intelligence and espionage. The
author is a former British intelligence agent.

6. RUSSIA

Australia, *Report of Royal Commission on Espionage*, Sydney,
Commonwealth of Australia, A. H. Pettifier, 1955.
A devastatingly documented account of Soviet espionage
operations conducted in Australia. Based on testimony from
former MVD agent Vladimir Petrov. An excellent sequel
to the Canadian report indicating types of Soviet intelligence
targets and the elaborate collection system employed by the
Russians.

Canada, *Report of Royal Commission to Investigate Disclosures
of Secret and Confidential Information to Unauthorized
Persons*, Ottawa, Clouthier, 1946.
A well-documented case study of Soviet methods, indi-

vidual agents, and organization emerges in this Royal Commission probe of atomic-espionage operations conducted through the USSR Embassy in Ottawa.

Congressional Investigations of Communism and Subversive Activities, Summary-Index, 1918 to 1956, United States Senate and House of Representatives, Senate Doc. No. 148, 84th Congress, 2d Session, Compiled by the Senate Committee on Government Operations, Washington, July 23, 1956.

Congressional investigations of Communist activity have ranged far and wide, particularly since World War II. This document contains an index and summary of all of these up to mid-1956. Investigations of Communist espionage have centered in the House Committee on Un-American Activities and the Senate Judiciary Subcommittee on Internal Security, but many other committees have probed into this matter from time to time.

Cookridge, Edward H., *Soviet Spy Net,* London, Muller, 1955.

A detailed and apparently competent account of modern Soviet secret intelligence and subversive activity, particularly espionage. It contains a brief history of Soviet espionage and a description of Soviet organization and activities since World War II.

Dallin, David J., *Soviet Espionage,* New Haven, Yale University Press, 1955.

A leading authority on Soviet Russia discusses in detail the Soviet espionage system, its evolution, its theory and its operational code. The book contains certain "area studies" of Soviet espionage, particularly Europe and North America. This is one of the most comprehensive and authoritative studies of the subject.

Heilbrunn, Otto, *The Soviet Secret Services,* New York, Frederick A. Praeger, 1956.

An analysis of cases involving Soviet espionage with special attention to Soviet espionage and subversion in Germany in World War II.

Hirsch, Richard, *The Soviet Spies: The Story of Russian Espionage in North America,* New York, Duell, Sloan and Pearce, 1947.

An early account of Soviet espionage during and immediately following World War II.

Kemp, Henry Werner, "Certain Aspects of Soviet Intelligence Activities," unpublished master's thesis, Columbian College, The George Washington University, June 8, 1955.

A useful descriptive survey of Soviet intelligence activities, with emphasis on the work of Soviet agents in the United States.

Liddell Hart, B. H. (ed.), *The Red Army*, New York, Harcourt-Brace, 1956.

This book contains a chapter on "The Soviet Intelligence Services," by Raymond L. Garthoff, pp. 265–274, which, although brief, is a relatively up-to-date description of the various Russian intelligence organizations.

Miksche, F. O., *Secret Forces*, London, Faber and Faber, 1950.

An analysis of the techniques of underground forces with emphasis on Soviet tactics and strategy of subversive operations.

Moorehead, Alan, *The Traitors*, New York, Scribners, 1952.

A British journalist describes atomic espionage and the roles played by such agents as May, Pontecorvo, and Fuchs.

Noel-Baker, Francis, *The Spy Web: A Study of Communist Espionage*, London, Batchworth, 1954.

Accounts of Communist espionage in Canada, Germany, Greece, and elsewhere.

Petrov, Vladimir and Evdokia, *Empire of Fear*, New York, Praeger, 1957.

Husband and wife Petrov shed additional light on activities of Soviet espionage in Australia in their life story.

Rastvorov, Yuri A., Series of three articles in *Life*, November 29, December 6, 13, 1954.

The first "How Red Titans Fought for Supreme Power," gives an account of Beria's downfall in Russia. The author was a member of the Soviet Secret Police for eleven years and became a "defector" in January 1954 while serving as a Russian intelligence agent in Japan. The second article "Red Fraud and Intrigue in the Far East," contains information on Soviet intelligence recruiting methods and a general account of intelligence activities. The final article is an account of Russian intelligence operations in Japan and a narrative account of events leading up to his defection to American authorities.

NOTES

CHAPTER I

Intelligence in the Nuclear Age: Introductory

1. This was the normal practice during the first five years of the Eisenhower Administration.

2. Commission on Organization of the Executive Branch of the Government, Hon. Herbert Hoover, chairman, *Intelligence Activities*, Report to Congress, June 1955, p. 26.

3. Remark attributed to Admiral Arthur Radford, in *Time*, February 25, 1957, p. 27.

4. *Dictionary of United States Military Terms for Joint Usage*, Washington, Departments of the Army, Navy, and Air Force, May 1955, p. 53.

5. *Intelligence Activities*, p. 25.

CHAPTER II

The Nature of Intelligence

1. In *U.S. News and World Report*, Copyright Interview, March 19, 1954, p. 65.

2. Sherman Kent, *Strategic Intelligence*, Princeton, New Jersey, Princeton University Press, 1951, p. viii.

3. George S. Pettee, *The Future of American Secret Intelligence*, Washington, Infantry Journal Press, 1946. See also Mark S. Watson, *The War Department: Chief of Staff, Prewar Plans and Preparations*, Department of the Army, Office of the Chief of Military History, Washington, Government Printing Office, 1950, pp. 505–519.

4. In *U.S. News and World Report*, March 19, 1954, p. 65.

5. William J. Donovan, "Intelligence: Key to Defense," *Life*, September 30, 1946, p. 114.

6. Harold Nicholson, "Intelligence Services: Their Use and Misuse," *Harper's Magazine*, November 1957, pp. 18–19.

7. Captain Ellis M. Zacharias, USN, *Secret Missions, the Story of an Intelligence Officer*, New York, G. P. Putnam's Sons, 1946, pp. 117–118.

8. Senator Richard B. Russell, *Congressional Record* (daily edition), April 11, 1956, p. 5413.

9. Quoted in *U.S. News and World Report*, May 25, 1956, p. 52.

10. Details of this affair are given dramatically but with apparent authenticity in L. G. Moyzisch, *Operation Cicero*, London, Wingate Press, 1950. When this book was published, British Foreign Secretary Ernest Bevin admitted that these events had occurred in Ankara, during the war. See *The Times* (London), October 19, 1950; also *The New York Times*, same date.

11. In *U.S. News and World Report*, March 19, 1954, p. 62.

12. See the *Report* of the Canadian Royal Commission to Investigate Disclosures of Secret and Confidential Information, Ottawa, 1946; also *Report* of the Australian Royal Commission on Espionage, Sydney, 1955; also for details on United States, *Subversive and Illegal Aliens in the U.S.*, Progress Report of Senate Internal Security Subcommittee, 82nd Congress, 1st Session, Washington, 1951.

13. *The New York Times*, August 8, 1957.

14. *The New York Times*, August 10, 1957. For a detailed description of Abel and his activities, see Frank Gibney, "Intimate Portrait of a Russian Master Spy," *Life*, November 11, 1957, pp. 123–130.

15. See Robert Eunson, "How We Nabbed Russia's No. 1 Spy," *Saturday Evening Post*, September 25, 1954, pp. 27 ff. See also "How Red Titans Fought for Supreme Power," *Life*, November 29 and December 6, 1954, pp. 18–21, pp. 174–176.

16. Quoted in *Subversive and Illegal Aliens in the United States*, p. 1.

17. *Congressional Record* (daily edition), May 6, 1953, pp. 6547–6548.

18. Senator Leverett Saltonstall, *Congressional Record* (daily edition), April 9, 1956, p. 5291.

19. Harry S. Truman, *Memoirs*, Vol. I, *Year of Decisions*, Garden City, New York, Doubleday and Co., 1955, p. 226.

20. Hanson W. Baldwin, *The Price of Power*, Council on Foreign Relations, New York, Harper and Bros., 1947, p. 205.

21. See, for example, Baldwin's article "Myopia on Intelligence," *The New York Times*, June 3, 1954.

22. Harry S. Truman, *Memoirs*, Vol. II, *Years of Trial and Hope*, Garden City, New York, Doubleday and Co., 1956, p. 452.

23. Interview with Allen W. Dulles, "We Tell Russia Too Much," *U.S. News and World Report*, March 19, 1954, p. 62; see also Murray Green, "Intelligence For Sale at the Corner Newstand," *Air Force*, November 1955, pp. 82–86.

24. Quoted in Arthur W. MacMahon, *Administration in Foreign*

Affairs, University, Alabama, University of Alabama Press, 1953, p. 86.

25. For a detailed discussion of these categories see Kent, *Strategic Intelligence,* pp. 11–68.

26. Kent, *Strategic Intelligence,* p. 11.

27. Kent, *Strategic Intelligence,* p. 38.

28. For a discussion of this problem between members of Congress and Air Force officials in 1957, see *Hearings,* "DOD Appropriations for 1958," House Subcommittee on Appropriations, 85th Congress, 1st Session, Part I, Washington, 1957, pp. 1062–1064, 1121.

29. Hoover Commission, *Intelligence Activities,* p. 66.

30. For a full discussion of this system and the problems of evaluation see Kent, *Strategic Intelligence,* pp. 168–174. The system actually in use by CIA today is very likely more elaborate than the one here described.

31. Truman, *Memoirs,* Vol. II, p. 306.

32. Pettee, *American Secret Intelligence,* p. 78.

33. Admiral Arthur Radford, in *Hearings,* "Study of Airpower," Senate Armed Forces Subcommittee on the Air Force, 84th Congress, 2nd Session, Part XIX, Washington, June 21, 1956, p. 1460.

34. In *Time,* August 28, 1950; quoted in Alfred Vagts, *Defense and Diplomacy,* New York, King's Crown Press, 1956, p. 77, footnote 92.

35. *Report,* Joint Committee on the Investigation of the Pearl Harbor Attack, 79th Congress, 2nd Session, 1946, pp. 179–181.

36. *Report,* Pearl Harbor Attack, p. 225.

37. Walter Lord, *Day of Infamy,* New York, Henry Holt, 1957, pp. 174–175.

38. Truman, *Memoirs,* Vol. II, p. 58.

39. *Hearings,* "DOD Appropriations for 1958," House Appropriations Subcommittee, 85th Congress, 1st Session, Part I, Washington, 1957, pp. 962–963.

CHAPTER III

United States Intelligence - Historical Background

1. *Hearings,* "Department of Armed Forces," 79th Congress, 1st Session, Senate Committee on Military Affairs, October 18, 1945, Washington, 1945, p. 61.

2. Numbers 13: 20.

3. Michael Prawdin, *The Mongol Empire,* London, G. Allen, 1940,

p. 254, quoted in R. Ernest Dupuy and Trevor N. Dupuy, *Military Heritage of America*, New York, McGraw-Hill, 1956, p. 56.

4. R. V. Jones, "Scientific Intelligence," *Journal of Royal United Service Institution*, August 1947, p. 352.

5. Quoted in Alfred Vagts, *Defense and Diplomacy*, p. 62.

6. For a general survey of diplomacy, military intelligence, and espionage over the past several centuries, see Vagts, *Defense and Diplomacy*, pp. 61–71.

7. Garrett Mattingly, *Renaissance Diplomacy*, Boston, Houghton Mifflin, 1955, p. 260. Mattingly's book gives fascinating details throughout of intelligence operations as a part of "embassy routine" at the time of the beginnings of modern diplomacy. See also Lawrence Stone, *An Elizabethan: Sir Horatio Palavicino*, Oxford, Clarendon Press, 1956, especially chapter 6, "The Secret Agent." A three-volume biography of Walsingham has been written by Conyers Read, *Mr. Secretary Walsingham*, Cambridge, Harvard University Press, 1925.

8. Roger Hilsman, Jr., *Strategic Intelligence and National Decisions*, Glencoe, Illinois, The Free Press, 1956, p. 19.

9. Vagts, *Defense and Diplomacy*, p. 65.

10. Department of the Army, *American Military History, 1607–1953*, ROTC Manual 145–20, Washington, 1956, p. 491.

11. See Jacob D. Cox, *Military Reminiscences of the Civil War*, New York, Scribner's, 1900, Vol. I, pp. 250 ff; also Bruce Catton, *This Hallowed Ground*, Garden City, New York, Doubleday, 1956, pp. 87, 138; James D. Horan and Howard Swiggett, *The Pinkerton Story*, New York, G. P. Putnam's, 1951, especially chapter 4 on Pinkerton. For a colorful account of intelligence activities within the Confederacy, see Harnett T. Kane, *Spies for the Blue and Gray*, Garden City, New York, Hanover House, 1954.

12. Peyton C. March, *The Nation at War*, Garden City, New York. Doubleday, Doran, 1932, p. 226.

13. March, *The Nation at War*, p. 229.

14. General Orders No. 80, War Department, August 26, 1918, quoted in Otto L. Nelson, *National Security and the General Staff*, Washington, Infantry Journal Press, 1946, p. 264.

15. General Orders No. 80, quoted in Nelson, *National Security and the General Staff*, p. 265.

16. "The Military Intelligence Division," *Journal of the United States Artillery*, April 1920, p. 296, quoted in Nelson, *National Security and the General Staff*, p. 265. For a fuller discussion of military intelligence, but one which did not appreciate the need for co-ordinated, national intelligence, see, Lt. Col. Walter C. Sweeney, *Military Intelligence*, New York, Stokes, 1924.

17. Dwight D. Eisenhower, *Crusade in Europe,* Garden City, New York, Doubleday, 1948, p. 32.

18. Eisenhower, *Crusade in Europe,* p. 32.

19. Sir John Slessor, *The Central Blue,* London, Cassell, 1956, p. 402.

20. Quoted in Pettee, *American Secret Intelligence,* pp. 36–37.

21. Industrial College of the Armed Forces, *Emergency Management of the National Economy,* Vol. XV, "Economic Intelligence and Economic Warfare," Washington, 1954, p. 37.

22. Elias Huzar, *The Purse and the Sword,* Ithaca, Cornell University Press, 1950, p. 211.

23. General Omar N. Bradley, *A Soldier's Story,* New York, Henry Holt, 1951, p. 33.

24. John P. Marquand, *Melville Goodwin, U.S.A.,* Boston, Little, Brown, 1951, p. 346.

25. See, *Report,* Joint Committee on the Investigation of the Pearl Harbor Attack, 79th Congress, 2nd Session, Senate Doc. No. 244, July 20, 1946. See also Samuel Eliot Morison's account in his *History of United States Naval Operations in World War II,* Vol. III, "The Rising Sun in the Pacific," Boston, Little, Brown, 1941, chapter V. A large number of other books deal with this episode.

26. The degree of surprise is clearly seen in Walter Lord, *Day of Infamy.*

27. For a detailed account of naval intelligence available prior to the attack, see Walter Millis, *This Is Pearl!* New York, Morrow, 1947; also Ellis M. Zacharias, *Secret Missions,* pp. 253 ff.

28. *Intelligence Activities,* pp. 29–30.

29. For an account of the intelligence failure at Pearl Harbor, see Rear Adm. Robert A. Theobald, *The Final Secret of Pearl Harbor,* New York, Devin-Adair, 1954, especially pp. 32–125. One need not accept his implausible thesis regarding President Roosevelt's motives in this episode in order to appreciate his detailed account of events.

30. Donovan, "Intelligence: Key to Defense," p. 110.

31. See "Unification of the War and Navy Departments and Postwar Organization for National Security," Report to Secretary of the Navy [Eberstadt to Forrestal], Committee Print of the Senate Committee on Naval Affairs, 79th Congress, 1st Session, Washington, 1945. Hereafter cited as Eberstadt Report. See especially pp. 159–163.

32. For a brief review of these arrangements, see Eberstadt Report, pp. 159–163.

33. See Dulles' book, *Germany's Underground,* New York, MacMillan, 1947.

34. An interesting post-factum intelligence operation was the

United States Strategic Bombing Survey, which surveyed Allied bombing in Europe, following closely behind advancing Allied armies. The aim was to produce intelligence useful in the strategic bombing of Japan. But victory in the Pacific soon followed and a comparable USSBS study was made in Japan. The resulting analyses comprise 208 separate published items for the European Theater and 108 for the war in the Pacific. For a concise analysis of these surveys, see Bernard Brodie, *Strategic Air Power in World War II*, Research Memorandum 1866, RAND Corporation, Santa Monica, California, February 4, 1957.

35. For an argument, bitterly stated, that adequate intelligence was available prior to the "Battle of the Bulge" but commanders ignored it, see Robert S. Allen, *Lucky Forward*, New York, Vanguard, 1947, pp. 206–217.

36. See Louis Morton, "The Decision to Use the Atomic Bomb," *Foreign Affairs*, January 1957, pp. 342–344.

37. These are the words of Stewart Alsop and Thomas Braden in their *Sub Rosa*, New York, Reynal and Hitchcock, 1946, p. 23.

38. Henry A. Murray and others of the assessment staff, Office of Strategic Services, *Assessment of Men*, New York, Rinehart, 1947, 1950, p. 10.

39. For personal and somewhat melodramatic accounts see: Stewart Alsop and Thomas Braden, *Sub Rosa;* Corey Ford and Alastair MacBain, *Cloak and Dagger*, New York, Random House, 1946; and William J. Morgan, *The OSS and I*, New York, Norton, 1957.

40. For details, see Alsop and Braden, *Sub Rosa*, pp. 228, 230.

41. See Alsop and Braden, *Sub Rosa*, p. 15. Later, in 1951, MacArthur reportedly took a dim view of CIA agents operating within his Far Eastern Command. For an explanation of MacArthur's attitude, see Maj. Gen. Charles A. Willoughby and John Chamberlain, *MacArthur 1941–1951*, New York, McGraw-Hill, 1954, pp. 144 ff. Willoughby was MacArthur's intelligence chief. The book also contains a detailed account of the so-called Allied Intelligence Bureau (AIB) which operated in the Southwest Pacific during the war.

42. Baldwin, *The Price of Power*, p. 205. Baldwin's reference to Switzerland is an implicit tribute to Allen W. Dulles.

43. Baldwin, *The Price of Power*, p. 205.

44. Baldwin, *The Price of Power*, p. 206.

45. John Chamberlain, "OSS," *Life*, November 19, 1945, p. 119.

46. Truman, *Memoirs*, Vol. II, p. 56.

47. Truman, *Memoirs*, Vol. II, p. 56.

48. Eberstadt Report, p. 163.

49. Eberstadt Report, p. 163.

50. See Truman, *Memoirs*, Vol. II, p. 57.

51. Walter Millis, ed., *The Forrestal Diaries*, New York, Viking, 1951, p. 37.

52. A document which figured importantly in these events was "Intelligence and Security Activities of the Government," Report to the President by the Bureau of the Budget, Washington, September 20, 1945.

53. Truman, *Memoirs*, Vol. II, p. 58.

54. *Hearings*, "National Security Act of 1947," House Committee on Expenditures in the Executive Departments, 80th Congress, 1st Session, 1947, p. 121.

CHAPTER IV

The Central Intelligence Agency: Basic Functions

1. Congressman Fred Busbey asked this question of James V. Forrestal, then Secretary of the Navy, in *Hearings*, "National Security Act of 1947," House Committee on Expenditures in the Executive Departments, 80th Congress, 1st Session, Washington, 1947, p. 120.

2. C. Northcote Parkinson, *Parkinson's Law*, Boston, Houghton Mifflin, 1957.

3. Title I, Section 102, 61 *Stat.* 495.

4. 63 *Stat.* 208, approved June 20, 1949.

5. The CIA is said, however, to have taken administrative measures to control strictly its expenditures, and to require a complete accounting for the use of all its funds, vouchered or unvouchered. Information about this system and details on use of funds are supplied each year to appropriations subcommittees of the House and Senate. See Senate Report No. 1570, 84th Congress, 2d Session, "Individual Views of Mr. Hayden," February 23, 1956, p. 26.

6. For an example of such speculation see Hanson W. Baldwin, *The New York Times*, articles on June 3 and August 3, 1954.

7. See Kent, *Strategic Intelligence*, pp. 91–94, a part of his brilliant and provocative chapter "Intelligence is Organization."

8. General MacArthur described such allegations as "pure bunkum," but they have perisisted. See *Hearings*, "Military Situation in the Far East," Senate Armed Services and Foreign Relations Committees, Part I, Washington, 1951, p. 241.

9. *U. S. News and World Report*, March 19, 1954, pp. 63–64.

10. Donald Robinson, "They Fight the Cold War Under Cover," *Saturday Evening Post*, November 20, 1948, p. 191. For a later ac-

count, along similar lines, see Richard and Gladys Harkness, "The Mysterious Doings of CIA," a three-part series in *Saturday Evening Post*, October 30, November 6 and 13, 1954.

11. Enno Hobbing, "CIA: Hottest Role in the Cold War," *Esquire*, September 1957, p. 31.

12. For a journalistic account of some of these and other CIA maneuvers in international politics, see Richard and Gladys Harkness, "The Mysterious Doings of CIA," November 6, 1954, pp. 66–68; see also other articles in this series on October 30, and November 13, 1954. For an account of earlier CIA overseas ventures see Donald Robinson, "They Fight the Cold War Under Cover."

13. Truman, *Memoirs*, Vol. II, p. 372.

14. Kent, *Strategic Intelligence*, pp. 90–95.

15. Kent, *Strategic Intelligence*, pp. 95–96.

16. Hilsman, *Strategic Intelligence and National Decisions*, p. 33.

17. The CIA does not officially admit engagement in espionage or overseas political action. Yet these clearly are functions of the agency, performed under explicit or tacit National Security Council directive.

18. Russell Baker, "The Other Mr. Dulles — Of the C.I.A." *The New York Times Magazine*, March 16, 1958, p. 17.

19. Quoted by Warren Unna, in "CIA: Who Watches the Watchman?" *Harper's*, April 1958, p. 46. For a detailed statement of Mr. Dulles' views on CIA, as of 1947, see Appendix A.

CHAPTER V

The Intelligence Community: Other Principal Members

1. *Intelligence Activities*, p. 13.

2. *Hearings*, "Department of Defense Appropriations for 1958," Senate Appropriations Subcommittee, 85th Congress, 1st Session, Washington, 1957, p. 796.

3. For a detailed account of G–2 structure and function during World War II, see Nelson, *National Security and the General Staff*, pp. 521–535.

4. For a detailed account of the concepts underlying the 1944 reorganization, see Nelson, *National Security and the General Staff*, pp. 527–531.

5. For a chart of this organization, see Nelson, *National Security and the General Staff*, p. 333.

6. Hoover Commission, *National Security Organization*, Appendix G, Washington, January 1949, p. 77.

7. *Hearings*, "Department of Army Appropriations for 1956," House Appropriations Subcommittee, Washington, 1955, p. 518.

8. These data are based on information given in *Hearings*, "Department of Defense Appropriations for 1958," Senate Appropriations Subcommittee, 1957, pp. 795–796.

9. This information is based upon details given in *Hearings*, "Department of the Army Appropriations for 1957," House Appropriations Subcommittee, 84th Congress, 2nd Session, pp. 409 ff.

10. See *Hearings*, "Department of the Army Appropriations for 1957," p. 396.

11. See, for example, *Organization of the Army*, Report of the Advisory Committee on Army Organization, Paul L. Davies, Chairman, December 18, 1953, p. 33.

12. *Hearings*, "Department of Defense Appropriations for 1958," Senate, p. 796.

13. *History of United States Naval Operations in World War II*, Vol. II, "Operations in North African Waters," 1947, p. 26.

14. Zacharias, *Secret Missions, passim.*

15. Zacharias, *Secret Missions*, p. 82.

16. Zacharias, *Secret Missions*, p. 83.

17. Morison, Vol. III, "The Rising Sun in the Pacific," p. 134.

18. Hoover Commission, *Intelligence Activities*, pp. 37–38.

19. Wesley F. Craven and James L. Cate (eds.), *The Army Air Forces in World War II*, Vol. I, "Plans and Early Operations," Chicago, University of Chicago Press, 1948, p. 625.

20. Gen. Henry H. Arnold, *Global Mission*, New York, Harper, 1949, p. 169.

21. Craven and Cate, *The Army Air Forces*, Vol. VI, "Men and Planes," pp. 480–481.

22. Air University, Research Studies Institute, "Development of Intelligence Function In U.S.A.F., 1917–1950," by Victor H. Cohen, Special Studies Report, January 1, 1957. The study itself is classified SECRET.

23. These quotations are from *Third Report of the Commanding General of the Army Air Forces*, to the Secretary of War, Washington, November 12, 1945.

24. For a review of World War II problems in processing intelligence data see Maj. Charles H. Barber, "Some Problems of Air Intelligence," *Military Review*, August 1946, pp. 76–78; see also Constance Babington-Smith, *Air Spy*, New York, Harper, 1957. For an analysis of factors influencing the selection of targets see Col. John H. DeRussy "Selecting Target Systems and Targets," *Air University Quarterly Review*, Spring 1947, pp. 69–78.

25. *Intelligence Activities*, pp. 41–42.

26. *Intelligence Activities*, p. 41.

27. For details, see "Jet-Speed Intelligence," *Air University Quarterly Review*, Spring 1957, Parts I and II, pp. 71–84.

28. For details of cryptography in the Renaissance see Garrett Mattingly, *Renaissance Diplomacy*, pp. 247–250; also J. W. Thompson and S. K. Padover, *Secret Diplomacy, A Record of Espionage and Double-dealing: 1500–1815*, London, Jarrolds, 1937, especially Appendix, "Cryptography," pp. 253–263.

29. Timothy W. Stanley, *American Defense and National Security*, Washington, Public Affairs Press, 1956, p. 27, fn. 24, and p. 35.

30. See *The New York Times*, November 10, 1954.

31. See Herbert O. Yardley, *The American Black Chamber*, Indianapolis, Bobbs-Merrill, 1931.

32. James L. McCamy, *The Administration of American Foreign Affairs*, New York, Knopf, 1952, p. 282.

33. Quoted in John Osborne, "Is the State Department Manageable?" *Fortune*, March 1957, p. 112.

34. Letter reprinted in *Hearing*, "Interlocking Subversion in Government Departments," Senate Judiciary Internal Security Subcommittee, 83rd Congress, 1st Session, Part 13, Washington, June 25, 1953, p. 870.

35. Hoover Commission, *Foreign Affairs*, Task Force Report, Appendix H, January 1949, p. 91.

36. *Foreign Affairs*, Task Force Report, pp. 92–93.

37. *Foreign Affairs*, Task Force Report, p. 93.

38. For a detailed argument on this and related points see McCormack's State Department Memorandum of February 12, 1946. This is reproduced as Exhibit No. 264, *Hearing*, "Interlocking Subversion in Government Departments," Part 13, pp. 856–860. See also counter-arguments of Donald Russell and others, pp. 865–869 and *passim*.

39. Hilsman, *Strategic Intelligence and National Decisions*, pp. 51–55.

40.. *Foreign Affairs*, Task Force Report, p. 94. See also Zara S. Steiner, "The State Department and the Foreign Service, The Wriston Report — Four Years Later," Princeton, Center of International Studies, Memorandum No. 16, Princeton, New Jersey, March 1958, especially pp. 38–41.

41. Statement of W. Park Armstrong, Jr., Special Assistant for Intelligence, *Hearings*, "State, Justice, Judiciary and Related Agencies, Appropriations for Fiscal Year 1957," Senate Committee on Appropriations, Washington, 1956, p. 503.

42. *Foreign Affairs*, Task Force Report, p. 95.

43. *Intelligence Activities*, p. 43.

44. See Don Whitehead, *The FBI Story,* New York, Random House, 1956, pp. 166–167 and *passim.*

45. For details, see Whitehead, *The FBI Story,* pp. 210–220.

46. Whitehead, *The FBI Story,* especially footnote 3 at p. 347.

47. Other agencies playing an important, if lesser, role in intelligence include the Treasury Department, with its numerous sub-agencies; the Department of Justice; Post Office Department; Interior, Agriculture, and Commerce Departments; the International Cooperation Administration; the Federal Communications Commission; and, not the least in importance, the United States Information Agency.

CHAPTER VI

Intelligence End Product: The National Estimate

1. In *The New York Times,* August 28, 1957.

2. For details on powerful long-range radar units based in Turkey and tracking Russian missile launchings, see "How U.S. Taps Soviet Missile Secrets," *Aviation Week,* October 21, 1957, pp. 26–27.

3. See Vagts, *Defense and Diplomacy,* p. 72.

4. News conference, October 30, 1957, transcribed in *The New York Times,* October 31, 1957.

5. See Winston S. Churchill, *The Grand Alliance,* Boston, Houghton Mifflin, 1950, pp. 356–358.

6. This issue was touched on at the 1956 Symington Hearings when General Twining was testifying on Soviet air capabilities. Remarked Senator Symington: "We want no intelligence that is not national intelligence." See *Hearings,* "Study of Airpower," Senate Armed Services Subcommittee on the Air Force, 84th Congress, 2nd Session. p. 1814.

7. In *U.S. News and World Report,* March 19, 1954, p. 66.

8. For details, see Robert J. Donovan, *The Inside Story,* New York, Harper, 1956, pp. 40–41.

CHAPTER VII

Surveillance by Congress: The Issue Debated

1. In *U.S. News and World Report,* March 19, 1954, p. 67. For a detailed, formal statement of CIA's official relations with Congress, see Appendix B for letter of Lt. Gen. C. P. Cabell, Acting Director, to

Senator Mike Mansfield on September 4, 1953. Reprinted in *Congressional Record* (daily edition), March 10, 1954, p. 2814.

2. *Congressional Record* (daily edition), April 11, 1956, p. 5424. All *Congressional Record* references in this chapter are to the daily edition.

3. S. Con. Res. 2, 84th Congress, 1st Session, January 14, 1955.

4. For a more recent bill see, among fifteen others, H.R. 211, 85th Congress, 1st Session, January 3, 1957, by Rep. Marguerite Stitt Church, "To Establish a Joint Committee on Foreign Intelligence." Senator Mansfield, with 20 co-sponsors, had introduced a similar resolution in the 83rd Congress.

5. *Senate Report No. 1570,* "Joint Committee on Central Intelligence Agency," Committee on Rules and Administration, 84th Congress, 2nd Session, February 23, 1956, p. 2.

6. *Senate Report No. 1570.*

7. *Senate Report No. 1570,* pp. 17–18.

8. *Senate Report No. 1570,* pp. 19–20.

9. Quotation from a letter of Senator Richard B. Russell to the Chairman of the Senate Committee on Rules and Administration.

10. *Senate Report No. 1570,* p. 24.

11. *Senate Report No. 1570,* p. 24.

12. *Senate Report No. 1570,* p. 28.

13. Quoted in *Senate Report No. 1570,* p. 24.

14. *Senate Report No. 1570,* p. 28.

15. *Congressional Record,* April 9, 1956, p. 5298.

16. *Cong. Rec.,* April 9, 1956, p. 5297.

17. *Cong. Rec.,* April 9, 1956, p. 5290.

18. *Cong. Rec.,* April 9, 1956, p. 5294.

19. *Cong. Rec.,* April 9, 1956, pp. 5305–5306.

20. *Cong. Rec.,* April 9, 1956, p. 5305.

21. *Cong. Rec.,* April 9, 1956, p. 5419.

22. *Cong. Rec.,* April 9, 1956, p. 5413.

23. *Cong. Rec.,* April 9, 1956, p. 5292.

24. *Cong. Rec.,* April 9, 1956, p. 5291.

25. The Armed Services subcommittee was composed in 1956, of Senators Russell, Byrd, Bridges, Saltonstall, and Lyndon Johnson. The Appropriations subcommittee included Senators Saltonstall, Hayden, Chavez, Russell, and Bridges.

26. *Cong. Rec.,* April 9, 1956, p. 5416.

27. *Cong. Rec.,* April 9, 1956, p. 5415.

28. *Cong. Rec.,* April 9, 1956, p. 5415.

29. *Cong. Rec.,* April 9, 1956, p. 5431.

30. William S. White, *The Citadel, The Story of the U.S. Senate,*

New York, Harper, 1956, p. 87. As Senator Mansfield later explained his measure's defeat: "What you had was a brash freshman going up against the high brass." Quoted in Warren Unna, "CIA: Who Watches the Watchman?" p. 46.

CHAPTER VIII

Intelligence and National Policy Making

1. The 1955 Hoover Commission made 62 recommendations for changes in the intelligence structure and procedure within the Department of Defense alone. A majority of these changes, most of which are classified information, had been made by early 1957. See *Hearings,* "Department of Defense Appropriations for 1958," House Subcommittee on Appropriations, Washington, 1957, Part I, p. 166.

2. A director of the Department of State's policy planning staff from 1953–1957 has disclosed that the policy-making process starts with an "appraisal of the external situation. This is known as intelligence." For development of this point see Robert R. Bowie, "Analysis of Our Policy Machine," *The New York Times Magazine,* March 9, 1958, p. 16. For more theoretical discussions of decision making, see, among others, R. C. Snyder, H. W. Bruck, and Burton Sapin, *Decision-Making as an Approach to the Study of International Politics,* Foreign Policy Analysis Project, No. 3, Princeton University, 1954.

3. Statement at Press Conference, quoted in *U.S. News and World Report,* March 8, 1957, p. 59.

4. For an authentic account of this cleverly devised and executed operation, see Ewen Montagu, *The Man Who Never Was,* Philadelphia, Lippincott, 1954.

5. Admiral Arthur Radford, in *Hearings,* "Study of Airpower," Part XIX, June 21, 1956, pp. 1467–1468.

6. For a discussion of the 1956–1957 controversy over intelligence on Soviet air power, see "A 900 Million Dollar Bobble," *U.S. News and World Report,* March 8, 1957; "Hitting the AF Below the Belt," *Air Force,* May 1957, pp. 42–43; and *Hearings,* "Department of Defense Appropriations for 1958," House Subcommittee on Appropriations, 85th Congress, 1st Session, Washington, 1957, Part I, pp. 926 ff and *passim.*

7. "U.S. Army Credits Soviet With Lead," by Jack Raymond, *The New York Times,* July 7, 1957.

8. Address before the Los Angeles World Affairs Council, April 13,

1956; reprinted in *Department of State Bulletin,* May 7, 1956, p. 758.

9. *Intelligence Activities,* p. 14.

10. *Hearings,* "Department of Defense Appropriations for 1957," Senate, Appropriations Subcommittee, 84th Congress, 2nd Session, June 7, 1956, p. 941.

11. "The National Estimate," Joseph and Stewart Alsop, *New York Herald Tribune,* January 8, 1956.

12. *Hearings,* "Study of Airpower," p. 1675.

13. *Hearings,* "Study of Airpower," p. 1329.

14. *Hearings,* "Study of Airpower," pp. 1329–1330.

15. For an incisive account of intelligence use and abuse in this period of the Korean War, see S.L.A. Marshall, *The River and the Gauntlet,* New York, Morrow, 1953, especially pages 1–17.

16. Robert E. Merriam, *Dark December,* Chicago and New York, Ziff-Davis, 1947, p. 99.

17. Truman, *Memoirs,* Vol. II, p. 331; for another side of this story, see Willoughby and Chamberlain, *MacArthur, 1941–1951,* pp. 354 ff.

18. "Intelligence," first of a series of five articles, *The New York Times,* July 20–25, 1948.

19. *Intelligence Activities,* p. 70.

20. For a detailed account of the selection and training of OSS agents in an earlier decade, see "A Good Man is Hard to Find," *Fortune,* March 1946, pp. 92–95 ff; also Murray *et al., Assessment of Men.*

21. *Intelligence Activities,* p. 70.

22. *Intelligence Activities,* p. 59.

23. Task Force Report, *National Security Organization,* Appendix G, January 1949, p. 76.

24. *Intelligence Activities,* p. 14.

25. *Intelligence Activities,* p. 14.

26. *Senate Report No. 1570,* p. 14. In addition to Mr. Killian, who in the fall of 1957 became the President's Special Assistant for Science and Technology, the Board as originally appointed was composed of Admiral Richard L. Conolly, Lt. Gen. James H. Doolittle, Benjamin F. Fairless, General John E. Hull (chairman after February 1958), Joseph P. Kennedy, Robert A. Lovett, and Edward L. Ryerson. The Board is assisted by a three-man staff, and its reports to the President are not publicized.

27. Others were William H. Jackson, New York lawyer and wartime intelligence officer, and Mathias F. Correa, a former OSS official.

28. For background information on these disputes see Hanson W. Baldwin, series of five articles on "Intelligence," *The New York Times,* July 20–July 25, 1948.

29. Other members were William B. Franke, former Assistant Secretary of the Navy; Morris Hadley, New York lawyer; and William D. Pawley, former Ambassador to Brazil.

30. *The New York Times,* October 17, 1954.

31. *The New York Times,* October 20, 1954.

32. *The New York Times,* October 24, 1954, Section IV, p. 2.

33. *Intelligence Activities,* p. 15.

34. *Hearings,* "Department of the Army Appropriations for 1957," House Appropriations Subcommittee, 84th Congress, 2nd Session, p. 413.

35. Allen W. Dulles, "The Communists Also Have Their Problems," address before the Advertising Council of San Francisco, September 19, 1957; reprinted in *Department of State Bulletin,* October 21, 1957, p. 639.

CHAPTER IX

Intelligence and Security: Retrospect and Prospect

1. See, particularly Henry A. Kissinger, *Nuclear Weapons and Foreign Policy,* New York, Harper, 1957, especially chapter 10, "The Strategy of Ambiguity." More direct sources revealing Communist techniques include, among numerous others, V. I. Lenin, *Selected Works,* New York, International Publishers, 1943 and various dates; Mao Tse-tung, *Selected Works,* New York, International Publishers, 1954 and various dates; Raymond L. Garthoff, *Soviet Military Doctrine,* Glencoe, Illinois, The Free Press, 1953, and the same author's *Soviet Strategy in the Nuclear Age,* New York, Praeger, 1958.

2. *Hearings,* "Military Situation in the Far East," Senate Committees on Armed Services and Foreign Relations, 82nd Congress, 1st Session, May 5, 1951, Part I, p. 240.

3. *Hearings,* "Military Situation in the Far East," p. 240.

4. "Mansfield Calls Intelligence Lax," *The New York Times,* November 19, 1956. Senator Mike Mansfield, Democrat, Montana, made these remarks in a television broadcast on November 18, 1956.

5. *Hearings,* "The President's Proposal on the Middle East," Senate Committees on Foreign Relations and Armed Forces, 85th Congress, 1st Session, Part I, p. 446; see also pp. 453, 464.

6. For a discussion of these and other points, see Harry Schwartz, "Intelligence and 'Moon,'" *The New York Times,* October 7, 1957.

7. Quoted in Churchill's *The Gathering Storm*, Boston, Houghton Mifflin, 1948, p. 352.

8. Allen W. Dulles, speech in New Haven, Connecticut, February 3, 1958.

9. Address at the Tenth Anniversary of the Russian Research Center, Harvard University, Cambridge, Massachusetts, January 30, 1958. Similarly perceptive comments on this general problem are found in Don K. Price, *Government and Science*, New York, New York University Press, 1954, particularly chapter V, "The Machinery of Advice," pp. 124–259.

10. Speech in New Haven, Connecticut, February 3, 1958.

11. For some of the ideas in this section, I am indebted to my senior Defense Studies colleague, W. Barton Leach, Professor of Law at Harvard University.

12. *U.S. News and World Report*, March 19, 1954, p. 67.

13. *U.S. News and World Report*, March 19, 1954, p. 64.

14. Speech in New Haven, Connecticut, February 3, 1958.

15. Speech in New Haven, Connecticut, February 3, 1958.

16. James Reston, Washington correspondent for *The New York Times*, testimony in *Hearings*, "Availability of Information from Federal Departments and Agencies," House Government Operations Subcommittee on Information, 84th Congress, 1st Session, Part I, November 7, 1955, Washington, 1956, p. 27.

17. *Hearings*, "National Security Act of 1947," House Committee on Expenditures in the Executive Departments, 80th Congress, 1st Session, Washington, 1947, p. 12.

18. Dulles, *Germany's Underground*, p. 70.

19. See Walter Schellenberg, *The Labyrinth*, New York, Harper, 1956.

20. Walter Millis, "Individual Freedom and the Common Defense," New York, The Fund for the Republic, November 1957, p. 73.

21. Greater centralization of United States national security organization and reassignment of armed service roles on the basis of functions to be performed will not be easily achieved. But when these changes are made, probably some years hence, they will have profound impact upon the national intelligence function. A rationally conceived statement of defense organization requirements for the nuclear age is contained in *International Security: The Military Aspect*, by Henry A. Kissinger and others, Rockefeller Brothers Fund, Special Studies Report II, New York, Doubleday Headline Publications, 1958, Chapter VI.

22. These words are from James A. Perkins' Address at the Tenth Anniversary of the Harvard Russian Research Center.

23. Bruce L. and Chitra M. Smith, *International Communication and Political Opinion*, Princeton, New Jersey, Princeton University Press, 1956. See also, among others, Stephen K. Bailey, and others, *Research Frontiers in Politics and Government*, Washington, Brookings Institution, 1955; Heinz Eulau, Samuel J. Eldersveld, and Morris Janowitz (editors), *Political Behavior, A Reader in Theory and Research*, Glencoe, The Free Press, 1956; and Leonard D. White, *The State of the Social Sciences*, Chicago, University of Chicago Press, 1956.

24. Pendleton Herring, "Expand the School!" *The Saturday Review*, February 1, 1958, p. 39.

25. See his *Strategic Intelligence and National Decisions*, especially pp. 141–175. It should be noted, however, in fairness to the intelligence community, that Hilsman's interviews on which his book is based were conducted some years ago, when the intelligence community was still in adolescence.

26. An earlier acute critique of intelligence doctrine is found in Willmoore Kendall's "The Functions of Intelligence," *World Politics*, July 1949, pp. 542–552.

Index

A–2 (Assistant Chief of Air Staff, Intelligence), 111–112

A–2, Air Corps, performance of in World War II, 111

Abel, Col. Rudolph Ivanovich, 24

Acheson, Dean, 52

Acquisition and Distribution, Division of, Department of State, 123

Administrative organization, chart, 139

Administrative problems, 162–163, 166, 177

AEC. *See* Atomic Energy Commission

Africa, North, World War II, 105–106

Air Corps, Information Division, 110

Air Corps Board, 110

Air Defense Command, 114

Air Force, Long Range Detection System, 32

Air Force, Secretary of the, 112

Air Force, U.S., intelligence role and organization, 110–116, 139; intelligence requirements, 111–112; Assistant Chief of Staff for Intelligence, 112; attaché system, 112; Electronics Intelligence Coordinating Group, 112; Policy and Management Group, 112; radar tracking stations, 112; Russian missile tests, tracking of, 112; Directorate of Collection and Dissemination, 112–113; Assistant Chief of Staff, Intelligence, Office of, organization, 112–114; *Air Intelligence Digest,* 113; Directorate of Estimates, 113; Indications Center, 113; military capabilities, east, 113; military capa-

bilities, west, 113; Watch Committee, 113; *Bombing Encyclopedia,* 113–114; physical vulnerability division, 113–114; Targets Directorate, 113–114; Counter-intelligence, 114; Inspector General, 114; target materials division, 114; prestige of intelligence, 115

Air Forces, U.S. Army, intelligence, World War II, 61–62; work with OSS, 69

Air Intelligence Digest, 113

Air Technical Intelligence Center, 114

Allies, U.S., 156–157; problems of intelligence co-operation, 70

Alsop, Joseph and Stewart, 171

Alsop, Stewart, 64 n 37

American misgivings, espionage and secret operations, 26

Analysis and evaluation, intelligence, 36–41

Analysts, intelligence, 176–177

Ancient function, intelligence as, 45–47

Appropriations Committees, U.S. Congress, 157

Appropriations subcommittees, U.S. Congress, 154

Ardennes Battle, 173–174; intelligence regarding German counter-attack, 61

Area study, 211

Armed Services Committees, U.S. Congress, 157

Armed Services subcommittees, U.S. Congress, 154

Armstrong, W. Park, Jr., reference to, 125 n 41

Army Intelligence Board, 101

Army Intelligence Center, 100–101

Malenkov, Georgi, 140–141
Man Who Never Was, The, 168–169
Manchuria, 89
Mansfield, Senator Mike, on CIA, 146, 152; on increased executive power, 152; on intelligence "failures," 189; letter to Director, CIA, Appendix B, 225–226
Mansfield (Senator Mike) Resolution, 146–150
Maps, Coordinator of, State Department, 123
Maquis, France, 65
Marine Corps, U.S., 95 n, 107 n
Marquand, John P., quoted, 53
Marshall, General George C., 42, 45, 122, 158
Marshall, S.L.A., reference to, 173 n 15
Mattingly, Garrett, on Elizabethan intelligence system, 48
Medical Intelligence Subcommittee, Joint, 139
Merriam, Robert E., on "Battle of the Bulge," 173–174
Middle East, crisis of 1956, 90, 189
Midway Island, Naval intelligence at, 60
Miles, Brig. Gen. Sherman, 42
Military Intelligence Division, U.S. Army, 50
Military Intelligence Service, U.S. Army, 98–99
Military Personnel Act of 1947, 109
Millis, Walter, on Dreyfus case, 48; on secrecy, 208
Missiles Panel, CIA, 132
Mistakes, CIA, 200–201
Mongols, 46
Monitoring foreign radio broadcasts, 86
Montagu, Ewen, reference to, 168–169
Morison, Samuel Eliot, quoted, 106
Morse, Senator Wayne, 152–153
Moses, 45
Mossadegh, Premier, 88

Murray, Professor Henry A., reference to, 65 n 38, 70

Nagasaki, 61–62
Nasser, President Gamal Abdel, 190
National Estimates, 2, 179
National Estimates, Board of, 90, 134–137, 139, 199
National Estimates, Office of, 134, 139
National Indications Center, 139, 140–141
National Intelligence Authority, 75, 121
National Intelligence Community, Chart, 139
National Intelligence Estimate, Chapter VI, 132–142
National Intelligence Survey (NIS), 31, 90, 103–104
National Intelligence Survey Committee, 103, 139
National Security Act of 1947, 76, 78–80
National Security Agency, 2, 116–118, 139
National Security Council (NSC), 1, 186, 198; members, 82–83; Intelligence Directives, 83; reports to, 138–139; planning papers, 202–203, 205
National security policy, role of CIA in creation of, 203–205
NATO, 35
Naval District intelligence, officers, 108
Naval Intelligence, Director of (DNI), 107–108
Naval Intelligence, Office of, 106–109; staffing of, prior to World War II, 53; World War II, 61–62; contribution to National Intelligence Surveys, 109
Naval intelligence corps, need for, 109
Navy, U.S., views on post-war intelligence system, 72; intelligence role and organization,